D0583353

CHAMPION
OF
SOUTHERN FEDERALISM

KENNIKAT PRESS

NATIONAL UNIVERSITY PUBLICATIONS

SERIES IN AMERICAN STUDIES

General Editor
JAMES P. SHENTON
Professor of History, Columbia University

JOSEPH W. COX

CHAMPION
OF
SOUTHERN FEDERALISM

Robert Goodloe Harper of South Carolina

National University Publications
KENNIKAT PRESS
Port Washington, N.Y./London/1972

Library of Congress Catalog Card No: 78-189554
ISBN: 0-8046-9025-1

Manufactured in the United States of America

Published by
Kennikat Press, Inc.
Port Washington, N.Y./London

This book is dedicated to the three generations of Coxes.

Contents

Preface

In the usual view, Federalism is considered in terms which suggest that it was nearly a sectional party with northern leadership, northern orientation, with programs and ideological positions designed to protect and advance the interests of the section it generally represented. With but few exceptions, the great names associated with Federalism are northern and any discussion of the period seems inexorably to center around Alexander Hamilton and the High-Federalists.

Lisle A. Rose in *Prologue to Democracy: The Federalists in the South* (Lexington: University of Kentucky Press, 1968) has done a splendid service by resurrecting Southern Federalism and this study ought to prove a turning point in the historiographical rediscovery of this neglected aspect of the early national era.

Robert Goodloe Harper, congressman from South Carolina's Ninety Six District from 1795 until 1801, is usually included in this interpretation of the period. He is generally represented as the stereotype of the very worst in Federalism, the nativistic, archly militant field-marshal of the reactionary Federalist forces in the House.

The writer challenges both this oversimplified interpretation of Harper's congressional career and the stereotyped northern image of Federalism. The process by which Harper reached the House and his years as a national political figure illustrate the fundamental differences between Federalism and southern Federalism.

The Federalist party was a viable force in southern politics at least until the internal security program of 1798 backfired in the faces of its authors. Southern Federalism never really fit the northern mold and was thus somewhat suspect in northern party circles. Southern Federalists tended to be less doctrinaire and rather eclectic in ideological matters. Prior to the French Crisis of 1798 they were, in general, a good deal more tolerant of their Republican opponents and not nearly as frightened of Thomas Jefferson as their northern counterparts.

There also existed a strikingly different orientation with respect to the third great section of the nation—the West. North-

erners regarded the western territories as something of an unpleasant burden that had to be borne and a reservoir of potential
troubles, which the abortive Whiskey Insurrection clearly
demonstrated.

Southern Federalists, on the other hand, viewed the West in
quite a different way. The territories held enormous promise for
the future and consequently represented a national blessing
rather than a burden to these agrarian-minded southerners. Harper shared this opinion and manifested a healthy and constructive interest in the development of the American West.

Nevertheless, in the crucible of the French Crisis Harper and
his fellow southern Federalists put aside all that had set them
apart from their northern cousins, and indeed, in their conversion
to High-Federalism they became more extremist than many of
the Hamiltonians. The roots of the tragedy of southern Federalism lay in the morbid, terrifying fear of racial conflagration
which the prospects of French invasion suggested. All moderation was cast aside in the rush to defend America from all
enemies foreign and domestic. Harper the moderate Southern
Federalist became Harper the extremist, with the result that by
1800 he no longer represented the views of his constituents, and
he quit both South Carolina and Congress rather than stand for
reelection.

The author wishes to acknowledge his indebtedness to several
individuals and institutions. My debt to Professors Aubrey C.
Land and E. James Ferguson, under whom I was privileged to
study, is inestimable.

I am also especially indebted to the staff of the Maryland
Historical Society, the Manuscripts Division of the Library of
Congress, and the South Carolina State Archives at Columbia for
making the research and preparation of this study possible. I wish
to thank the *Adams Manuscript Trust* for permission to use and
quote from the Adams Papers.

To Myron Scholnick, friend and colleague who read and criticized this manuscript several times, and to Miss Anita Mattucci,
who expertly prepared it, I am particularly grateful.

Joseph W. Cox
Baltimore, Maryland

CHAMPION
OF
SOUTHERN FEDERALISM

General Robert Goodloe Harper
From a Portrait by Charles B.J.F. de St. Memin,
in the collection of the Maryland Historical Society
who graciously allowed its use here.

1
Genesis:
The Revolution to Princeton

It was Friday morning, January 14, 1825. The gallantly dressed, distinguished southern gentleman stood reading his newspaper in front of the fireplace in his tastefully elegant Baltimore home. Also in the room was his nineteen-year-old son, whom everyone considered a fine young man of great promise, and a little Negro boy who sat waiting, eager to satisfy his master's needs for his hat, cloak or riding crop. The gentleman standing before the fireplace had every reason to be in good spirits that morning. He was sixty years old but still in excellent health. Had he not just the day before made one of the best arguments in court he had ever delivered, a presentation of some three hours length. And had he not then gone to a ball that evening in a mood uncommonly gay and agreeable, and enjoyed himself as if he were twenty years younger and this morning after breakfast felt none the worse for wear. It was not just his health he had reason to be grateful for. He could feel justly proud that his life and career had been marked with better than average success. He had a splendid legal practice and was recognized as one of the three giants of the Baltimore bar. A powerful congressman during one of the most important periods in his nation's history he had also achieved political prominence in the two states he had resided in. And certainly not the least of his accomplishments was the fact that he had married the daughter of one of the wealthiest men in all America, an event which had brought in its wake impeccable social position and a splendid family. No one would have criticized the gentleman if that morning he had paused to reflect upon an eminently successful life.

Then without the slightest warning and without a word Robert Goodloe Harper collapsed and was dead before he reached the floor, probably the victim of a massive coronary attack. A friend remarked that his family and friends were "dumbstruck at the suddenness of his passing."[1]

Robert Goodloe Harper was and still is characterized by those who find reason to mention him in discussing the era in which he

3

lived as the perfect example of the nativistic paranoia of the extreme Federalists of the Pickering or Cabot variety. Particularly since the 1950s, Harper has been used as an archtype of the xenophobic hysteria of the 1790s, a period which legitimately begs comparison with the 1950s. There is, of course, a degree of validity to this traditional interpretation of the man and his era. However, the author believes that a careful review of Harper's career forces the student to modify seriously, if not completely, this never-challenged interpretation.

It would be, of course, impossible to maintain that Robert Goodloe Harper was anything other than a firm Federalist. Indeed, one of his valid claims to historical treatment is the tenacity with which he clung to his beliefs into a period when to be so labeled was to be reviled by one's contemporaries. To be a Federalist required a belief in an ordered society. Nature presented man with massive obstacles and challenges which could only be met successfully if the individual recognized his true place in society, a place which ideally, but unfortunately not always, depended upon a balance of the individual's capacities and aspirations. There is an almost platonic quality to Federalist beliefs, most notable in the often expressed ideal of every man doing that which he was best-qualified to do, and that which he was somehow happiest doing, for society. Society was distinct from the individuals who made it up and this organic understanding of society was central to the structure of Federalist ideology.[2] Equality and democracy were simply incomprehensible to the Robert Goodloe Harpers, for all their experience had strengthened their conviction that man's basic nature was anything but benign. It is interesting to speculate whether the eighteenth-century "liberal" who so condemned this conception of human nature has been supported or undermined by the experience of civilized man in the twentieth century.

There is something else to be considered here. Despite Republican charges and accusations of monarchist plots and "creeping aristocracy," one fact must never be lost sight of—that is, that Federalism has too often been explained on the basis of the opinions and correspondence of some of its more extreme adherents. The result is the impression that a small class of conspiratorially minded men dominated if not dictated American development in the period 1789-1800. This is to completely overlook the fact that these men who sat in the national councils in New York and Philadelphia and for a few months in Washington, not to mention the state legislatures, were elected in duly constituted and open elections. They could not have been elected if only the "better sort of people" had voted for them. Federalism had a genuine appeal to a great many people below the topmost rungs of the social ladder. It was, after all, in tune with the colonial experience and one should not lose sight of the fact that even Thomas Jefferson scarcely went beyond government of and for the people; it would be left to the Jacksonians to add the "by." It would not be until the late 1790s, or even the early years of the next century, that the Jeffersonian party could woo away the great majority of the American people from this older understanding of the good government.

For a time, this conception of good government was the mainstream of American political thought, and Robert Goodloe Harper was squarely in the middle of the stream. In the second half of the Federalist decade, not merely the extremist leadership, but the bulk of the nation itself veered drastically to the right in a fit of hysteria engendered by fear and suspicion of a foreign revolution which in the minds of the many, not the few, constituted a threat to the American experiment. And in that moment of fear Robert Goodloe Harper too veered sharply to the right to engage in excesses which the nation and he would later regret. Harper, in the opinion of the author, has been not falsely but improperly understood. He is most often placed in the category of ultra-Federalist when in fact that label is inappropriate for much of his career in Congress. Prior to 1798 he more accurately belongs in the company of the moderate southern Federalists. However, the political mainstream again shifted noticeably in 1800 and the Robert Goodloe Harpers found themselves isolated on an island now bypassed by the mighty river as it churned on into the nineteenth century. They waited, sometimes not too patiently, for the stream to resume its true and ancient course but it never did.

Sixty years before that fatal Friday in 1825, near Fredericksburg, Virginia, Robert Goodloe Harper was born to Jesse and Diana Goodloe Harper, the only boy in a covey of girls. Jesse Harper was by trade a cabinetmaker who by his son's account was possessed of a small but independent estate in land and slaves acquired partly by his marriage and partly by his own industry. When the boy was four the family moved just across the line into North Carolina in Granville County, and it was here in this frontier environment that Robert grew up. Quite early Jesse

Harper informed his son that because of the size of the family, eight daughters plus Robert, and the small nature of his estate, "that I was to expect nothing from him, but such an education as the Country could afford."[3] His mother taught him to read and write and when he was ten years old he began attending a grammar school in the neighborhood.

The young frontier scholar's life continued uninterrupted until the British army under Lord Cornwallis, after defeating General Gates at Camden, invaded and overran North Carolina. Harper was fifteen, and like countless other boys up and down the rebellious colonies, begged his parents to allow him to join the militia unit forming in the area and do his part in freeing the colony and ridding North Carolina of the invading tyrant. Against the wishes of his parents "whose religious character rendered them extremely apprehensive of the effects of a military life . . ." the boy left school and joined a volunteer corps of cavalry with which he served under General Greene until the enemy left the state and was shut up in the Yorktown Penninsula.[4] After the British had been driven out of North Carolina, Harper returned home on leave exceedingly taken by the military life. As he himself later wrote, "I returned home with my fondness for a military life greatly inflamed by the notice of the officers, and the promotion I had met with in the Corps."[5] Jesse Harper, greatly concerned that his only son was about to throw away his chances for an education, promised that if Robert would continue his education until he was twenty, he would attempt to secure a higher commission for him and assist him in preparing for a military career. To this proposal, Harper eagerly consented and it can be assumed spent too much time daydreaming about the military future which stretched before him, no doubt seeing in himself characteristics similar to those of the great victor of Yorktown. But alas, to Harper's dismay and his father's delight, "the Peace soon taking place, put an end to my military projects."[6]

The impression made upon the boy by his revolutionary experience was quite profound, and this early ingrained fascination for the military life and his respect and deference for military men never left Harper. It characterizes him as it did so many others of the Federalist persuasion. The fascination with the image of a sword, a white charger, and ten thousand troops was no more potent an influence on Alexander Hamilton than it was upon Robert Goodloe Harper.

His experiences in the revolution also imbued him with a profound and militant sense of patriotism. His sister remarked later that "love of Country was a principle that he cherished from the time he lern'd to think."[7] In its finest form this principle acting upon men can move them to exalted acts of sacrifice for their country, and in its least acceptable form men can be driven to commit acts designed to subvert the constitutionally chosen government of the state they believe they are saving from destruction either from without or within. With the Harperian variety of militarily-minded men it acted more in the former context than the latter.

After the war, Harper drifted seemingly aimlessly, searching for the substitute for the military career which was now closed to him. There is good reason to believe that his life involved mostly gambling and a period of general dissipation. He had been hired in 1783 by John Henderson, the pioneer of Kentucky and Tennessee, to help survey some land given to Henderson's company by the states of Virginia and North Carolina. "This expedition gave me a considerable knowledge of the Western Countries, and a turn for land speculations, which had no inconsiderable influence on my future affairs."[8] He purchased some western lands but because of a fraudulent survey and the fact that his career turned in another direction he was prevented from deriving any benefit from them. After he returned from the West, by his own admission, he spent his time

for nearly six months, in idleness and dissipation. A fondness for gaming, which had early shown itself, and was too much favoured by the manners of that Country, began to assume an alarming appearance; and joined to a taste for fashionable gaiety, called for pecuniary supplies which my father's situation could illy [sic] afford.[9]

Evidently, Jesse Harper had had enough and flatly told his son that he must choose a career and begin supporting himself in some respectable profession. The elder Harper encouraged the boy to try college, the boy later recalled, and knowing that his father could not contribute too substantially to the project, he thought he could support himself by acting as a tutor as he had done in the local grammar school. "I therefore accepted the small sum which he offered me, less than one hundred dollars, and set out for Princeton in June 1784. I was then nineteen years and six months old."[10]

The young man's stay at Princeton is not very well documented but some aspects of his college career are evident. By more careful management of his funds than he had evidenced heretofore in life, his money lasted until winter, but he then had to apply to President Witherspoon for a position teaching a grammar school which was then part of the college. His tutoring duties and his small charges occupied eight hours of his day and the remainder he devoted to his studies. In the spring of 1785, possibly through his father's supplications, he was advanced a sum of money by Governor Spaight of North Carolina. "With this I returned to college, and resolved to bring into the remaining half year, the studies of the Junior Class, to which I belonged, and those of the Senior Class too; and to present myself for examination and a degree with that class." [11] He gave up all extracurricular employment and buried himself in his books. Harper's efforts were successful, for he received his degree with the senior class that year and was awarded a gold medal annually offered for the best essay written by a member of the graduating class.

The only intimation concerning Harper's relationship with his family comes from a series of letters between the family and the young man at Princeton. There are of course the familial expressions of regret at seeing him leave home although it was not the first time. His father promised to look after his affairs and exhorted him not to forget to write home as often as he could, an exhortation which apparently did not have the desired effect, for Harper's letters were few and infrequent.

There is besides all of this, running all through the series of letters from home, a familial concern for Harper's spiritual welfare and evidence of the deeply felt religious convictions of the elder Harpers. His father wrote in 1784, "and now My Dear Child suffer me to put you in mind that an awfull eternity is before us, & that the Judg [sic] stands at the dore [sic] to whom we must all give account. . . . Beg the Almighty for his Grace to assist you . . . to shun & avoid Every Appearance of Evil. . . ." [12] Later that year, his father wrote again telling him that he was not well and beseeching him to promise that in case of the elder Harper's death Robert would live near- "yr Mammey & sisters to comfort & assist them when I am gone. . ." and again there is almost a verbatim repetition of the warning concerning the health of his soul. [13] His sister Letty wrote telling him how much she missed him but that she looked forward to corresponding with him. As was the fashion she asked him to "inclose a lock of your hare . . . & I shall esteem it as the Richest juel [sic]."[14] He also received letters from his sister Frances and brother-in-law, Robert Hyde, all of them criticizing him for not writing to the family and expressing concern for his soul.

As in the family correspondence of all college boys, the subject of money often arose in Jesse Harper's letters to his offspring at Princeton. In one instance the younger Harper had left home after informing his creditors that his father would settle his accounts for him. The father, after encountering the creditors, wrote to his son demanding an accounting and blamed the young man for some "abusefull language" he had received on his son's account. [15] Once the circumstances of Robert's debts were straightened out the major source of family criticism of young Harper was his failure to write home and the concern this caused his family. Sister Letty complained, in May 1785, that they had not received a single letter from him in eight months and later in October of the same year, his sister Frances complained of not receiving a line in over a year. [16] The pleas for letters continued to reach Harper but apparently to no avail, for his letters home remained infrequent.

While at Princeton, Robert Goodloe Harper apparently made several decisions which would determine the course his life and career were to follow. The evidence documenting his college years is slight, but certain influences are definitely discernable and are worthy of at least cursory attention. Robert had arrived at Princeton in a financial state that made his academic career tenuous at best. His background and family connections were, by the standards of the frontier, better than average but he certainly lacked entrée into the influential social and economic inner circles of American society, and he had no sponsor to recommend him. Harper had always had a taste for the good life; college and his association with the more affluent and distinguished of his classmates convinced him that the life of the gentleman was the only thing he would settle for. A letter from a Princeton chum tells us that the young man joined one of the more important societies in the college community but unfortunately not which one. [17] Harper's friends were quite aware of his financial hardships and several encouraged him to remain in college no matter how great the material hardships. They were particularly gratified when windfalls came Harper's way for he was a good student and they felt assistance was justified. One

James Morris of Albany, a recent graduate, wrote Harper entreating him to stick it out, saying that "it would be much to your advantage to stay at Princeton [for] certainly the opportunities for improvement there are very great, and more especially for you who have a disposition for study. I admire the goodness of your friend Col. S[paight] it is what every Gentleman ought to do: but few would. . . ."[18]

There are indications in the student's correspondence that he, and those of his friends who had also sprung from humble beginnings, came to feel themselves a bit above the rural districts which had produced them. This might explain why Harper virtually cut himself off from his family, scarcely wrote and to my knowledge never returned home after 1784. One of his friends who had gone to upstate New York to study law wrote to Harper at Princeton describing life in what he evidently considered "uncivilized America." He described how a local attorney had recently come "nigh being assassinated by two or three ruffians . . ." after winning an unpopular court decision.[19]

The Princeton years were significant for yet another reason, for it was there that Harper came to the realization that his education had not really fitted him for any particular profession. Sometime in between those long hours of study and tutoring in the grammar school Harper decided that after graduation he would turn to the study of the law and seek his fortune before the bar. There was really nothing surprising about the decision. His first love, a military career, being closed to him, and considering Harper's conception of the good life, the law was just about all that remained open to this increasingly ambitious young man. Had he had connections which would have made a career in the business world more attractive the decision might have been quite different. But during Harper's lifetime it was the world of politics and not that of the counting house which attracted the bright, ambitious college graduate and legal practice was the surest entrée to political circles. In the new nation no one could say just how far a bright and talented young lawyer might advance himself. However, once Harper had made his decision he faced the task of convincing his parents and family that the law was the right pursuit for their kinsman.

Just what the family's objection to the law or lawyers was is not clear. Their objection to Harper's earlier dreams of a military career were apparently based upon religious convictions, although whether or not they were pacifists is unclear. Their objections to the law may have been nothing more than the belief that interpreting the law for profit too often involved chicanery and made it difficult for the virtuous man to avoid compromising his principles, something they would have desired to avoid at all cost.

At any rate, a letter written much later to Harper's son recalled how Harper while still in college had, in one of his rare letters home, detailed the great and good works of a prominent lawyer in one of the eastern states. The writer, clearly a relative or friend of those early years, stated that "this letter was written [by Harper] to reconcile the family to his study & practice of the law, to which, from previous considerations, they were opposed." [20] Most probably with a good deal of misgivings, the family reluctantly agreed to accept Robert's chosen profession. There is no indication that their continued opposition would have made any difference anyway.

Once the decision was made, the only question remaining was where Harper would study law. Why he chose Charleston remains a mystery, but the decision to go South rather than North needs little explanation. He was after all a southerner and the choice was logical. North Carolina offered little opportunity for a student to prepare himself but might later have promise for a lawyer who had studied and been admitted to the bar in one of the major southern cities. Charleston was thus the logical choice. There is also the possibility that Harper, while serving with General Greene during the war, may have drifted down into South Carolina and resolved to return someday to seek his fortune. In his autobiography Harper recalled the decision this way.

> Leaving College, my desire to see the world, and to obtain opportunities for improvement which the interior Country of North Carolina did not afford, induced me to form the resolution of visiting Charleston; where I hoped to obtain the situation of Tutor in some private family . . . until I could become qualified for the Bar. It was my intention to return home then and establish myself in North Carolina. [21]

And thus, in the fall of 1785, this young aspirant to legal fame and fortune set off southward to begin his assault upon that very formidable Charleston society with no one to recommend him, no law office to enter, and little more than his determination and ambition to sustain him. A friend did get off a letter to a cousin visiting in Charleston telling him to look Harper up, but other than that he was entirely on his own.[22]

The new adventure had begun under slightly less than auspicious circumstances but there is no reason to believe that Harper was anything less than confident. Money, background, and powerful friends might not have been too evident but confidence in himself was something Robert Goodloe Harper never lacked.

NOTES

1. John P. Kennedy, *Memoirs of the Life of William Wirt, Attorney General of the United States* (New York: G. P. Putnam and Sons, 1872), II, 169.

2. Rowland Berthoff, "The American Social Order: A Conservative Hypothesis," *The American Historical Review*, LXV (April, 1960, 495-514.)

3. Much of the information concerning the first years of Harper's life comes from an unpublished account which I have entitled his "Autobiographical sketch." It was written for Charles Carroll of Carrollton in 1801 and hereafter will be referred to as Autobiography. It is located in the Harper-Pennington MSS in the Maryland Historical Society.

4. Autobiography, p. 2.

5. Ibid.

6. Ibid.

7. Elizabeth Hyde to C. C. Harper, Harper-Pennington MSS, MHS, April 30, 1825.

8. Autobiography, Harper-Pennington, III, MHS.

9. Ibid.

10. Ibid.

11. Ibid.

12. Jesse and Diana Harper to RGH, July 14, 1784, Harper-Pennington MSS, MHS.

13. Jesse Harper to RGH, October 20, 1784, Harper-Pennington MSS.

14. Letitia Harper to RGH, November 20, 1784, Harper-Pennington MSS.

15. Jesse Harper to RGH, November 21, 1784, Harper-Pennington MSS.

16. Letitia Harper to RGH, May 25, 1785, Harper-Pennington MSS; Frances Harper to RGH, October 9, 1785.

17. John Henry to RGH, September 26, 1784, Harper-Pennington MSS, MHS.
18. James Morris to RGH, June 5, 1785, Harper-Pennington MSS, MHS.
19. John Henry to RGH, October 17, 1785, Harper-Pennington MSS, MHS.
20. Anonymous to Charles Carroll Harper (no date, but written after RGH's death in 1825), Harper-Pennington MSS III, MHS.
21. Autobiography, p. 3.
22. John Henry to RGH, October 9, 1785, Harper-Pennington Papers.

2

South Carolina

South Carolina took no detectable notice of the prospective law student when he arrived in Charleston in November of 1785, but it is unlikely that Harper was as oblivious of the city as it was of him. South Carolina's largest and most famous city had been known throughout the colonies as one of the most impressive of American cities. The young provincial who had been so impressed by Princeton must surely have been struck by the crown jewel of the South. A young man who arrived from the North at almost the same time has left us an excellent description of Harper's Charleston. The city's streets were straight, generally regular but very narrow. Pedestrians were granted the rare luxury of about four feet of pavement and brick on either side of the street. The street proper, between the pavements, was left in its natural sandy condition. This made crossing the street disagreeable but it also insured that carriages made little noise moving along the avenues "and one's ears were not strained as they were in New York. . . ."¹ The major disadvantage of this arrangement was the swirls of dust the wind often stirred up. The houses themselves were even more scattered than in Philadelphia, which allowed "the free circulation of air." Though many of the dwellings were of wood, most were of brick one to three stories high, none being higher. The inhabitants of these dwellings were protected by a police force that the traveller characterized as "pretty good."

However, a city is not her buildings but her inhabitants, and Charleston was set apart from her rivals up and down the Atlantic seaboard by her people and not by her four-foot sidewalks. Our traveller was struck by the affluence of the city, the two sources of which he took to be "the planting interest" and commerce. This affluence, he felt, had had a very great influence upon the customs and manners of the citizens.

> The inhabitants possess not that keeness & sagacity which are visible in countries more difficult to subsist in; and which tends to make them famous for ingenuity & improvements. Pleasure becomes in a great measure their study. Science but little patronized or pursued, & activity

to habits of study looked upon as the retreats of the tasteless or
melancholy resorts of the needy . . . manufactures are neither patron-
ized encouraged or pursued; and they seem to be perfectly content to
supply themselves from foreign markets.[2]

Timothy Ford, our observant visitor, went on to note that "the
military art goes fast to decay; [and the citizens] . . . seem willing to forget the dangers & hardships of war amidst the alluring
baits of pleasure . . . ," and after all these, students of the classics
ought to have recalled the example of the fall of Rome.[3] The
northerner also confided to his diary his opinions concerning the
extreme pretentions of the wealthy and that despite their "for-
mality and scrupulosity to a considerable extreme, there was a
dearth of religion" and many travellers labeled Charleston as a
"seat of wickedness."[4]

It must be suggested that Charleston's affluence and wickedness was more apparent than real. Several years later, Aedanus
Burke, in a speech before the first session of the national legislature, made reference to the superficial wealth of South Carolina.
"Though it is true, that there are men there who live in affluence,
are rich in land and . . . servants, yet I believe they are universally
in debt."[5] This could be inferred, he continued, from the laws
the South Carolina legislature had passed to aid debtors. It would
take the citizens of South Carolina a dozen years to pay off their
state and private debts, "especially when their produce is so
fallen in price as not to pay the expense of cultivation."[6] A later
spokesman of the South concluded that the general depression in
the state reached its worst point in 1785 and 1786 and that it
was not until the middle nineties that South Carolina began to
recover from the effects of the war and the depression which
followed in its wake.[7] The "Critical Period" interpretation of the
1780s has come under a great deal of attack but South Carolina
does not provide as convincing evidence for the revisionist historian as states further northward.

General prosperity did not return to South Carolina until the
1790s and then it was not so much the Hamiltonian financial
program which brought about the recovery but rather the cultivation of cotton which gradually took up the slack in the state's
economy. The first step was taken with the introduction of the
sea-island variety in 1786 in Georgia and a year or so later in
South Carolina. With the invention of the cotton gin in 1793 the
new industry moved inland beyond the coastal districts into the

middle country and eventually even into the up country which Harper would represent in Congress in the late 1790s. By 1794, cotton was being raised in the Orangeburg District and by 1796 in the High Hills of Santee in Camden, both middle country areas.[8]

But when Harper arrived in 1785, he must have realized that he might possibly have chosen a more auspicious locale in which to commence his career. At least, this must have been his first reaction. Fortunately, economic prosperity did return and his fortunes rose with it.

Thus far, the discussion has revolved largely around Charleston, quite logically of course, for Charleston was the center of all South Carolina's important activity. There was, however, another South Carolina, a South Carolina quite different from the coastal areas typified by St. James Creek Parish or Christ Church Parish. This was a South Carolina which a visitor to Charleston might not even come into contact with. The reference is of course to the back country, or as it was called in South Carolina, the up country. In 1785, this would have included the territory of Ninety Six, Camden, and parts of Orangeburg, and Cheraws Districts. The most obvious difference between the two areas, upper and lower South Carolina, is evident from the first census of 1790. The three lower districts of Beaufort, Charleston, and Georgetown, the low country, had a white population of 28,644 as compared with the 111,534 white people in the up country. Then too, the vast majority of slaves were owned in the three lower districts.[9]

The discrepancy in white population and slave ownership, however, was not the only difference between the two areas, and it should be noted that emancipationist sentiment was no stronger in the back country than it was in Charleston District. Two distinct societies existed. The up country was settled much later and by an entirely different stock. Western South Carolina had been peopled by that great eighteenth-century "Scotch-Irish" migration which had followed the Appalachian range and touched every colony from Pennsylvania to Georgia. The migrants were welcomed to the region but not expected to participate in the colony's government "and strange as it may seem a similar attitude was held by the newcomers themselves. They were half apologetic and seemingly conscious of being a different social group."[10] Since they did not immediately take up the customs and institutions of the earlier settlers, the distinctiveness of the up country was even more pronounced when they came to outnumber the coastal inhabitants.

In the 1780s and early 1790s the up country residents began to ask for their rights as citizens of the state. The situation was made acute by the fact that the section with four times the population of the other, was in a minority in the state legislature, representation being based on the "temporary" organization of the First Provincial Congress in 1774. The glaring inequity of representation is easily discerned by comparing three of the election districts. In the election of 1790, St. Stephen's Parish, low country, with 226 white inhabitants, elected three representatives and one senator, the same as Edgefield with 9,785, or Pendelton with 8,731 white residents, both up country districts. The entire upper division of the state with 111,534 whites, elected fifty-four representatives and seventeen senators, while the lower division with 28,644 whites elected seventy representatives and twenty senators respectively.[11] The low country, if it felt it needed justification for maintaining the status quo, could turn to tax statistics. The up country paid £8,390 in taxes in 1790 while the lower division paid £28,081, more than a third of which came from the city of Charleston alone.[12]

An interesting sidelight upon this situation is presented by a close look at the ratifying convention which met in Charleston in May 1788 to vote on the new federal Constitution. One South Carolina scholar maintains rather convincingly that "if the convention had been representative of the white population of South Carolina, it is doubtful whether ratification would have taken place at all."[13] The necessary supporting evidence is contained in the records of the convention proceedings. The delegates from the low country voted eighty-eight percent for and twelve percent against the new plan of union; while the middle section voted forty-nine percent for and fifty-one percent against. The delegates from the under-represented up country districts voted twenty percent for and eight percent against the Constitution.[14] The vote in the convention was as much a product of the sectional division of the state as it was opposition to altering the national government.

Before this conflict assumes the connotation of a South Carolina Bacon's Rebellion the account should be qualified by a mention of the unique nature of this sectional division. There were no hints of a march on the capitol, and no intimations of violence. This was not so much class struggle as a power contest between the older established aristocrats of the coast and the newly arrived back country "gentlemen." The back country advocates of legislative reform did not contend that they had been oppressed but rather voiced their concern about a future abuse of power by the dominant minority in the low country. Their printed arguments and broadsides were of course an attack upon the existing system of representation but their language was moderate and dignified. It would be difficult indeed to document an example of the arm-waving, red-eyed demagogue who whipped up the populace for the march on Columbia. This does not mean, however, that the movement for reform in the late 1780s and early 1790s did not disturb the low country planters, only that their fears were exaggerated.

So much space has been devoted to the topic of South Carolina's sectional problem because it is indicative of the state's condition when the prospective lawyer arrived, and for another even more important reason. In the early 1790s Robert Goodloe Harper attached himself to this legislative reform movement and rode the popular cause first into the state legislature, then two months later, into the federal House of Representatives as a congressman from one of the back country districts.

Soon after arriving in Charleston in November 1785, Harper looked up the father of one of his small pupils at Princeton, who having heard of him from his son, made Harper several loans that tided him over until he found employment. Shortly thereafter, he was teaching in a large grammar school in Charleston owned by a Mr. Thompson. As compensation for his teaching duties Harper received 40 guineas per annum, board, lodging and washing.

The Schoolmaster introduced his young assistant to two of his former pupils by the name of Parker who were commencing their legal practice with "great reputation." "They received me into their office at all my spare hours, and furnished me with books," Harper remembered nearly twenty years later. [15] Sometime later a friend went out of his way to introduce Harper "to several persons of distinction, and among others to General [Charles Cotesworth] Pinckney and Mr. Edward Rutledge, both of whom gave me assistance and direction in the study of law." [16] His sister, writing in 1825, thought he had been taken into the office of Edward Rutledge, but this is doubtful, for had it been the case Harper would certainly have mentioned it in his autobiographical sketch. [17] At any rate, one year after his arrival Harper was admitted to the bar. From one standpoint Harper had arrived in Charleston at the right time, at least insofar as his admission to the bar was concerned. In the late colonial period admission to the Charleston bar had been governed by rule of court "which required membership for five years in one of the four inns of court in England, and having kept Commons for eight terms." [18] These requirements had all been changed by an Act of 1785 which required judges to grant licenses to persons whom, upon examination, they considered to be qualified in knowledge and character. Some formal preparation or legal apprenticeship was expected but not required. So, Harper was fortunate at least in this respect.

Apparently, too, his first case was a success. A friend, from those early Charleston days, recalled that Harper's speech before the court, in the oratorical style which was to remain his trademark, "caused tears to flow in profusion throughout the House." [19] Tear-producing eloquence, however, was not quite enough to guarantee a beginning lawyer's success in Charleston in the 1780s and Harper decided to leave the city and try his luck in the up country where the prestige of being attached to an established Charleston law firm did not matter as much as it did in the tidewater. In the extreme southwestern corner of the state lay the district known simply as Ninety Six, the largest in the state, which stretched from the Broad River to the Savannah. The center of the district was a small community called Cambridge in Abbeville County on the site of Old Fort Ninety Six, and it was here that Harper decided to establish his practice.

Fort Ninety Six occupied a very prominent place in the history of the South Carolina frontier. The fort was of purely local construction and importance until the British and Loyalist troops seized it during the Revolution. A force of Whig Carolinians had then laid siege to the fort and the struggle became something of a back country epic. [20] The old town of Ninety Six was destroyed by the British when they evacuated and Cambridge had grown up upon the ruins of the old fortress. The best description of the country town dates from 1805, but rural villages do not change considerably in nineteen years and Harper probably found the town in pretty much the same condition. Not really a town but rather a country village, Cambridge contained about fifteen or twenty houses, stores and taverns located at the top of a small hill. At the center stood the old brick courthouse and slightly down the hill was the jail. Also in the community was a small college conducted by the Reverend John Springer, a Presbyterian divine formerly of Princeton, who became Harper's close friend. Springer's college never consisted of more than "log studies temporarily thrown up till better ones could be errected. . . ."[21] Though no degrees were ever conferred, the college flourished for a time and local recollection had it that Harper was once an instructor in the school, but we have no indication as to what subjects he is supposed to have taught. It would not have been unlikely that the young lawyer, who had had some experience as a teacher, might have sought some sort of supplement to his meager income, and the college would have provided a likely opportunity.[22]

In selecting Cambridge Harper had not made a bad choice because the town flourished until a change in the South Carolina judiciary system moved the courts to Abbeville. The twenty-five-year-old counselor plunged into his professional activities, and from the spring of 1787 when he opened his practice until the latter part of 1789 he stuck it out in Cambridge trying to make a success of his new career. He certainly did not lack for clients and he was constantly employed, but they could pay him only pitifully small fees or neglected to pay him at all, and he became disillusioned. The country was still too backward and he had not the time to wait for its improvement to catch up to his ambitions. In the fall of 1789 he left Cambridge and resolved to return once more to Charleston. In later life Harper completely wrote off those two years in Cambridge and felt that his return to the coast in 1789 should "be regarded as the commencement of my practice at the Bar."[23] In yet another way his departure from the up country closed a chapter in the lawyer's life. Both his parents had died in 1788 and now his life was entirely his own to direct.[24] If he had indeed felt an obligation to return one day to his home in North Carolina, it now counted for naught, and Harper may have experienced along with his grief an understandable sense of release and relief. Had his parents survived, Harper might have felt obligated to return home to look after them.

The chronicle of Harper's career must now wend its path through what is probably its most shadowy and fitfully documented phase—Robert Goodloe Harper and his misguided plunge into the intoxicating, appealing, and dangerous world of the land speculator. The South Carolina years left two indelible marks upon Robert Goodloe Harper; his dabbling in western lands was nearly as significant in influencing his later life as was his introduction to politics and his election to Congress. Both activities appealed to the flamboyant, ambitious, gambling strain in his character and it would not be too far-fetched to suggest that he entered politics not merely in search of fame and attention but because the guaranteed income might enable him to extricate himself from the humiliating debts his speculative ventures had heaped upon him.

From 1789 to 1794, it appears that Harper's major occupation was land speculation, in which he acted either as an agent for others or for himself. That it did little to advance his law practice is obvious, and the extant records of court proceedings in South Carolina for this period show only infrequent and insignificant references to Harper the courtroom lawyer. They usually show him acting as the agent in the sale of a slave or being granted power of attorney to sell property. [25] No criminal court records survive, but there is no indication that Harper appeared significantly in criminal actions in the period in question. This is not to imply that Harper did not practice in Charleston during these years but only that he was not a leading attorney. Certainly his practice neither occupied all of his time nor satisfied his desire for worldly gain.

As a lawyer, however, Harper was brought into association with the courthouse group, and no doubt had access to information concerning the most profitable areas of land speculation in the state. A list of his acquisitions between 1789 and 1795 would be risky due to incomplete land records, and misleading because, as in the case of many speculators, most of his purchases were made on credit and involve no real increase in capital investment or actual personal wealth. Like a great many other South Carolinians, Harper took advantage of the South Carolina Land Act of 1785, which allowed for the purchase of vacant lands at ten cents per acre. His purchases under this act and his other ventures in western lands were undoubtedly made largely on credit, for he had no other way of obtaining the necessary capital. Harper's purchases were of necessity never made in large blocks of lands.

He began by investing in sound, improved property. As early as 1791 he leased a house and lot to one Susan Wilkinson, and if more of the land records existed other similar small acquisitions and leases would likely appear. [26] Harper also made purchases of small blocks of land in areas which he suspected would quickly develop. There are references to the purchase of 182 acres in

Ninety Six in 1790, 185 acres in the same district in 1794, and the same amount in Spartanburg County, also in 1794.[27] In all these transactions Harper apparently acted on his own behalf. Had he been satisfied to continue operating on this level he might have avoided the financial overextensions and failures that plagued him for the next twenty years of his life. But the heady lure of easy wealth and great adventure proved too potent and the small-time speculator was drawn into one unsuccessful scheme after another.

It began in 1791 when he was employed by one of the four Yazoo land companies then negotiating with the Georgia legislature for the purchase of large tracts of territory on the Mississippi. His function was "to arrange, methodize, and manage their business . . . ," for which he was to receive a share equal to one-twentieth of the purchase.[28] After arranging the necessary details, preparing a prospectus and arranging for the sale of stock, Harper was supposed to go to Philadelphia to act as the company's agent and chief salesman. This particular Yazoo company had been organized in 1788 and was headed by Major Thomas Washington, with Alexander Moultrie, William Clay Snipes, and Isaac Hugher as major partners. Some light is shed upon its operations by the documents arising from the impeachment proceedings against Moultrie in 1798 for having, while a state official, misused South Carolina funds, specifically state indents, in connection with the Yazoo land deal.[29]

In 1789 Thomas Washington, acting for the company, had applied to the Georgia state assembly to purchase land claimed by that state on the Mississippi River. Altogether, the four Yazoo companies bought some thirty-five million acres in Mississippi and Alabama for 500,000 dollars, at about one and one-half cents an acre. The transaction was completed in 1795 and finalized by a subsequent legislature in 1796. The Washington-Moultrie company had paid 66,964 dollars, Georgia Rattlesnake money, for its share of the territory, and according to Moultrie's statement at his impeachment John Nicholson of Philadelphia was a party to the transaction.[30] The firm of Morris and Nicholson was indeed involved in this as well as many other southern speculations.

Harper entered the operation after the founding of the company and before the sale was consummated. His task was to go to Philadelphia to sell stock in order to help raise funds to pay for the company's purchase in the Yazoo country. Having spent some time in Philadelphia, Harper must have known that any prospective buyer of any consequence had most likely vacated a city so inhospitable in the summer months, but he went north anyway. It may have been that Harper planned to acquire an office and organize his operation for a fall promotional campaign when Congress returned. At any rate, the promoters in South Carolina decided upon "other means which they thought sufficient," which may have been Moultrie's plan to use state funds. They informed Harper and he returned to South Carolina. Apparently, he had no further dealings with this particular Yazoo company. He did, however, note the significance of the episode in his autobiography, commenting that "this incident initiated me again into land speculation, diverted my mind . . . from my professional pursuits . . ." and gave him a "relish for the northern states which contributed not a little . . . towards inducing me to accept a seat in Congress."[31]

Returning to Charleston, Harper plunged still more deeply into land speculation, purchasing in 1793 some seven thousand acres of land in Charleston District.[32] That same year, he contracted to buy over one thousand seven hundred additional acres in the Charleston District in partnership with James Thompson, Jr.[33] If he had stopped at this point he would still have been in a position to extricate himself from debt. But in 1794 he joined Wade Hampton, an individual who had both greater capital reserves and greater accumen in speculative ventures than himself, in a plan to sell lands to Morris and Nicholson of Philadelphia at what they hoped would be a tremendous profit. Harper later claimed that Hampton had talked him into the plan but it is unlikely that Hampton had to do much persuading. Robert Morris and John Nicholson agreed to buy all the land Hampton and Harper could supply at one shilling per acre, payable in five equal annual installments with interest for the last three years. Although Hampton and Harper were to be paid in Morris and Nicholson's notes, the plan seemed sound enough. Morris and Nicholson were a nationally known firm and their notes were "known to pass current in Philadelphia and Charleston, as cash. . . ."[34]

Hampton formed the company and Harper busily contracted for all land he could get his hands on for sale to the Philadelphians. In his autobiographical sketch, written for his future father-in-law, Harper conservatively estimated the amount of land he transferred to Hampton's company for sale to Morris and

Nicholson at one hundred and fifty thousand acres. [35] The South Carolina records show that, in one instance alone, Colonel Jacob Rumph of Orangeburg gave a power of attorney to Harper to sell a tract of land Rumph owned in the Edisto River area containing two hundred and eighty thousand acres. Harper was to receive a commission on the sale. [36] He purchased for himself 58,587 acres of South Carolina lands in Camden and Cheraw Districts from a John Swepson of Greene County, Georgia, in the fall of 1794, doubtless also for sale to the Pennsylvania buyers. [37] As Harper later recalled, "Hampton assured me that there was no doubt of this land being sold . . ." and very advantageously. [38] Harper stood to make nearly £4,000 from the sale of Colonel Rumph's land alone and he hoped that this along with business debts due him "would place me in a situation to justify my giving up my profession for public life. . . ." [39]

At about the same time, perhaps blown up by the certainty of success and great wealth in the Hampton undertaking, Harper joined in forming a separate company for land purchases in Georgia. Besides himself, this venture included Mordecai Gist of St. Andrews Parish, William Clay Snipes of St. Bartholomews, who appeared earlier as a major partner in the ill-fated Washington-Moultrie Yazoo company, and Peter Belin of Camden County, Georgia. The articles of agreement for the company have survived and outline the plan of operation. The backers proposed to survey and obtain grants for the greatest possible quantity of vacant lands in the state of Georgia in the area of the Satilla River, the Turtle River, the Saint Marys River and the Altamaha. [40] Several of the parties to the agreement had already obtained grants for large tracts, although it is not known whether Harper was one of them.

Snipes and Belin, who knew the country where the company hoped to buy land, were detailed to go there and attend to the surveying and obtaining of the necessary grants. Mordecai Gist and Harper, who apparently knew very little about surveying, were to remain in Charleston "to render any such services and perform such business as may be necessary for perfecting the objects . . ." of the company. [41] Harper's remaining in Charleston was made even more necessary by the fact that he was apparently the only lawyer in the group.

NOTES

1. "Diary of Timothy Ford, 1785-1786," *South Carolina Historical and Genealogical Magazine*, XIII (1912), 145.
2. Ibid., pp. 203-204.
3. Ibid.
4. Ibid., pp. 190-191.
5. Aedanus Burke in House of Representatives, Gales and Seaton, *Annals of Congress*, 1C2S, May 7, 1789, pp. 296-297.
6. Ibid.
7. Ulrich B. Phillips, "South Carolina Federalist Correspondence," *American Historical Review*, XV (1909), 529-543.
8. David Duncan Wallace, *South Carolina: A Short History, 1520-1948* (Columbia: University of South Carolina Press, 1961), p. 364.
9. John H. Wolfe, *Jeffersonian Democracy in South Carolina* (Chapel Hill: University of North Carolina Press, 1940), p. 5.
10. Ibid., pp. 5-7.
11. Wallace, pp. 356-360.
12. Ibid.
13. Wolfe, p. 37.
14. Ibid.
15. Autobiography, p. 3.
16. Ibid.
17. Elizabeth Hyde to Charles Carroll Harper, April 30, 1825, Harper-Pennington Papers, III.
18. Wallace, pp. 409-410.
19. Partial letter anonymous to Charles Carroll Harper, 1825. The friend referred to is the Rev. Mr. Springer of Charleston, Harper-Pennington Papers, III.
20. James F. Jameson (ed.), "The Diary of Edward Hooker, 1805-1808," *Annual Report of the American Historical Association for 1896* (Washington: The Association, 1897), p. 884.
21. Ibid.
22. Ibid.
23. Autobiography, p. 3.
24. Diana Harper to RGH, February 10, 1788, Harper-Pennington Papers.
25. South Carolina Miscellaneous Records DDD, pp. 543-544, January 1785. South Carolina State Archives Department, Columbia.
26. Charleston County Land Index, II (1764-1800), L.H. 3724, 179. South Carolina State Archives Department, Columbia.
27. Ibid., XXVII, 340, and XXXVI, 177. Also, State Records, XXIX, 242.

28. Autobiography, pp. 3-4.
29. Legislative Papers Folder, "Impeachment—Moultrie Case." South Carolina State Archives, Columbia.
30. "Thomas Washington Estate," Inventories B-1783-97, pp. 526-527. South Carolina State Archives, Columbia.
31. Autobiography, p. 4.
32. Charleston Land Grants Index, September 2, 1793, pp. 58-65.
33. South Carolina State Records, XXX, 114, 128.
34. Autobiography, p. 4.
35. Ibid.
36. South Carolina Miscellaneous Records, A, 250-251, August 22, 1794.
37. Ibid., pp. 262-266, November 25, 1794.
38. Autobiography, p. 5.
39. Ibid.
40. South Carolina Miscellaneous Records, CCC, 105-107. While the territory of the Satilla, the Turtle and Altamaha rivers was within the general Yazoo country claim, this was not one of the major Yazoo land companies and the writer could find no connection between it and the Yazoo fraud.
41. Ibid.

3
Speculator Turned Politician

With the certain view that his speculative undertakings would
at least make him financially secure, Robert Goodloe Harper
decided that he should now enter politics and actively seek
office. Once again, in the summer of 1794, he journeyed across
the state to the District of Ninety Six. There he offered himself
as a candidate for a seat in Congress in the fall general election.
This procedure was perfectly legal and acceptable, for South
Carolina law provided that a man might offer himself for office
in any district where he owned property and Harper had owned
land, clear of debt, in Ninety Six for several years. This time,
however, he planned to settle permanently in the district. He
must have been extremely confident about his success in the fall
election, for he purchased, on credit, a plantation valued at some
three thousand five hundred dollars and announced that he
planned to live on it and work it. After his election Harper
returned to Charleston to practice law until it was time to take
his seat in Congress in the fall of 1795. However, he could not
resist the temptation of yet another speculation and soon after
his return to Charleston he became involved with a Mr. Price of
that city in a plan to purchase large quantities of South Carolina
and Georgia lands which Harper was to sell in Philadelphia.[1]

At this point the narrative reaches one of the most confusing
aspects of his South Carolina career, his dual election to Congress
in 1794. Indeed, the details of the election are so fuzzy that both
the *Dictionary of American Biography* and the *Biographical
Directory of Congress* are inaccurate in their handling of this
phase of his career. The impossibility of separating his speculative
activities from his initial entry into politics, coupled with the
unusual South Carolina electoral laws, and the fact that Harper
seemed to be forever moving around the state make confusion
inevitable. An investigation of all the relevant information concerning Harper in this period, however, solves the mystery of the
dual election.

The fact is that Harper sought the two seats in Congress
independently of one another. The possibility of running for a

second seat did not occur to him until after the first, representing
Ninety Six District, was assured. After returning to Charleston
and entering into the land scheme with Mr. Price, the possibility
of the second congressional seat arose. Harper said later that he
was "induced" by Mr. Price to stand for the seat representing
Orangeburg District which had been left vacant by the death of
the former congressman, Alexander Gillon. Gillon's term would
expire at the end of the session then convened in Philadelphia
and before Harper was to take his seat representing Ninety Six. [2]
He would thus go to Philadelphia earlier than he had planned, to
serve out the remainder of Gillon's term and, it may be suggested, attempt to sell as much of the land he and Price had
purchased as possible.

The problem was that all of his elaborate plans for a political
career, an independent financial position, and his plantation in
Ninety Six depended, to a considerable extent, on the money
owed him by Wade Hampton. "I then proceeded on my jour-
ney," Harper wrote, "not doubting, that in the course of the
following Winter or Spring, I should get my notes out of Hampton's hands." [3] Even though the notes in which Hampton was to
pay Harper were depreciating at a rapid rate Harper was confident that together with the lands he held clear of debt, he would
have assets to meet all his engagements. Hampton was also in
Philadelphia the winter of 1794, and all that winter and spring
Harper attempted unsuccessfully to get Hampton to surrender
the notes. Harper was not satisfied with either Hampton's conduct or reasons for not giving up the notes but lamented that
since there was no possibility of bringing a suit against Hampton,
he was forced to submit.

Meanwhile, as so often happened to the luckless speculator
who had overextended himself, Harper's debts began coming due.
His plantation and much of his lands had all been purchased on
credit and time was fast running out. As the possibility of
collecting from Hampton grew more hopeless, Harper began
grasping at straws. Using the South Carolina lands purchased
together with Price as security, he invested 4,500 dollars in a
cargo of wine to Charleston which yielded only 1,400 dollars and
he sank still deeper into debt. Hampton never delivered the notes
due Harper, who later claimed that he had proof that as early as
the winter of 1794 Hampton had paid them out "in those
purchases of Georgia lands, out of which has arisen the greater
part of whatever fortune he possesses." [4]

So ended Harper's career as a western land speculator. The
results of his fling at speculation are impressive considering his
start with almost nothing. Along the way Harper managed to
contract considerable debts. To the Philadelphia firm of Nicklin
and Griffith he was indebted for 9,000 dollars. To those people
who had contracted for the first and second Georgia purchases he
recognized debts of some 2,200 dollars and to two friends for
money loaned to him 2,050 dollars. Altogether, he stood indebted for some 13,450 dollars. His assets were of small help to
him and he had to pledge the eighty thousand acres of South
Carolina lands for the Nicklin and Griffith debt.[5] These debts
would saddle him for years to come. They provided the major
obstacle to his marriage to Charles Carroll of Carrollton's daughter in 1800. As late as 1801 he was still nearly 14,000 dollars in
debt. Some men, the truly fortunate, emerged from the speculative wars wealthy, respected, and victorious. Most left the field as
Harper did—on his shield.

Harper's abysmal failure as a land speculator is redeemed,
however, by his rise to prominence in South Carolina politics. In
light of the fact that less than ten years after he first stood on the
Charleston dock as an impoverished nonentity Robert Goodloe
Harper represented his adopted state in the Congress of the
United States, the failures in land speculation do not seem quite
as important. After Harper was unsuccessful in his first period of
residence in Ninety Six he had returned to the low country
resolved to seek his fortune in Charleston. As he himself had
explained later, his career should be dated from his return to the
coast, which the extant Charleston records indicate was in 1791.
One year later Harper had made enough of an impression upon
the controlling interests in Charleston to wangle an appointment
as a quorum justice for that district.[6] Launched in a small way
on a political career, he might possibly have worked his way up
into the permanent class of public officials in Charleston. However, this was a long and laborious process and long suffering
patience was not one of this aspiring politician's virtues. When
major political success did come to him it would be via another
and more rapid route.

Before Harper's political career can be pursued even one step
further, one of the most tangled and confusing controversies
surrounding the man must be cleared up as nearly as is possible.
The usual interpretation of the matter in question reads something to the following effect. Prior to his election to Congress in

1794, it is said, Harper was an enthusiastic republican and quite radical in his pro-French sympathies, vice-president of the Jacobin Club in Charleston, and a familiar of the French consul.[7] The story was given a novel twist when he was elected to Congress in 1794, as a "Republican," and upon arrival in Philadelphia he suddenly turned his coat to become an arch Federalist. This interpretation is far too simple. It presupposes party development in South Carolina far more sophisticated than actually was the case, and contains equal proportions of truth and error.

French partisanship was powerful and widespread in Charleston in the early 1790s. Citizen Genêt, quite understandably, chose to land there because of the enthusiastic reception which could be expected from the city's residents. One very reliable observer characterized 1794 as a year "when Sansculottes and their principles had great ascendency in Charleston—when the tri-colored cockade of France was the great badge of honour, and *Ca'ira* and the Marseillaise hymn the most popular airs—and 'Vive la république Française' the universal shout."[8] The French cause remained popular there long after Genêt had overplayed his hand. South Carolina's foremost historian David Duncan Wallace informs us just how potent was the impact of the French Revolution upon the down country city. "The zeal for France," stimulated by British depredations of American commerce and the profits in the French West Indian trade, "survived the fall of Genêt and the brutalities of the Terror."[9]

The rosters of Charleston's two Jacobin clubs were sprinkled with old and respected South Carolina names. In 1793 a two-day celebration was held to honor the French National Assembly and a great many distinguished citizens including the governor and members of the state judiciary paraded through the city streets proudly wearing the tri-color and marching in the company of French privateersmen. When the great reaction against revolutionary France and "Liberty, Equality and Fraternity" finally came, it was prompted by the disquieting news from the French West Indies and in particular from Haiti.[10] The refugees from Toussaint L'Overture's black revolution dealt the Francophile forces in Charleston an irreparable blow.

The question of Harper's association with Charleston republicanism and the truth or falsity of the "Jacobin Harper" image conveyed in the older interpretation of the man's career is more difficult to answer. The most complete assessment of just what Harper's relationship to the Francophile element in Charleston was comes from the *Annals of Congress* in the form of Harper's own explanation of his earlier actions. In the early months of 1798 amidst the fiercely partisan debates in the House of Representatives, William Branch Giles, the arch Republican from Virginia, hurled the "Jacobin Club charge" and the allegations concerning his earlier radicalism at Harper in an attempt to demonstrate his inconsistency of conduct and principle. The South Carolinian's defense of himself offers the only reasonable explanation to this particular Harperian riddle.

As for his alleged membership in the Jacobin Club, that was just "one of those falsehoods of party, which though known to be unfounded is still repeated." ¹¹ He readily admitted that as a young Charleston lawyer in need of both acquaintances and business he had joined a "Patriotic Society" and in the company of seven or eight other young lawyers had attended one or two meetings. But finding the society composed "of persons from whose society much improvement could not be expected they never went afterwards; and so anti-Jacobin was their conduct considered, that they merited and received expulsion from the society." ¹² He also admitted sympathizing with the French Revolution in its early stages, apparently not nearly as strongly as many other Charlestonians, but said that he soon came to a change of opinion. He came, he said, to realize that the principal actors were "a set of worthless scoundrels and mad-headed enthusiasts, who in endeavoring to reduce their fallacious schemes to practice, have introduced more calamities into the world than ages of good government will be able to cure." ¹³

Harper the "Jacobin" never existed in anything more than an early and fleeting sympathy with the principles of the French Revolution until it became apparent that it was not just another revolt in the American style. Perhaps his attachment to the revolution might have been stronger and more enduring if he had been more closely connected, as many in Charleston were, with the West Indian trade rather than western lands. Harper's explanation is of course debatable in light of the fact that congressmen occasionally stray from the path of veracity in the heat of debate.

Yet, this was an age in which men followed their representative's actions because they actually believed that he was their representative to the Congress of the United States. Harper, knowing that his South Carolina audience would read what he said in debate, would have been foolish to falsify his earlier relationship to Charleston republicanism. There were many Charlestonians who could quite easily have trapped him in a falsehood, yet no one came forth to expose the congressman's distortion of the facts. William Branch Giles to the contrary, Robert Goodloe Harper was not and had never been a Jacobin. In the middle nineties he led the up-country struggle to reapportion the eastern district-dominated legislature but this was scarcely a movement of the downtrodden and exploited small farmers against the rice-country aristocrats, and its leadership was definitely not of the arm-waving, fist-pounding demagogic variety.

In the early 1790s the movement to reapportion the state legislature in line with the westward shift in population to the middle and up-country came to life, and Harper, having moved once again to Ninety Six, attached his political future to the struggle, gambling that it would launch his political career. The movement failed in 1794 but it lasted long enough for Harper to ride the crest into political prominence. By the time the dust settled, with reapportionment having been successfully postponed by the eastern districts, Robert Goodloe Harper sat in the national House of Representatives in Philadelphia, where he remained until 1801.

What apparently sparked the movement for reapportionment was the first federal census of 1790. Once the statistics were collected their analysis suggested startling conclusions to the up-country people. The upper division contained four times the white population of the coastal region but held a minority of seats in the state legislature. The up-country reaction was the formation of the Representative Reform Association under the leadership of Wade Hampton, Ephraim Ramsay, Abraham Blanding, John Kershaw and Robert Goodloe Harper, with the stated intention of changing the basis of representation established by the Constitution of 1790. [14] This constitution, as David Duncan Wallace put it, had "closed the period of experimentation, and was mainly the work of the conservative classes, definitely protecting property and institutions against the 'mob'." [15]

There was, however, more to the struggle than Professor Wallace suggests. Had the Constitution of 1790 been merely a conservative counterrevolution instead of the compromise it was, the reapportionment movement of 1794 might indeed have been more of a republican uprising than it was. The Constitution of 1790 was instead a compromise in which the down-country made definite concessions to the more egalitarian elements to the

westward. One student of Jeffersonian democracy in South Carolina states that "although democrats and the inhabitants of the
up-country must have found the Constitution of 1790 disap-
pointing, the patient ones knew that something had been
gained."[16]

Religious qualifications for voting, Protestant qualification for
office holding and the control of elections by church wardens
were done away with. Primogeniture was abolished. The prospective voter found that he could substitute a three shilling tax for
the fifty-acre freehold qualification.

The reduction of property qualifications for office holding was
a definite concession by the down-country aristocracy. For
example, the qualification for the governorship was lowered from
£10,000 to £1,500, and that of a state senator from £2,000 to
£500. For the resident representative the requirements were
made more flexible. He had to be in possession of a settled
freehold estate of five hundred acres and ten Negroes or a real
estate valued at £150 sterling clear of debt.

However, despite these concessions the Constitution clearly
weighted representation in the state legislature in favor of the
low-country districts. The upper division found itself outvoted
seventy to fifty-four in the House and twenty to seventeen in the
Senate.

Harper established his claim to prominence in the movement
with his *Address to the People of South Carolina—by the General
Committee of the Representative Reform Association at Columbia.* Styling himself "Appius," Harper provided the most theoretical and forceful presentation of the up-country position. The
heart of his argument was that government, as the reformers
understood it, involved a compact which bestowed both rights
and responsibilities upon all concerned. In this compact individuals had given up certain rights and accepted the principle of
majority rule. At the same time, the compact granted political
equality to all citizens and this entailed representation according
to population.

Harper's argument made it quite clear that the back country
had not thus far been badly treated by the dominant down
country but that he feared future abuse. What really disturbed
the reformers was the fear, in the modern parlance, of "creeping
aristocracy."

The counterargument of the coastal region that property as
well as numbers should be represented was dismissed by Harper

as invalid on the ground that society and personal rights had existed long before property rights. The latter would exercise sufficient influence without being granted additional power in the apportionment of delegates to the state assembly. Harper argued that property ought only to be represented in one house of the bicameral legislature and that the lower house ought always be reserved to the people.

Harper and the reformers dismissed the argument that the wealthy section paid more taxes and thus deserved more representation. The reformers replied that if the wealthy paid more taxes they also received more benefit from the government. Moreover, the census of 1790 revealed a further inequity in representation, for a great deal of property owned by individuals in the low country actually lay in the up-country. On the basis of both property and population the upper region should have five representatives to every three for the low country.

The reapportioners also pointed out the even distribution of wealth in their region as contrasted with the older section; they worried lest inequality of wealth should someday result in inequality of condition. They proposed to end the sectional division in the state before the situation worsened.[17]

The low country spokesmen were quick to rise to the defense of the status quo. "Americanus, " a Charleston lawyer, Timothy Ford, in a series of newspaper articles later published as *The Constitutionalist*, publicly attacked the reform movement. "Americanus" recalled that before the Revolution when the strangers began moving into the back country, the coastal residents had welcomed them, allowing them natural rights but, of necessity, not political privileges. Had the strangers made known their doctrines of majority rule as expressed by "Appius, " the low country would have regarded every new settler "as a reinforcement to an internal enemy."[18] "Americanus" and other writers justified the existing system as fundamentally necessary to protect the peculiar interests of the low country.

Somewhat later Henry William DeSaussure, one of the most prominent of the coastal residents, called attention to the fact that no southern state had yet adopted proportional representation based on population. The real danger in granting the up-country the political control it demanded, he postulated, was that the lower region would then most certainly seek to become a separate state and the argument could result in civil war.[19] DeSaussure denied that equality was the natural condition of

man. If this were admitted, he said, the whites would be forced
to "instantly free the unfortunate slaves," and ruin both
races.[20]

The association of reapportionment with abolitionism was
probably the most devastating argument leveled at the reformers.
Timothy Ford, in an attempt to attack Harper's argument on a
somewhat higher level, concentrated on refuting the theory of an
original state of nature. "The rights of property as well as those
of life and liberty, are the gifts of nature. The end of civil society
is to guard them by stronger sanctions, the moral sense being too
weak and too unequal amongst men for that purpose."[21]

The reapportionment leaders may have taken the wrong course
when they attempted to present a slightly abstract argument
which frightened low-country leadership. In any case, the reapportionment movement was doomed from its inception by the
fact that, as in similar present-day situations, the reformers had
to appeal to a legislature dominated by the smaller section to
reapportion itself, a prospect which, barring divine intervention,
was highly unlikely.

It was at this point that Robert Goodloe Harper was elected to
both the state legislature and to two separate seats in the national
House of Representatives in that confusing multiple election. He
is supposed to have served several years in the state legislature
prior to being elected to Congress, specifically, from 1790 to
1794. However, in reality Harper only served two months in the
fall of 1794.

To recap his political progress again is to be reminded that
Harper was elected congressman from the Ninety Six Congressional District on October 13 and 14, 1794, for a term to begin
in March of 1795. On November 10 and 11 he was elected to
Congress from the combined districts of Beaufort and Orangeburg to fill out the term of the late Alexander Gillon. His
election to the state legislature from Spartanburg District occurred in the October 13 and 14 election.[22] The new state
legislator was slow in arriving in Columbia, not taking his oath in
the lower house until December 2, 1794.[23]

He served not quite two months and his career as a state
legislator was uneventful. On December 3, 1794, he was appointed to a "Committee to Review the Judiciary System of the
State." This was apparently his only major committee
appointment. [24] Several days later, he served on a committee to
"Enquire on what terms they can get the public Business printed

for."[25]   His voting record consists of voting nay on two motions
to raise the salary of the governor and aye to a motion to make
the chief justice's salary £600 per annum.[26]

His brief career in the lower house came to a close when the
move for reapportionment was handily defeated by the low
country delegates. The reapportionment petitions were presented
to the legislature on December 10, 1794, "stating to the House
the great Inequality of the Representation in the Legislature. . . ." [27] After some debate, the petitions were tabled until
the following morning. The next day, in a tie vote to refer the
petitions to a committee of the whole house, Harper voted nay
but the Speaker voted in the affirmative and the matter was again
postponed. The struggle was really over before it began. The
down-country had the votes. The committee of the whole house,
the following day, December 12,

> Resolved, that, . . . it is inexpedient to grant the prayer of the Petitions
> in as much as the Representation established by the present constitu-
> tion was founded in a Spirit of Compromise . . . of interests between
> the different parts of the state; and has been proved by Experience well
> calculated to preserve the Tranquility and advance the prosperity
> thereof.[28]

The resolution passed fifty-eight to fifty-three on a strictly sectional vote.

Meanwhile, sixteen senators and fifty-six representatives had
drafted another message to the people of the coastal region in
behalf of reapportionment. This address was undoubtedly the
least theoretical and most practical statement of the up-country
case yet delivered. They bitterly resented the charges that the
up-country merely wanted to seize control in order to avoid its
fair share of the tax burden. They denied that they had in any
way countenanced violence of any kind or had ever even been
disorderly. They felt themselves to be quite patient and that they
had clearly demonstrated that they cared for order as much as
anyone. If such had not been the case, they said, they might have
withdrawn from the legislature and established a rival government in the state.

There were three distinct sections of the state, their argument
ran, the upper, lower and middle and it was clear that in any new
arrangement the middle section would hold the balance between
the two more clearly distinct regions. Their proposals were designed to insure that natural balance, with the up-country having

fifty-nine representatives, the low country still retaining its sixty-eight, and the middle country possessing the balance with thirty-eight. This, the reapportioners said, would protect the interests of the older section, particularly concerning new amendments to the constitution, and would be more equitable to the up-country districts.

The most obvious reference to their opponent's charge that they were tainted by emancipation sentiment appeared in the latter part of the address and received great emphasis as the most serious charge hurled at them. This group of erstwhile reformers answered the charge in the only way they could, by parading themselves as even more staunch defenders of the institution of slavery than their attackers. They were, they said, already slaveowners and any up-country representative so bold as to question slavery stood likely to encounter tar and feathers from his constituents when he got home. The up-country had nothing to gain and a great deal to lose by emancipation. As taxpayers they were not eager to make up for the loss of revenue from the tax on slaves nor did they wish to raise taxes in other areas. In addition, if any threat to the institution did someday arise in the up-country, the balance provided by the middle section would certainly defeat it.[29]

The address ended with the customary plea for unity and the end to division in the state.

> Be just on your part; be candid and wise. . . . We shall then accept as a boon what we might claim as a right, and make you a rich return in confidence and attachment; so shall the wounds of our country be healed, the source of our differences forever dried up, and our public prosperity and happiness be fixed on a basis broad as our soil and firm as the everlasting foundations of truth and justice.[30]

Their efforts were to no avail. Petitions which continued to arrive in Columbia were ignored by the lower house of the legislature. Another vote on reapportionment was forced in 1796 but the result was another failure. Not until 1808 was a settlement pushed through the recalcitrant assembly and this "Great Compromise of 1808" occurred long after Robert Goodloe Harper left South Carolina.

The great reform movement stalled temporarily but as far as the young lawyer was concerned it had served its purpose. Harper took leave of the sectional squabbles in the Carolina legislature and departed to take his seat in Congress, where larger problems and grander things awaited him.

For all practical purposes, Robert Goodloe Harper was never to return to South Carolina.

NOTES

1. Autobiography, p. 5.
2. Ibid.
3. Ibid., pp. 5—6.
4. Ibid., p. 6.
5. Ibid., p. 7.
6. South Carolina Session Laws, 1791-1806, December 21, 1792, p. 74. The quorum justice present in several of the southern states was a carry-over from the colonial period. They were among the justices of the peace appointed for Charleston District. The presence of a minimum number of them was required for any meeting of the justices to be official.
7. J. G. deR. Hamilton, "Robert Goodloe Harper," *Dictionary of American Biography* (New York: Scribner's Sons, 1928-1932), VIII, 285-286.
8. Charles Fraser, *Reminiscences of Charleston*, 1785-1854 (Charleston: John Russel, 1854), pp. 35-36.
9. Wallace, p. 346. That there were economic undercurrents to Charleston's republicanism seems beyond any doubt. To again quote Professor Wallace, "Upon this revelry of republican enthusiasm and quick riches fell the shadow of Jay's treaty threatening the lucrative commerce with France and offending the South by denying it the British West Indian trade and forbidding its exporting cotton—clauses, which however, the Senate deleted." Ibid.
10. Ibid., and Phillips, p. 734.
11. *Annals of Congress*, 5C2S, March 29, 1798, pp. 1354-1355.
12. Ibid.
13. Ibid.
14. Wallace, pp. 354-360.
15. Ibid., p. 344.
16. Wolfe, pp. 46-47.
17. RGH *An Address to the People of South Carolina—By the General Committee of the Representative Reform Association at Columbia.* Columbia: 1794.

18. Wallace, pp. 356-360.
19. Ibid.
20. Wolfe, pp. 51-52.
21. Ibid.
22. Miscellaneous Records, Book A, pp. 266-267. South Carolina Archives. The election returns are quite spotty and incomplete.
23. Journal of South Carolina House of Representatives, pp. 44-45. South Carolina Archives.
24. Ibid., p. 58, December 3, 1794.
25. Ibid., p. 88, December 5, 1794.
26. Ibid., pp. 59, 62, 166.
27. Ibid., pp. 119-120, December 10, 1794.
28. Ibid., pp. 145-147, December 11, 1794. The vote was taken the next day.
29. *An Address of the Senators and Representatives of the Upper Division to the People of South Carolina* quoted in Wolfe, pp. 52-53.
30. The address was published in the Charleston *Columbian Herald*, October 29, 1795. RGH was responsible in part at least for the composition of this attempt to explain the position of the reapportioners to the people of the coastal districts.

4

First Days in Congress: Another View

South Carolina's newest contribution to the lower house of the American Congress took his seat in February of 1795 during the final session of the Third Congress. Harper was serving out the unexpired term of the late Alexander Gillon until the term to which he had been elected would begin with the convening of the Fourth Congress.

Since apparently the only soul he knew in Philadelphia was his ex-business associate Wade Hampton, Harper sought credentials, or at least letters of introduction, to his future political colleagues and to capital society. He was successful with at least one person, for on June 12, 1795, Pierce Butler, eminently respectable in Republican circles and an important United States Senator, wrote a letter to James Madison introducing and recommending the young congressman.

Butler began by informing Madison that Harper had entreated so earnestly for the introduction that he had been unable to refuse him. He admitted that he knew Harper only slightly but that he appeared to be ambitious, polite and generous in feelings.

However, Butler cautioned, he seemed to be a fellow to whom one ought not to bare one's political soul on short acquaintance. And finally, in his most telling and accurate observation, the perceptive Mr. Butler noted that the new congressman seemed "liable to impressions, and apt to be hurried away by the feelings of the moment." [1] Not too much later Butler was apologizing to Madison for ever having introduced, let alone recommended a young man who was accused, at the time and throughout his political career, of having turned his political coat.

Secondary political figures such as Harper have not aroused the historical curiosity they deserve. This is particularly true in the decade of the 1790s when the giants of the political arena overshadow the lesser lights whose careers and contributions are chronicled in terms of hearsay, cliché, and half-truths which few deem important enough to warrant examination. Harper thus

40

appears to the Jeffersonian inclined historian as the classic proto-
type of opportunistic, militant, and nativistic Federalism.

His sins were compounded by the fact that he was elected as a
staunch Republican and then almost immediately upon his arrival
in Congress became an equally devout Federalist. Contemporary
foes also made much of the charge that Harper had also undergone a miraculous transformation from ardent Francophile and
supporter of the French Revolution to Federalist blackguard who
was more monarchic in sympathy than the British minister. This
transformation too has been injudiciously accepted by later historians. Harper denied this interpretation of his conduct, but he
had as little success with his opposing colleagues as he has had
with later critics.

The classic statement of this transformation myth is to be
found in the *Dictionary of American Biography* article on
Harper.

> Up to the time of his election [1794] Harper had been an enthusiastic
> Republican. Madison, writing to Jefferson of his pleasure at his elec-
> tion, described him as "sound, able and eloquent." He had been radical
> in his pro-French sympathies and was Vice President of the Jacobin
> Club of Charleston, and in 1793 had almost haunted the French
> Consulate.

Once in Philadelphia, the article continues, Harper found the
great and powerful on the other side and began to shift his
position until he came full circle in displaying anti-French, pro-
British feelings. [2]

This view of Harper appears cogent and likely, considering the
state of American political flux in the early 1790s, until it is
subjected to close examination. When this is done it becomes
apparent that the origin of the explanation rests not on fact but
on the desperate straits in which the friends of France found
themselves in the wake of the XYZ disclosures when it became
necessary to counter by any means the Federalist demands for
retaliation against the French Republic.

William Branch Giles, the fiery Virginia Republican, was most
guilty of hurling this "turncoat" charge at Harper and historians
have too often accepted Giles' word on the matter. In the spring
of 1798, Harper, writhing under Giles' accusations that he had
forgotten his earlier commitment to the "rights of man," rose in
the House to answer once and for all the charge of apostasy. The

South Carolinian said that he had never been interested in the "rights of man," as the gentleman from Virginia understood the term, taking for granted that Giles meant sympathy for the French Revolution. He had, he stated, attended a meeting or two of a patriotic organization in Charleston, but had never in any way been connected with the Jacobin Club. At first he had considered the leaders of the revolution as high-minded men but had long since recognized his mistake and now looked on the entire movement as tragic in the extreme. "Charges concerning his earlier affiliation with radical groups were merely political propaganda which were known to be false but were repeated for party purposes." [3]

Republicans at that time, and most historians since, shrugged their shoulders and refused this obviously weak attempt at parrying such a sure and deadly thrust from the Virginian. Ulrich B. Phillips expressed this unquestioning acceptance of the charge when he declared that in some cases, "that of Robert Goodloe Harper, for example, the reaction [to Genêt] was so strong as to carry young men all the way from rampant democracy to fast conservatism and steady membership in the Federalist party." [4]

This explanation assumes, first of all, that Harper was a rabid defender of the French Revolution from its inception and that he later soured. The interpretation also accepts the notion that the reapportionment movement in South Carolina had been radical in goals and leadership; that Harper was a Jeffersonian Republican when he arrived in Philadelphia in 1795 and that he quickly "sold out" to the friends of the administration. Also suggested, of course, is that after deserting, Harper went on to become the "McCarthy of his age." [5] A recent account of the diplomacy of the Federalist Era relegates Harper to a footnote thus: "Robert Goodloe Harper is a good example of a pro-French Revolution politician whose views changed with the progress of the Revolution so that he became a vigorous anti-French Revolution Federalist." [6]

The evidence to support the older interpretation of Harper's attitudes toward the French Revolution is completely lacking. Harper's career in South Carolina has left not a single shred of evidence to confirm such a belief. Of even greater importance is Harper's denial on the floor of the House of the alleged association with the Charleston Jacobin Club. Harper offered a perfect opportunity in this instance, for anyone who cared, to disprove the congressman's claim and embarrass him publicly. This was an age when the proceedings in Philadelphia were avidly followed by constituents at home and if Harper was falsifying the record there would have been numerous individuals in Charleston who could have called him to account. Letters would have undoubtedly been sent off to one of the several South Carolina congressmen of Giles' persuasion supplying them with ammunition for use against the congressman from Ninety Six. It would seem that this would especially be the case if Harper had in truth also deserted the Republicans. Yet, there is not a single instance of any such missive flying to Philadelphia and despite the fact that Giles often castigated Harper upon the same grounds he never introduced new evidence to support the charge.

Indeed, it might be suggested that Harper, along with others of the Federalist persuasion, had not been nearly as friendly toward the French Revolution in its early stages as even they sometimes asserted. To this point Harper's career had scarcely touched international events but had revolved instead around purely local affairs. Harper may have indeed had an early flirtation with the revolution in France but the evidence that survives suggests that the romance was brief and never very ardent.

In the second instance, Harper is accused of having risen by way of a democratic movement to wrest control of the South Carolina Legislature away from the down-country planters in the early 1790s, and that having reached Philadelphia the first term congressman broke all ties with this popular movement and became a Federalist of the New England variety. As has been previously suggested, the reapportionment struggle in South Carolina was not by any stretch of the imagination Bacon's Rebellion reenacted. The aims of the reapportioners were really quite moderate and the leadership of the movement anything but radically democratic. [7] Indeed, the effort died a relatively quiet death in the legislature. Harper represented the more populous up-country in Congress but this is not to say that he arrived there by championing the cause of an irate, small farm, back-country constituency against the down-country great planters. As early as January 1793, he had received the recognition and support of some of the better sort of people. Alexander Gillon wrote to Wade Hampton "that great efforts have been and are still being made for Mr. Harper—and by some Men of influence." [8]

The third aspect of the Republican indictment, the charge that Harper ignored the political persuasion of those who had elected him, turned his coat and joined the Federalist camp is also open to review and serious revision. It seems doubtful that the labels Federalist and Republican would have meant very much in South Carolina politics in 1794, even more doubtful that these labels would have been closely analogous to the political divisions in the national congress. Harper had reached the House via a purely local issue and his statement that his "political connections and predilictions, as far as I had formed any before I went to Congress, were all on the popular side" was probably accurate. [9] Beyond that he could not be labeled. As Harper himself explained the state of South Carolina political development:

> The political parties, indeed, which then divided Congress . . . were hardly known in South Carolina, and not at all felt there, when I was first elected. But parties did exist in the State, which although confined to State objects, partook somewhat of the same character with those in Congress. [10]

He felt that he came to Congress unpledged, although he knew that his choice of "party" would have to be explained to his constituents and that the "popular side" would be easier for them to accept. [11]

He chose to align himself with the friends of the administration rather than with its critics, but this certainly, under these circumstances, did not amount to turning one's political coat. It seems, according to the prevailing interpretation, that the choice was motivated by Harper's ambition to advance himself but this could scarcely have been the case in 1794. Harper took his seat when the House was dominated by a Republican majority, the only such session during the Federalist period. Ambition, the fact that he represented the up country and the fact that he had been opposed by many of those who would soon find their way into the Federalist ranks in South Carolina, should have impelled him toward the Republican side. This did not occur and from the start he was voting with the Federalists.

The conclusions are obvious. If Harper had in truth changed sides he probably would have been defeated in 1796, but he won reelection then and again in 1798, from the Ninety Six District. There was more Federalist political strength in the up-country than many recent students of Federalism at the national level have suspected. The state and local scholars have begun to doubt the older interpretation. For example, a recent South Carolina historian has suggested that there was indeed "a sizable covey of Federalists in Ninety Six . . . by this time." [12] At any rate Harper found enough Federalist support in 1796 and again in the election of 1798 to justify his choice of that party. His career in Congress illustrates the error in explaining South Carolina politics during this decade in the simple positing of down-country Federalists versus up country Republicans. [13] It would also seem that if this much of the generally accepted interpretation of Robert Goodloe Harper's role in the events of this period is questionable, then the entirety of the explanation warrants review.

NOTES

1. Wolfe, pp. 87-88, quoting from the papers of James Madison, January 23, and June 12, 1795.
2. Hamilton, VIII, 285-286.
3. *Annals of Congress*, 5C2S, April 2, 3, 1798, pp. 1371-1376.
4. Phillips, p. 733.
5. David H. Fischer, *Revolution of American Conservatism* (New York: Harper and Row, 1965), p. 37.
6. Alexander De Conde, *Entangling Alliance: Politics and Diplomacy under George Washington* (Durham: Duke University Press, 1958), p. 181 fn.
7. This group included Charles Pinckney, Pierce Butler, Thomas Sumter, and Wade Hampton, hardly gentlemen ready or willing to lead the masses against their betters. Phillips, p. 735.
8. Charles E. Cauthen, *Family Letters of the Three Wade Hamptons, 1782-1901* (Columbia: University of South Carolina Press, 1953), p. 4.
9. RGH, letter to the *National Gazette* (Philadelphia), December 14, 1824.
10. Ibid.
11. Ibid.
12. George C. Rogers, Jr., *The Evolution of a Federalist, William Loughton Smith of Charleston*, 1758-1812 (Columbia: University of South Carolina Press, 1962), p. 285.
13. John C. Miller, *The Federalist Era, 1789-1801* (New York: Harper and Row, 1960), p. 125 offers the best example. "The Western part of the state was strongly Republican; only in Charleston and the lowland planting areas did Federalism hold its ground. Unhappily for the Federalists, the continuance of their rule depended upon maintaining a system of representation which discriminated against the western counties." As noted in Chapter III, this system of representation did continue to exist until well into the next century.

5

Harper and the West

The results of John Jay's mission had not yet reached American shores when Harper assumed his duties in February of 1795. The lame duck representative was allowed several months to acclimate and establish himself before the explosive news from England initiated one of the fiercest and most significant foreign policy debates in the nation's history. Had Harper arrived green in the midst of the Jay paroxysm, he would not have been quite so disposed to enter the contest as energetically as he did. His reputation was made in those encounters with William Branch Giles and the Pennsylvanians in late 1795 and early 1796. The fact that he appeared before the storm broke and had ample time to test himself on less important matters was quite significant, insofar as Harper's career was concerned. The questions with which he interested himself in those first few months are indicative of the state of his political development to that point.

He came as a southerner and a Federalist with an interest in the West and western development so often found in gentlemen from that region. Indeed, he was always to be considerably more interested in the very section of the United States most Federalists were either to neglect or write off as a liability. This interest in the West and its development represents one of the fundamental differences between Federalists and southern Federalists. The early months of 1795 gave Harper an opportunity to indulge that interest which manifested itself in advocating coastal and interior surveys, government purchase of reserve timber lands in the Southwest, strengthening of the western military establishment, the closer scrutiny of the organization of western trade and government, and among other things, offering himself as something of an authority on Indian affairs. '

When Harper arrived, the House was debating the western defense establishment, and his very first speech dealt with the problem of the western tribes. He told the House that he had a fair knowledge of the subject as a lifelong resident of the region. Indian troubles, he went on, arose generally from theft, either Indian from whites or vice versa, with the result being murder on both sides. He pointed out the difficulty of protecting the Indian's property as long as the frontiersmen universally believed that the red man was always guilty. Congressman Harper concluded by saying that he had a great respect for these white westerners, whom he represented, but that along with the great numbers of "worthy people among them, [there were] . . . likewise many others of a very different kind." [2] This is not to say that the Indians had found a defender but rather that Harper did not think it possible to protect them. That same day, he voted against a Senate Act entitled "An Act to Prevent depredations on the Indians South of the River Ohio." [3] Throughout his career in the House, Harper retained this attachment to the needs of his increasingly western-oriented constituents, the point being that this southern Federalist's perspective contrasted sharply with that of his northern brethren.

Harper's close association with the Yazoo Companies would not have been known to very many, if any, of his colleagues, but his enthusiastic interest in the southwestern frontier was readily apparent to all. He devoted a great deal of time and energy to the several proposals to survey the region and particularly to a request for national financial assistance for such a survey already under way in Georgia. William Branch Giles feared that there would be no end to such requests once one was granted and James Madison declared that such a survey, to be acceptable, had to extend to all the states. William Vans Murray, of Maryland, rejected the idea completely as being unconstitutional. Harper alone rose to speak for the request, saying that he was acquainted with the project and knew that the surveys were accurately executed. He noted that Georgia supplied the best timber for shipbuilding in the United States and that the commerce of that state would soon be a very great object. "If the Constitution of the United States forbade the granting of money in this way, there was an end of it. But if ever a deviation was to be made . . . this would be one of the most proper cases." [4] The proposal was recommitted over Harper's attempt to submit an amended resolution. Throughout the remainder of the session and into the next he attempted to have the survey plan brought up for discussion but without success.

The Georgia survey proposal died a quiet death in committee but another question involving the Georgia frontier refused to expire peacefully—the Yazoo land controversy which troubled the national government for a decade. The subject under discussion in early 1795 was not the legality of the Georgia land deal but the definition of the extent of the western area Georgia had previously claimed and now recently sold to the several Yazoo companies. The western boundary of Georgia's claims with publicly owned western lands was inexact and the national government was attempting to negotiate a settlement.

The House was debating a measure which would empower the executive to purchase a portion or all of the Georgia-claimed western lands. There was sympathy for giving the president carte blanche which Harper supported enthusiastically.[5] The congressman demonstrated not only his western interests but his commitment to Federalist attitudes toward government when he defended the carte blanche approach. Discretion and operating freedom were essential in such bargaining, and he believed that prior fixing of price "would be destroying the responsibility of the Executive."[6] The "transformation" from Republican to Federalist had apparently been quite complete.

Harper developed a detailed historical argument to prove that Georgia actually had a right to the lands in question but, he said, he wished it belonged to the United States, particularly since it involved thirty million fine acres. He envisioned the day when it would be worth one dollar an acre and a time when its settlement would open the Mississippi River. He concluded by remarking that if the Yazoo Companies had established their rights, he would advise the repurchase from them. Harper voted against limiting executive freedom of action, and he was in rather odd company in the minority with James Madison, a minority which did not include his Federalist friends from the northern states.[7]

Three years later, the House was again debating the settlement of the Georgia-United States land dispute, and in this instance Harper denied the authority of the House to discuss the validity of the claims of individuals upon part of the territory, saying that it was a matter for the courts to determine. He desired to placate the fears of these individuals, and thus to avoid arousing their objections to a federally negotiated settlement with Georgia. The individuals in question were the Yazoo claimants whose claims had already been challenged by a subsequent Georgia legislature and were a little later invalidated in the state's new constitution. Harper noted that "a powerful part of Georgia . . . are interested in these claims" and by holding out the possibility of an amicable settlement of their claims, he thought to enlist their support for the negotiation.[8] "Mr. Harper said he had no interest in these claims. There was a period in which he had an interest in them, but when there was a prospect in the year 1795 of the business coming before Congress, he gave up his right to them." [9]

The Republicans were aghast, particularly Abraham Venable and John Nicholas, who shouted that this proposal granted unheard of powers to the Federal Commissioners to bind the United States not only to Georgia but to private citizens. Nicholas ridiculed Harper's plan to buy the support of the Yazoo claimants for the Georgia cession, sardonically noting that, "it was a little remarkable that, for so little, the gentleman should be inclined to give so much." [10] Harper's plan was indefinitely recommitted. The problem was not solved until several years later, after Harper had left Congress, when in 1803 Georgia agreed to the cessation of the state's Yazoo claims with the federal government picking up most of the cost of settlement. [11]

Harper's sympathy for the western land speculator in trouble was not limited to southern land schemes. In the case of Robert Randall and Charles Whitney, accused of trying to bribe members of Congress in order to secure a large grant of land in the Great Lakes country, the South Carolinian rose to their defense. The two individuals were in custody awaiting Congressional indictment. Harper went out of his way to demand that the House follow the strictest of judicial porceedings, that counsel be provided for the defendants and that the rights of the accused be respected. [12]

With respect to the West, however, most of the time of the Congress was not taken up with untangling speculative schemes but rather with the much more basic problems of dealing with the Indians and providing for the settlement of the vast region soon to be enormously enlarged. Robert Goodloe Harper's ideas concerning these problems again demonstrate that in analyzing the distinction between northern and southern Federalists, the West provides a significant point of comparison. The debates in Congress show that section, not party, determined the positions most men took where the subjects of western lands, size of purchase, price, or Indian claims were concerned.

That the West was of crucial importance during this most critical of decades is obvious. The fact that the West accounted for five-sixths of the general government's expenses between 1790 and 1796 made the section's importance equally apparent to Harper's congressional colleagues. [13] General Anthony Wayne's victory at Fallen Timbers in August 1794 and the signing of the Treaty of Greenville in 1795 removed one frontier problem and revealed others just as difficult to deal with.

The Federalists found dealing with the red westerner considerably easier than with his white counterpart. Governmental Indian policy had three objectives, in addition to the primary objective of avoiding further warfare. First, and probably most important, was parrying British and Spanish influence among the western tribes; second, channeling the lucrative fur trade through American factors, and lastly, safeguarding the Indians from that abuse at the hands of unscrupulous traders which so often provoked red-white conflict. Prior to 1796 trade with the Indians had been conducted by private traders licensed and bonded by the general government. With the revamping of the federal western land program in that year, the Indian trade was also modified by the authorization of government owned and operated factories, each under the direction of a government appointed Indian agent.

Congressman Harper was quite emphatically opposed to this new innovation in the customary approach to trade with the savages. With reference to commerce in general, Harper declared that "public bodies never manage these matters without loss . . . all these objects [Indian trade to road repair] prosper under private individual direction, but when entered into by public bodies nothing is ever brought to perfection, and the public money is lost." [14] He suggested that private individuals be substituted for governmental participation; but the notion of private citizens trading on government loans was rejected by the House. William Branch Giles, and other southern members, agreed with Harper's doubts concerning the original bill and wanted to proceed very slowly, while Theodore Sedgwick, leading Massachusetts Federalist, scoffed at delay since, he said, the House had all the available information and delay was to no purpose. [15] Some northern Federalists agreed with Harper and Giles but most did not and the bill eventually passed the House.

The most difficult task Harper's Congress faced was, of course, the development of a new approach to disposing of the public lands. The Indians were no longer a serious threat in the Northwest and by the terms of the Jay Treaty Great Britain had agreed to surrender her western posts. The Northwest, once closed to settlement by circumstance, was now thrown open to occupation. In early 1796 the House Land Office Committee, chaired by William L. Smith, Harper's senior South Carolina associate, reported out a bill designed in Smith's words "to raise revenue, and to sell the land in such lots as would be most convenient to settlers," in tracts three miles square and at an upset price of two dollars per acre. [16]

Federal land policy was still not anchored to any concrete method of disposal or body of principles to guide land sale and settlement despite the Ordinances of 1785 and 1787. Alexander Hamilton as secretary of the treasury had departed from the 1785 ideal of accurate and uniform surveys and adopted an indiscriminate settlement approach, his object being revenue from sales not actual settlement. Indeed Hamilton's policy discouraged the latter by encouraging large sales of great tracts of western lands. [17] No one doubted that the sale of the western lands would produce revenue. But the two questions arose, how best to harvest this fiscal crop and was revenue the only consideration?

James Madison opened the debate by suggesting that the entire public domain should be thrown out for sale in the interest of filling the national treasury as rapidly as possible. He thus placed himself in a curious alliance with eastern speculative interests. Madison was simply reacting to an opportunity to erase that hated legacy of the Hamiltonian system, the standing national debt.

Albert Gallatin, who nearly alone of the Republicans was capable of dealing with the former secretary's creations on equal terms, hastily tried to correct Madison's well-intentioned error. The debt had to be eliminated as quickly as possible but the settler's interests required attention first. Anticipating Turner, Gallatin ventured that the true happiness of America depended upon a ready supply of cheap lands available to the poor, hopeful pioneer. [18]

What eventually emerged from the debate was a series of amendments to the Smith Bill which came to represent the frontier position. The amendments called for erasing the debt, the small tract approach, extended credit, the resettlement of the eastern poor and the channeling of the profits into public rather than private treasuries. The amendments also provided for a branch land office west of the mountains to facilitate purchase by the small settler. [19]

Robert Goodloe Harper rose to speak in favor of the last point particularly and said that he had not a single objection to any of Gallatin's amendments, although he did remark that revenue was not as important to him as it was to the Pennsylvanian. He was concerned with another objective as well, that of providing a method of sale and settlement which would preserve law and order and "give a stable and orderly system of government to this new society." Consequently he proposed to release part of the land to be sold immediately and more as the demand increased. [20]

Harper was concerned with selling to the "ultimate cultivator," as he called him, not with casting odium upon land speculation. Land was just as fair an object of speculation as anything else. He was, however, concerned about orderly settlement, about carrying law and order and defense to the settlers and about avoiding future jurisdictional difficulties among the new states to be created out of this territory. Harper also reminded the members what throwing all of the land up for sale at once would do to the price. [21] Republican sympathy was, however, for throwing the entirety of the land on the market and Harper's amendment was lost.

In an attempt to appeal to the veteran vote, Harper made a plea for the acceptance of Revolutionary Land Warrants in exchange for these western lands. The soldiers would be rewarded and the value of the land warrants raised. William Findley of Pennsylvania questioned Harper's sincerity saying that he had heard many false pleas in the name of veterans, but Harper's soldier's amendment passed on April 6, 1796.

The land bill with the Gallatin-Harper amendments passed the House with the nearly unanimous support of the frontier congressmen, notably those from New York, Pennsylvania and Virginia, including Robert Goodloe Harper. It really was for naught since the Federalist-dominated Senate emasculated the House bill, amending most of the "small purchaser" facets of Gallatin's proposals. The Federalist Land Act of 1796 failed to accomplish any of William Loughton Smith's objectives, for it produced scant revenue from the sale of only fifty thousand acres by 1800. Neither did it settle the northwest. [22] The important point is that this failure was the responsibility of Harper's eastern party associates and occurred despite the efforts of those, both Federalist and Republican, who better understood the West and its needs.

Also of interest in this discussion of Federalism and the West is Harper's role in and reaction to the Blount Conspiracy in the spring of 1796. While Harper had nothing to do with this tangled and confusing scheme hatched by the former governor of the Tennessee Territory to enlist the aid of the British government for an invasion of the Floridas and Louisiana by a force of American backwoodsmen, he played an important role in the impeachment attempt which followed the revelations of Blount's activities. Particularly interesting is the fact that Blount had been elected as a Federalist senator from Tennessee and had upon election promptly become a Republican. Even after Blount's expulsion from the Senate in 1796 the House decided to continue with the impeachment proceedings, and Harper was appointed one of the managers of the impeachment as a member of the prosecution committee.

In a letter to his constituents in July 1797, a back-home technique which he developed to a more impressive degree than any other representative of his political generation, Harper explained the conspiracy to the folks in Ninety Six. He was convinced that Blount deserved impeachment and he was especially concerned about the effect the episode had upon American neutrality, for he feared that it might result in Spain's refusing to honor her recently accepted treaty obligations with the United States.[23]

There is also good reason to suspect that Harper's objections to the conspiracy stemmed from Blount's detection and failure and not from any great opposition to the idea of seizing Spanish territory, particularly since the air was filled with rumors about a transfer of much of the Spanish West to France which posed all sorts of disturbing problems to the western-oriented congressman. Harper corresponded frequently with a friend and former Philadelphia acquaintance William Sullivan and in reply to a letter from Harper, Sullivan wrote in July 1797:

> It is generally believed that we shall fight the French or Spaniards or both very soon. The people have not been more ready to fight anytime for 20 years past. We may acquire an immense Southern territory and possession of the gold and silver mines.—What we may lose we can state more accurately when lost. . . . I am pleased to see you are on the Committee in Blount's affair. This will accord with yr. views as well as the public interest. [24]

Most northern Federalists, with the exception of Alexander Hamilton, were embarrassed by and opposed to the whole Blount affair, with most of them going to extraordinary lengths to excuse England from any complicity, convince the Spanish they had been misinformed concerning an exaggerated threat, and punish the painfully unrepentant Blount. [25]

Harper demonstrated his independence from the views of his northern friends by refusing to allow the trial to be conducted in Blount's absence. He argued that Blount had to appear to answer charges. To proceed in his absence was a violation of the individual's basic rights and a fateful departure from the basic tenents of Anglo-American judicial procedure. The first step away from that tradition might be difficult but each subsequent departure would be increasingly easy and the end result would be legal proceedings both inquisitorial and nothing less than tyrannical. "If, . . . we depart from the maxims of experience, we subject ourselves to the domination of our passions—to revenge on one side, or to favoritism on the other, and our reasonings will lead us this way or that according to our enmity or affection toward the party accused." Harrison Gray Otis, Massachusetts Federalist, saw no merit whatsoever in Harper's argument and, he commented, "let us not suffer this State criminal or any other to escape from any needless attention to form." ²⁶ This disagreement is distressingly modern and it saw Harper cast in the role of civil libertarian in opposition to his fellow Federalists.

Blount, meanwhile, had fled to Tennessee, where he was received like a returning conquering hero even though he did not quite fit the part, and he refused to return to Philadelphia to answer charges. The House was spared any further annoyance on Blount's account by the gentleman's premature death in 1800.

Most congressional difficulties with the West dealt not with conspiracies, although it sometimes seemed that way, but rather with surveys, organization of territories and preparation for statehood. The only state to be created out of the western territories during Harper's term in Congress was Tennessee, which entered the Union in 1796 while the House was debating the land act of that year. As happened so often when the subject of debate was the West, Harper found himself in the company of Madison and Gallatin rather than Goodrich and Otis. Again, the determinant was not party attachment but provincial interests and local attitudes. Northern Federalist opposition to hasty admission of these new western states was to a great extent based on the belief that the older states would thus be surrendering their hold on the central government, a development which in time seemed inevitable with the increase in the number of states.

However, opposition also stemmed from the mistaken fear that the Federal party lacked ability to garner votes and win elections in these frontier regions. There was living proof to the contrary in the person of Robert Goodloe Harper and others in the House, and the elections of 1796 and 1798 brought additional evidence of the party's rural strength. The Federalists were eventually defeated when they dismissed this ability which they had prematurely despaired of losing. Unable to trust the inhabitants of western, rural America, they came to fear them. When this occurred, the Federalists threw themselves out of the path of the future and were everlastingly consigned to the past.

Harper had not yet joined the rest of his party in their fortress of little hope and in May of 1796 he rose in the House to challenge the arguments of the opponents of Tennessee's admission to the Union. He was willing to wink at the hastily drawn state constitution but he was concerned about the proper apportioning of federal representatives and wanted an accurate census taken first. He saw "no inconvenience [to the older states] to admit them [Tennessee] into the Union." On the contrary, admission "would add to its strength and resources; [and] would increase the public happiness and prosperity." He did feel that the right to demand admission was debatable and he personally favored admission simply on the grounds that the people of Tennessee wanted it. On the final vote for admission Harper voted with the largely Republican majority while most prominent Federalists voted against the measure. [27]

This tendency to divide sectionally rather than on a partisan basis over western questions was most clearly illustrated by an episode in 1797 involving the extension of slavery into the Southwest and the new Mississippi territories. Congressman George Thacher, Federalist from Massachusetts, during one of the numerous discussions of the Georgia western lands question, suggested that the Northwest Ordinance prohibition of the extension of slavery ought to be extended to the newly created Southwest territory. Harper felt obliged to correct the gentleman's mistaken, though well-meant, motion in defense of the rights of man. Such a regulation respecting the Northwest was quite proper since the people who settled there came from regions where slavery had not existed and thus was not likely to take root in any settlements they founded.

However, the new Mississippi territory was considerably different, for slavery already existed there and had existed, indeed was essential, in the regions from which these people had migrated. Thacher's suggested corollary was thus improper because it "struck at the habits and customs of the people."

Harper's reply to Thacher heralded a heated debate, yet with both sides obviously wary of approaching the problem of slavery in the territories. Harrison Gray Otis and several of the northern Federalists bent over backward in their overdone, passionate defense of southern property rights, but it was again a sectional rather than a party affair. The division found Gallatin and Thacher on one side and Giles and Harper on the other, with the suggested resolution drawing only twelve supporters. Harper was continuing to vote his southern and western attitudes on this most crucial of all sectional questions. [28]

Despite the shortcomings of the 1796 land law the West did make some progress during the latter part of the Federalist decade. By 1799, the Northwest had moved to the second stage of territorial organization, under the terms of the 1787 Act, and had elected William Henry Harrison its first representative to the Congress. As was to be expected, Harrison made himself the champion of the interests of the frontier and became particularly involved with rewriting the Federalist land act of 1796. After acquiring the chairmanship of the House Land Committee, Harrison reported out a bill reflecting western interests even more clearly than the Gallatin-amended bill of 1796. The leading historian of western land policy calls the 1800 act "one of the most important measures in Public Domain history . . ." particularly in light of the very liberalized credit system it established. [29] This republicanized land law passed Congress in the spring of 1800, enacted by one of the last Federalist congresses, not in 1801 after Jefferson's inaugural, and it was enacted by the very same House of Representatives which had passed the Sedition Act.

The Harrison bill retained the minimum price of two dollars an acre but reduced the minimum purchase to three hundred twenty acres, with an eight percent discount for cash payment, and a four year credit arrangement with but one-quarter of the total purchase price due as the down payment and one-quarter each year thereafter. The bill also carried provisions for preemption and the establishment of several new land offices west of the mountains. [30]

Harper had supported nearly everything the Harrison bill incorporated, from the basic provisions of the new law to the Land Committee's suggestion that the Northwest Territory was too large and unmanageable and ought to be divided into two smaller regions for the sake of administrative efficiency. Even here, in the last year of his congressional career, after all that had happened during 1797 and 1798, Harper again joined with Gallatin, Harrison, Nicholas and company, and he urged the prompt adoption of this greatly revised approach toward the West. In a speech in April of 1800, Harper noted that the most serious failure of the 1796 law was that it had produced neither revenue nor settlement and he hoped that this new bill which favored the small settler, rather than the large scale speculator, would remedy both deficiencies. Once again, with southern and western votes, the land bill passed the House and this time the Senate as well without major changes, and although the final vote in the House was not recorded there is no reason to doubt that Harper voted with the majority. [31]

Yet when all the evidence is in, there remains the basic fact that the Federalists, with whom Harper must be included, failed to deal adequately with the West. There is also little doubt, however, that this failure was probably unavoidable. It was not simply a matter of distance and communication but also a question of time. The central government had precious little time to devote to any western affairs that were less than critical. The office of the secretary of state was entirely too overburdened with diplomatic difficulties, with a succession of foreign crises, between 1789 and 1801 to give more than token attention to its lesser domestic responsibilities. When State's attention was drawn to the West it was quite often because of some grander matter of Anglo-American or Spanish-American disagreement, not the day-to-day matters of governing and developing the hinterland.

One historian of the Federalists as administrators suggests that the Federalist record of western accomplishment would have been more comparable to their fiscal and organizational attainments if only the energies of the first secretary of the treasury had been set at revealing the possibilities of the West. [32] Things might have gone fairly well under the direction of a Robert Goodloe Harper, certainly far better than they did under the supervision of that considerably less western-oriented Federalist Timothy Pickering. Even so, Harper's attention was soon to be turned away from the western forest with all its constructive promise for the future. The nation was succumbing to the French hysteria which damned individual and party reputation alike and brought the entire Federalist system under the severest criticism.

NOTES

1. *Annals of Congress*, 3C2S, February and March 1795.
2. Ibid., February 27, 1795, pp. 1268-1269.
3. Ibid., p. 1256. The action would have been favorable to both the interests of his constituents, himself, and the shareholders of the Yazoo Land Companies.
4. Ibid., February 1795, pp. 1249-1250.
5. Ibid., March 2, 1795, p. 1277; pp. 1278-1285. 4C1S, December 16, 1795, p. 149.
6. Ibid., March 2, 1795, p. 1278. Harper's attitude toward limitations upon the freedom of the executive never varied. This was true even during the administration of John Adams, whom Harper greatly disliked and on occasion opposed.
7. Ibid., p. 1280.
8. Ibid., 5C1S, March 20, 1798, pp. 1277-1278.
9. Ibid., p. 1278. As has already been noted, there was more to Harper's "giving up his rights" to the Georgia lands than a desire to avoid charges of personal interest.
10. Ibid., Nicholas, p. 1278, and Venable, p. 1283.
11. The settlement was held up in 1806 when John Randolph of Roanoke led House rejection of the arrangements for cession of the lands to the central government. The rights of the Yazoo company claimants remained in doubt until the *Fletcher v. Peck* decision in 1810. The central government eventually voted some four million dollars to settle their claims.
12. *Annals*, January 1796, pp. 227-229. The two were discharged when it proved impossible to determine what law they had violated. Needless to say, the grant they sought was never obtained. Harper's attitude here and in the Blount Conspiracy was in marked contrast to his northern Federalist fellow congressmen.
13. Samuel Flagg Bemis, *Jay's Treaty: A Study in Commerce and Diplomacy* (New Haven: Yale University Press, 1962), pp. 177-183, 263-264.

14. *Annals*, 4C1S, p. 283.
15. Ibid., p. 289. See also Lenonard D. White, *The Federalist: A Study in Administrative History* (New York: The Macmillan Company, 1956), for an extensive evaluation of the Federalist approach to the West and its shortcomings. Actually, in this particular instance, two such government trading houses were established at a cost of one hundred fifty thousand dollars, one in Georgia and one in Tennessee. During Jefferson's first term a report was issued which demonstrated that the trade operations had been honestly and capably managed to the advantage of the Indians, and to the government as well since a profit was shown. White, pp. 383-386.
16. *Annals*, 4C1S, pp. 267, 331.
17. *American State Papers: Documents, Legislative and Executive of the Congress of the United States* (38 vols.; Washington: Gales and Seaton, 1832-1861), I, 8. See also Vernon Carstensen, *The Public Lands: Studies in the History of the Public Domain* (Madison: University of Wisconsin Press, 1963), pp. xviii-xix; and Roy M. Robbins, *Our Landed Heritage: The Public Domain 1776-1936* (Gloucester: Peter Smith, 1960), p. 14.
18. Raymond Walters, Jr., *Albert Gallatin: Jeffersonian Financier and Diplomat* (New York: The Macmillan Company, 1957), p. 95.
19. *Annals*, 4C1S, pp. 328-331, 338, 355, 402-423, 856-868.
20. Ibid., p. 350. This would have amounted to approximately one and one-half million acres out of the total of twenty million acres to be sold.
21. Ibid., pp. 351-352. Harper continued, "Perhaps . . . the most important differences which had arisen betwixt the different States in America, was owing to the different methods adopted in their original settlement. If a settlement was commenced by degrees order begins at first, and grows with its growth but if a country be settled before any regular order takes place, if a good government is ever established, it is by strugglings with a variety of difficulties." It must be admitted by the author that Harper's emphasis upon orderly settlement is in the northern rather than the southern tradition, see Robbins, p. 7. However, contrast Harper's pronouncements with those of Chauncey Goodrich, Federalist Representative from Connecticut. "A Land Office bill is before us, and has been several days in discussion, to bring to market our western lands. . . . It will be carried, if the crude schemes and local views of the abettors of this measure can fix any mode of compromise. One most pernicious idea is held out to give it popularity; that it is a fund for the redemption of the public debt. It is glossed over with the pretense of accomodation to the agricultural interests. Past experience of the expense attendant on the rude, unsocial, and discontented inhabitants of the new country makes no impression." Goodrich to Oliver Wolcott, Sr. (father of Adams' Secretary of the Treasury), February 21, 1796, George Gibbs (ed.), *Memoirs of the Administra-*

tions of Washington and John Adams from the Papers of Oliver Wolcott (2 vols.; New York: William Van Norden, 1846), I, 303-304.

22. *Annals*, 4C1S, p. 418; Robbins, pp. 15-17.

23. RGH to his constituents, July 24, 1797, Elizabeth Donnan (ed.), "Papers of James A. Bayard, 1796-1815," *Annual Report of the American Historical Association for the Year 1913* (Washington: The Association, 1915), p. 40. Also interesting is a letter from Carlos U. de Yrujo to President John Adams, April 21, 1797, in which de Yrujo expressed concern about reports of an army forming under General George Rogers Clark in Georgia. The Spaniard represented the anger of his government in the strongest terms and demanded that "the US take the necessary measures to cause their neutrality to be reflected. . . ." Adams Papers, Incoming, no. 384, L.C.

24. William Sullivan to RGH, July 23, 1797, Sullivan Papers, L.C.

25. See Timothy Pickering to Andrew Ellicott, July 28, 1797, Pickering Papers, XXXVII, 219, Massachusetts Historical Society.

26. *Annals*, 5C2S, December 21, 1798, pp. 2476-2478, p. 2479.

27. *Annals*, 4C1S, May 5, 1796, pp. 1305-1306, 1327-1329. What Harper was concerned about here was the question of whether or not a territory could demand admission to the Union. Harper had doubts about answering the question with an unqualified yes. Rather, he preferred to consider admission to the Union as a matter of securing the mutual consent of both territory and the states already in the Union.

28. Ibid., 4C2S, pp. 1306-1309. William B. Giles' reasoning for his opposition to the suggested prohibition of the extension of slavery is more than interesting. He thought that "If the rights of man was the desired objective, then let slavery be moved westward . . . if the slaves of the Southern States were permitted to go into this Western country, by lessening the number in those states, and spreading them over a large surface of country, there would be a greater probability of ameliorating their condition, which could never be done whilst they were crowded together as they are in the Southern States." Ibid.

29. Robbins, pp. 18-19; *Annals*, 6C1S, March 14, 1800, p. 625.

30. *Annals*, p. 652.

31. Ibid., March 28, 1800, p. 649, and April 2, 1800, pp. 651-652. The Land Act of 1800 passed the Senate one month later on May 10, 1800.

32. White, p. 386.

6

Jay's Treaty
to the Election of 1796

"YES, Sir, You have bitched it; you have indeed put your foot in it Mr. Jay—for shame, Sir,—" expressed the reaction of one American to the treaty John Jay, late of the Supreme Court, had brought back from England in March of 1795.[1] The writer was not alone in his opinion of the most detested single diplomatic arrangement in American history. Robert Goodloe Harper had nothing to do with the formulation of the envoy's instructions, or the negotiations, but he did play some part in the great national foreign policy debate which followed Jay's return. Of particular importance for this study are Harper's reaction to the treaty itself and to the attempt by the House of Representatives, or at least its Republican members, to force a far larger role for themselves in the conduct of American foreign policy. This "decade of precedents" witnessed no more important clash than the head-on encounter between the executive and legislative branches of the new government, and the fact that the legislative branch involved was the more popularly elected one added to the significance and excitement of the power struggle.

As with so many other facets of constitutional assignment of responsibility, the formulation and conduct of foreign policy was open to a certain amount of debate. The role of the Senate of the United States seemed relatively clear-cut in that senators were to be asked for their advice and consent, the only difficulty being whether the emphasis was to be placed on the former or the latter function. Was the Senate, in other words, to have a part in the instructing of ministers, in the creation of policy guidelines, etc., or was its role to be simply one of approving or disapproving the finished product obtained by the executive branch or its agents?

Until the Jay Mission to England in 1794 the Senate had played this dual role as a matter of course and few persons thought very much about the upper house's participation. The executive had not objected to this procedure because the Senate had been overwhelmingly proadministration in its sympathy, and the details of the instructions could be worked out amicably within the confines of the administration party. However, the composition of the Senate had changed by 1794 and by that year one-third of its members were antiadministration men. When this occurred, the president ceased seeking the "advice" of the senators and thenceforth asked only for their "consent" to the agreements brought home by the diplomats. Executive diplomatic prerogative was thus greatly strengthened.

There seemed to be little opportunity for problems to arise concerning the responsibilities of the House of Representatives in this increasingly executive area. The Constitution assigned no direct responsibilities to the House and none seemed likely considering the already established roles of the Senate and the chief magistrate. On the other hand, House involvement in the foreign policy area was not without precedent. Since 1789 the House had taken an active role in foreign affairs on at least five major occasions.

The fundamental act of creating the Department of State rested with the House in 1789. The establishment of the Post Office in 1792 marked yet another instance, for the postmaster general had been authorized by the House to make arrangements with foreign powers for the reciprocal delivery of the mails, which resulted in the first executive agreements. The House had openly debated Washington's controversial Neutrality Proclamation in 1793 and had enacted the first Neutrality Law in 1794. In that same year the House had agreed to a temporary embargo on all ships bound for foreign ports and authorized the president to lay another embargo pending the next session of Congress.[2]

These instances, of course, refer only to the most important events and take no account of the frequent floor discussions regarding this or that foreign power or event abroad and its effect upon the United States. Jay's Treaty offered those who sought to expand the role of the House a perfect opportunity. Although the attempt, when it came, originated in partisanship and not in a deeply believed commitment to such aggrandizement upon constitutional or ideological grounds.

John Jay's mission and the treaty he negotiated lie outside this study, but South Carolina's and Harper's reaction to the Chief justice's accomplishment are quite germane. The attempt to settle several difficult problems in Anglo-American relations outstanding since the Revolution along with several newer ones had been authorized in April of 1794 and the negotiations completed on November 19 of the same year. Copies of the treaty arrived in the United States in March 1795 but were kept closely guarded until the special session of Congress convened in June. The Senate ratified the treaty June 8, 1975, by a purely party vote, although many Federalist Senators were more than a little disappointed at Jay's handiwork. Immediately thereafter, the treaty "leaked" to Benjamin Franklin Bache and the whole abomination appeared in the Republican *Aurora*. The public outcry, as illustrated by the quotation opening this chapter, was at first disbelief and then a popular howl of outrage. Even President Washington had his doubts about signing the treaty and left for Mount Vernon in early July without formalizing the agreement nearly nine months old.[3] Had it not been for the Fauchet-Randolph revelations of late July 1795, a marvelous trump withheld by the British government until it would do the most good, the president might have been dissuaded from ever signing the treaty. Pressured by the knowledge that eventual war might be the alternative to a ratified bad treaty, and prodded by the specter of French machinations in internal American affairs, Washington signed the Jay Treaty on August 12, 1795. The supporters of the treaty had apparently scored a fait accompli while the Jay critics were left to stew throughout the winter and into the next spring.

The reaction in South Carolina to the "Jay Betrayal" was scarcely equaled for severity and the undiluted scorn heaped upon Great Britain, Mr. Jay, and their creation. In Charleston, the British flag was dragged through the streets and burned before the door of the British consul by a mob of irate citizens.[4] On July 11, 1795, Charlestonians of anti-Jay sentiments gathered at Saint Michael's church to listen to a host of leading citizens harangue against the treaty. The newly appointed, although never confirmed, Chief Justice of the United States, John Rutledge, delivered a remarkable "spell binding, hour-long speech, which one listener reported as sufficient to raise the tombstones in the nearby graveyard," and no doubt the hackles of northern Federalists as well.[5] Charles Pinckney termed the treaty "ungrateful to our allies" and the state's newspapers carried even more damning opinions.[6] A meeting in Camden declared that "war, with all its horrors, ought to be preferred to peace upon such disgraceful and dishonorable terms."[7] The further west one moved in the state the more extreme the denunciations became. At a meeting in Edgefield, in Harper's district, effigies of the hated Jay and the state's Federalist Senator Jacob Read were strung up and then burned.⁸ Republican societies in the western counties proclaimed their sympathy for the French cause and exclaimed that this treaty would force Americans to recognize just who the nation's true European friends and enemies were.⁹

The lower house of the state legislature, in which Harper had served briefly, resolved that the treaty was "highly injurious to the General Interests of the Said [United] States" and that the president and the Senate had overstepped their authority in ratifying such an agreement. ¹⁰ Harper's colleague William Loughton Smith was also hung in effigy for his support of the treaty, which probably had little effect on the congressman, for he was accustomed to receiving expressions of lack of public confidence. For example, Smith was sent the following message:

> Wm. Smith Your aristocratical behavior in Congress had introduced us to form a conspiracy against you and for that toryism you shall fall by the hands of private murder and nobody shall know who committed it—for all American Sons are crying out against you—you rascal. You shall fall—and so beware of your life—for we are determined to mangle your body. . . .
>   [signed] Fifteen Republicans and boys to extirpate torys¹¹

Robert Goodloe Harper, freshman congressman, managed to buck this tide of anti-Jay, Francophilic sentiment, strongest perhaps in the very part of the state he represented, write a pamphlet defending the treaty which underwent fifteen editions and not simply survive but win reelection twice. ¹² His approach, that of a frontal assault with flags flying, was risky considering the explosiveness of the subject but it succeeded. Throughout his career in Congress Harper was a warm advocate of presenting all manner of problems to the people, providing them with ample accurate information and then trusting them to make the correct decision, another trait that set him a bit apart from many northern members of his party. He took his case to his constituents, presented them with the facts and then left them with the decision of either turning him out or reelecting him.

Harper began by stating that no treaty could possibly be as bad as some of the Jay Treaty's critics made it out to be. He did not believe, he said, that it prostituted American sovereignty or that it was a wanton sacrifice of the rights of this free nation, or that it was so pregnant with evils that it threatened to ruin the nation forever. If for one instant he thought that these charges were true, Harper assured his constituents, he would commit all his strength to fighting the treaty in Congress and if that failed he should have felt obligated to "return among you, sound the alarm, and join you in a resort to the last expedients for preventing the execution . . . of a contract which was to place the legislative functions of the Union under the control of a foreign government. . . ."[13]

He based much of his defense of the treaty upon his trust in the character of George Washington and Thomas Pinckney, who had both approved it. Harper denied that the treaty provisions were hostile to France or that it compromised American neutrality. The charge that the appointment of John Jay while he was still chief justice was unconstitutional might easily be tested, Harper said, by calling for impeachment proceedings.

He realized that while his position was opposed by many of the people who had elected him to the office he held, he still welcomed reelection if his constituents saw fit to accept his views. Nevertheless, this in no way meant that he had altered his stance or that he no longer supported the treaty and the administration and he warned them that his future actions would be as independent as in the past.[14] He had gambled that the people in Ninety Six would respect and honor the brash "I'd rather be right than congressman" stance of their new representative.

In April of 1796, a public meeting in Newberry responded to the communication from their congressman by informing Harper that, while they thought the treaty a bad bargain they nevertheless preferred such a treaty to war. Harper was congratulated for his sincerity and courage, especially his refusal to modify his position after learning that nine-tenths of the people in his district opposed the treaty.[15] So far as can be determined, he was not burned in effigy but instead was reelected in 1796 by a greater majority than he had won in 1794. The gamble obviously paid handsome dividends at home as well as in Philadelphia, for Harper's Jay Treaty address was reprinted and greatly enhanced his reputation in and out of Congress.[16]

It was the first session of the Fourth Congress which saw the entire Jay affair brought to a climax in the lower house and there was far more involved than Anglo-American relations. For the most part, Jay Treaty scholarship has concentrated upon the causes of the crisis, the negotiation of the treaty, the role of American political figures such as Hamilton or Washington, or the impact of the issue upon domestic party development.[17] Each of these approaches has validity but not for the purposes of

this particular study. The approach to the Jay Treaty most valid
here is an examination of the event as one of the most important
battles in the continuing undeclared war between the legislative
and executive branches of the American government, with the
stakes of victory being a much larger role for the House in the
conduct of American foreign policy. Harper entered the fray a
private and emerged as an important Federalist commander by
virtue, so to speak, of a battlefield commission.

It began while the House was debating a proposal providing for
the appropriation of the necessary funds to establish the several
arbitration commissions established by the terms of Jay's Treaty.
It was all rather a mechanical reaction to the Senate ratification
of the treaty until Congressman Edward Livingston, a Republican
from New York, threw the matter open to debate with the
introduction of his famous set of Jay Treaty resolutions. Included in Livingston's demands was the call for the president to
lay the papers of the negotiations before the House. Livingston
based the call upon the House's incomplete knowledge of a
treaty for which they were being asked to appropriate public
monies.[18] The Republican House dominated by antitreaty sentiment adopted Livingston's call for the Jay Papers by the stag-
gering vote of sixty-two to thirty-seven, which has to represent
one of the strongest diplomatic no-confidence votes ever adopted
by the House.

From the instant the Livingston resolutions touched off the
debate, Harper and William Loughton Smith split with the rest of
the South Carolina delegation over the fundamental question of
the right of the House to make such a demand upon the executive branch of the government. Harper's earlier expressed feelings
about a strong unencumbered executive became even more
apparent.[19]

William Loughton Smith, not Harper, at this point acted as the
leading southern Federalist spokesman in the House and was so
regarded by the northern wing of the party. Northern correspondents wrote to Smith, not Harper, providing him with additional
intellectual armament for the battle raging in Congress, the most
important correspondent being Alexander Hamilton, who offered
Smith his own very narrow interpretation of the foreign affairs
role of the House. There was not at the time or in the future to
be any such thing as the "Hamilton-Harper" correspondence.
After Smith left Congress Hamilton turned to other southern

correspondents and the absence of frequent exchanges between Hamilton and Harper is not insignificant.[20]

Of the two South Carolinians Smith was clearly the more acceptable to the northern element of the party. William Loughton Smith's credentials and connections were Charleston, mercantile, all with the better families; his father-in-law was Ralph Izard and one did not do much better than that. There was nothing about Smith that could in any way make him suspect in the party's northern circles. The same thing could not be said for Robert Goodloe Harper.

The Federalists in the House responded to Livingston's original resolutions by attempting to restrict the discussion to very narrow, specific questions and especially to the question should or should not the House make the appropriations required by the treaty? In a speech on the floor of the House Harper delivered a classic statement of the problem as the Federalists understood it. "The question was, whether the Treaty be so bad that the public welfare requires it to be broken; whether it is less evil to abandon our national faith—to destroy the respectability of our Government in the eyes of foreign powers . . ."; whether it was more dangerous to risk a power struggle between the branches of government or to execute the treaty? There were no other questions to be decided by the House, Harper asserted, and the Jay Papers were unnecessary to decide the matter.[21] Gallatin, Madison, Livingston, and the treaty opponents saw no reason to so limit the discussion and the debate was thus expanded until the question of appropriations stood in some secondary relationship to the real objective of the Jay critics from the beginning, which was the defeat of the treaty itself, and it was apparent that there were more than sufficient votes in the House to accomplish the task.[22]

After the debate had gone on for a considerable length of time Harper rose again to note that the discussion had completely shifted ground from the original question, which brought loud coughing, shuffling of feet and other assorted noises from Republican members of the House. He made it quite clear that he understood why the opposition had altered the attack, and he pointed out that Gallatin himself had stated "that a Treaty is not valid, does not bind the nation . . . till it has received the sanction of the House of Representatives."[23] Nothing could be further from the truth, Harper said, for the treaty-making and legislative powers were entirely independent of each other. Each power was exercised in a different orbit where it was supreme and controlled only by the Constitution. Treaties simply did not operate in the manner of laws, and acts of the legislature were obviously not operative as treaties. Thus, Harper concluded, the power to negotiate could in no way invade the legislative domain and neither could the legislature interfere with or restrict executive conduct of foreign relations—the only check being Senate concurrence.

After consulting his cabinet advisors the president flatly refused to deliver the papers to the House and on March 25 so informed the critics of his foreign policy, citing the prerogative of the executive and the absence of any real necessity for the House to see all the materials. This rejection was promptly followed by a Madison-directed House disapproval of Washington's position and the introduction of another resolution on the question of putting the treaty into operation. The Jay critics were confident of eventual victory and their strength in the House reinforced that belief. Harper had correctly identified the real crux of the debates as control over foreign policy and he believed, he said, that the president had likewise seen through the subterfuge of the Virginia and Pennsylvania critics' arguments— for which he was again called to order.[24] At any rate, George Washington did not need Robert Goodloe Harper to tell him what the real issue was.

It is not necessary here to recount the details of the defeat in early March 1796 of the antitreaty forces, notwithstanding their overwhelming numerical strength. In what for that day was a massive lobbying operation, the friends of the treaty and the administration threw their weight and influence against the block of opposition votes in the House, with the result that Madison saw his expected twenty-one vote majority dwindle away. Clergymen were in the forefront of the treaty party, as they were politically active later during the French scare of 1798, and doubtless the anticlericalism of the revolution in France contributed to their motivation in both instances. Powerful mercantile interests and supporters of the Hamiltonian economic system, fearful of the effects of war with Britain on commerce and debt payment, along with others in Anglophilic sentiment, brought pressure to bear on stragglers in the congressional ranks. However, this was only part of the explanation.

The question was so framed and presented to the American

public that the only two apparent alternatives were the treaty, bad as it was, or war with Britain. The choice was distasteful but clear, as the Federalists presented it, and the representatives in Congress read public opinion accurately. Samuel Smith, Maryland Republican, noted the direction the struggle was taking when he wrote, "This people believe that under *all* the present circumstances it will be desirable to make the necessary appropriations. . . . Yet [those who] think farther than their immediate private interests are highly satisfied with the principles supported by the [Republican] majority." Smith felt that the American people were prepared to acquiesce in probable evil rather than risk war or an open split between the branches of government, which might be just as destructive.[25]

The Marylander was quite correct, for by April 29 the votes to block the treaty appropriations were no longer there, and in committee of the whole the House voted fifty to forty-nine, with the Federalist speaker voting, to make the necessary expenditures. The following day, the House sitting as a legislative body voted fifty-one to forty-eight on the same question, and in this way the Jay Treaty was carried into effect.[26] Thus, one of the most momentous foreign policy debates in the nation's history ended with this triumph for executive autonomy.

Ironically, the Federalist position was based upon the most narrow interpretation of the Constitution's foreign affairs provisions possible, and this fundamental constitutional question was decided along purely partisan lines. The Federalists found it expedient in this instance to adopt the extremely narrow approach to the Constitution of their opponents for the simple reason that both the executive branch and the Senate were safely in the hands of the "friends of government," while the lower house was dangerously inclined toward the antiadministration view. Had the composition of the executive or legislative branches of the government been reversed the "fundamental" constitutional positions of Federalists and Republicans would have been different as well.

Harper had not accepted the ridiculously narrow view of the role of the House advocated by some northern Federalists, a view so narrow that it virtually denied the lower house any foreign policy prerogative, even that of discussing past or projected treaties. He had instead taken the view that departing from the already established constitutional guidelines was dangerous and that for the function allocated to the House the papers of the negotiation were not really necessary. Harper noted that if the House was contemplating impeachment proceedings against the negotiator or the president, then a call for the complete diplomatic record was justifiable, but that such intent needed to be expressed in the resolution before the House.[27]

In writing to his constituents, Harper was quick to present the peace, bad as it was, or war choice. Somewhat later, again writing home, he explained why the vote had turned as it did, and he noted that of the six-man South Carolina delegation he and Smith alone voted for the treaty appropriation. "Vast numbers of petitions came in, from all parts of the country, praying that the Treaty might be carried into effect. This, I believe [Harper wrote] was one principal cause why it was done," with many of the most resolute opponents being brought over by such pressure.[28] Harper's explanation was accepted by the people in Ninety Six or at least by enough of them to elect him again in 1796.

These letters home were used for much more than explaining the congressman's behavior or voting record. Quite often Harper took the opportunity to inform the citizens of Ninety Six about the recent events in Europe, the state of British financial affairs, the rise of Napoleon, or any number of interesting subjects. For example, in the March 9, 1796, "newsletter" Harper ranged all the way from the Italian campaigns, to the price of bread in France, and the prospect of French peace with the Austrians. In this same communication Harper had some extremely unkind things to say about "some very tyrannical bills brought into Parliament by the minister [Pitt] for preventing meetings of the people," and he expressed a view of the Treasonable Practices Act and the Seditious Meetings Act which was warmly shared by his constituents.[29] Harper somewhat regretted having made these remarks after the American Congress had enacted similar legislation.

Be that as it may, this innovation in voter relations won Harper great notice beyond the borders of Ninety Six, indeed even beyond the boundaries of the United States itself. Part of the reputation this correspondence and its publication won for Harper stemmed from the fact that these arguments were always closely reasoned, lucidly presented, and above all, representative of a quite moderate, reasonable viewpoint. For instance, during the heat of the Jay Treaty debates in the House some Federalist members and protreaty men among the Republicans were so brash as to threaten to scuttle the highly profitable and popular Pinckney Treaty with Spain if the Jay appropriations did not pass. Harper reproved both these individuals and the Republicans who attempted to take political advantage of these intemperate remarks by commenting that he certainly hoped that members were not reacting like angry children who because they could not get all they wanted would have none at all.[30]

Harper's defense of the Jay Treaty published along with his general reflections on Franco-American relations was the most famous of these pamphlets and was widely circulated in Europe as well as the United States. John Jay thought Harper's pamphlet the fairest justification ever given to his much maligned treaty, and he wrote Harper thanking him and saying that "had all the publications . . . been written with equal knowledge . . . or with equal candour and decorum, more truth would have been disseminated, and less irritation excited."[31]

There were, however, those Federalists who remained unsatisfied with what had been an extremely satisfactory session of Congress. One of these gentlemen thought it shameful that following the Jay struggle the exhausted Congress had been quick to move for adjournment instead of staying on to complete the remaining business. He did concede that "more mischief has been prevented, than could have [been] expected and the most essential laws have been passed to keep the government moving."[32]

The gentleman might have excused the haste of the lawmakers to get home had he remembered that 1796 was a presidential election year—possibly, although no one was certain in June, the first such election without George Washington as a candidate.

The campaign of 1796 marked the first real presidential encounter between the two parties, with foreign policy being a key issue, and the first real test of the Federalist organization now denied the Washington magic to carry the rest of the party's candidates. It was also the first time that Robert Goodloe Harper's controversial record went before the voters of Ninety Six.

The summer of 1796, however, found Harper in serious financial straits and there was some doubt in his mind whether he should even stand for election. Wade Hampton had not turned the notes due Harper over to him and he "resolved to quit Congress, and engage . . . in profession of the law."[33] Harper went to New York and spent several weeks in the city, staying with Aaron Burr, although how they first met is unknown. Burr urged him to move to New York and open practice there,

assuring him that the city held much promise for such a bright
and ambitious young man. The New Yorker was then retiring
from active practice and offered to assist in setting Harper up.[34]

Burr's interest was quite flattering and Harper did need to
improve his financial position, but his decision to stand for
reelection was based on something more than economic necessity. Apparently pricked by the "antis" charges concerning his
change of coat and its effects on his chances of ever being
returned to Congress from his district, Robert Goodloe Harper
chose to run again, perhaps partly to prove that the Republican
claims were false and possibly to satisfy himself that he could
win. Aaron Burr's kind tender of assistance to Harper's New
York legal career was turned down, and the South Carolinian
turned his efforts to the election.

Federalist election hopes in South Carolina revolved around
the figure of Thomas Pinckney, whose successful negotiations
with Godoy had added greatly to his political stature. The hope
was that Pinckney as a vice-presidential candidate would draw
some Carolina electoral votes in Mr. Adams' column and possibly
make up partially for Jefferson's strength in the upper South.
Ralph Izard, William Loughton Smith, and Harper managed the
Federalist campaign in the state with the former two gentlemen
exercising most of the leadership. Smith urged his father-in-law
to visit the state capitol and exert as much influence as he
possibly could upon the legislators.[35] The leading obstacle in the
course of this Pinckney strategy was the intended vice-
presidential candidate himself and what might be called the
Pinckney family pride.

Thomas Pinckney had some cause to doubt northern Federalist sincerity. He had been American minister to England and by
all rights ought to have been entrusted with the mission given to
John Jay. Instead, Pinckney had been hurried off to Spain,
removed from the more important stage to play a role in a lesser
diplomatic drama and upstaged by the chief justice.

However, there was more involved than pique at past in-
justices. Pinckney suspected that he had not necessarily been
added to the Federalist slate because he had any real chance of
winning, but rather in order that he might split the southern
vote, which otherwise was likely to fall entirely to Jefferson.
Knowing full well how far northern Federalists were willing to go
to secure the Virginian's defeat, the Federalist vice-presidential
candidate was aware that further sacrifice of the Pinckney honor

might well be considered by northern party leaders part of the price of victory. South Carolina Jeffersonians took advantage of the Pinckney vanity and playing upon that, attempted to induce him to retire from an electoral contest he could not win, which could do nothing to advance his political position and possibly very much harm it.[36] Federalist affairs in South Carolina were so shaky that Pinckney was on the verge of withdrawing on election eve.

Harper, who spent the election in North Carolina visiting friends, kept in touch with events in South Carolina by corresponding with Smith and Izard among others. He seemed to be more concerned with Thomas Pinckney's election than with John Adams' chances or, indeed, even with his own. His election prognosis demonstrated that he knew whereof he spoke and that his interest in Pinckney was grounded on much more than a casual reading of the political stars. He knew that the up-country, or the "upper country" as he called it, was generally inclined toward Jefferson, but he felt certain that Adams and other Federalist candidates might, nevertheless, pick up a fair number of votes there. Harper predicted that the real key lay in the way Pennsylvania voted and the results bore him out.

The fact that he remained reasonably rational on the subject of Thomas Jefferson is significant. Harper's moderate attitude toward Jefferson may simply have been due to the state of political opinion in the South Carolina back-country, and then again, it may have reflected the fact that southerners, Federalists as well as Republicans, did not react to national elections and candidates as seriously or as emotionally as their northern political cousins. Southern Federalists naturally preferred the election of someone else to the chief magistracy, but at the same time there was general agreement that the republic was not without hope if Thomas Jefferson was elected.

One of the more important southern Federalist objections to Jefferson was of peculiarly southern origin and nature. Some of Jefferson's pronouncements regarding the permanence of slavery and the prospects for an emancipation movement disturbed the deeper South, and there were those who hoped to turn this to Federalist advantage particularly in South Carolina, where the transition to cotton culture was most highly developed and slavery thus most economically necessary.[37]

Harper's correspondence with Ralph Izard concerning the campaign was positive rather than negative; that is, he attempted to

emphasize the necessity of electing Thomas Pinckney and not
merely the defeat of Jefferson. His concern was that Edward
Rutledge and others might persuade Pinckney to quit the contest, which had to be prevented at all costs. Harper wrote to
Izard in November asserting that "Major Pinckney may be assured, I speak from the most certain knowledge, that the intention . . . was to make him President, and that he will be supported with that view . . ." by Federalists in the North. [38] He did
not go so far as to say that a majority of "the eastern people"
preferred the South Carolinian to Adams, but that Pinckney
could count on their support as another means of electing a
Federalist president and that he had a good chance of winning if
he remained in the race.

So far as the elections in South Carolina were concerned,
Harper was willing to follow the advice of gentlemen on the
scene but he did have some definite opinions on that subject.
There had been talk in the upper country of Pierce Butler's
making an attempt for the governorship and that move, he felt,
had to be thwarted. He suggested several possible opposing candidates, among them John Ewing Colhoun. Harper also pressed
for the selection of a candidate to stand for Butler's Senate seat
and thought the irascible Dr. David B. Ramsay might prove a
good choice. Dr. Ramsay had previously irritated South Carolinians with his public antislavery views, but Harper had heard that
Ramsay had recently become a large slaveholder in Georgia and
thought that that had likely brought the doctor to a right view of
the matter. [39]

Above all else, the congressman from Ninety Six desired the
defeat of Charles Pinckney, especially if Pinckney stood for
national office. Harper shared the nearly universal, bitter hatred
for Charles Pinckney so rampant in down country South Carolina
circles. Harper reasoned that it was perhaps the lesser of two evils
to allow Pinckney to be elected governor in order to prevent him
from becoming a United States senator. [40]

If all went according to plan, South Carolina was to play an
important part in the Federalist scheme of things for the fall
national elections. Involved here was the High-Federalist attempt
to move Thomas Pinckney ahead of John Adams in the choice of
a new chief magistrate. Never enjoying great popularity, even in
his own lifetime, "His Rotundity" was aware that persons in his
own party were not convinced he could win or perhaps suspected

that even if he did win he was not enough of a "party man" to be trusted.

It was impossible to drop Adams openly as the party's first choice since this would mean the loss of nearly all of the New England, Adams votes. Thus a scheme was worked out to support Pinckney quietly at John Adams' expense. Simply stated, the idea was that Adams and Pinckney were to be supported equally by the New England and middle states electors and in this way Pinckney was certain to be assured the presidency by Federalist strength in South Carolina. Thus, Pinckney would become president and John Adams would remain in the second office for another four years.[41]

Robert Goodloe Harper's extreme interest in Mr. Pinckney's campaign suggests that he was well acquainted with and most likely party to the Carolina end of the scheme, although since he spent the election months in North Carolina he could have played only a peripheral role. It was Harper who in correspondence with Ralph Izard stressed the necessity of Pinckney's remaining in the election race and who stated that Pinckney was intended for more than merely picking up South Carolina electoral votes for John Adams.[42] Harper was not in direct communication with Alexander Hamilton but William Loughton Smith was. The two Federalist congressmen must certainly have exchanged information, and Harper's "most certain knowledge" of the affair was no doubt from Alexander Hamilton by way of Smith.

Fortunately for John Adams the entire attempt failed because the South Carolina electors refused to vote on a strictly partisan basis, particularly since a favorite son was entered in the contest. They voted instead for Adams and Pinckney or Jefferson and Pinckney. What took place in Columbia was the result of Jeffersonian strength in the state, regional attachment for the two southern candidates, and possibly a manifestation of southern Federalist rejection of northern attempts at manipulation. For whatever the reason, the state's electoral votes were evenly divided between Federalist and Republican tickets, and Thomas Pinckney was denied any national office at all even though he ran stronger than the rest of his party in the state.[43]

Harper made no secret of his admiration for Thomas Pinckney. In another letter home dated January 5, 1797, after the results of the election were public, he said so. "I am one of those who

would have preferred Major Pinckney to either [Adams or Jef-
ferson] . . . conceiving him to be possessed, in a higher degree
than either, of those qualities which fit a man for holding the
reins of government. . . ." [44] He thought Jefferson to be deficient
in most of the requisite attributes of discretion, coolness, firmness of character, and uniformity of conduct.

> He possesses much knowledge, chiefly of the scientific kind, the least
> useful for a statesman; whose business it is to judge and act, not to
> write books; No one will deny him the praise of considerable literary
> genius; and for his diplomatic writings he has been greatly . . . com-
> mended. But for his public conduct, I take him to be of a weak
> wavering indecisive character; deliberating when he ought to act, and
> frequently acting . . . without steadiness of judgment . . . always pur-
> suing certain visionary theories of the closet, which experience con-
> stantly contradicts . . . like most literary men . . . so devoted to popular
> applause, that he cannot be relied on . . . to risk it, by a manly decisive
> conduct in difficult situations. With this opinion of Mr. Jefferson, I
> might think him fit to be a professor in a college, President of a
> Philosophical Society, or even Secretary of State; but certainly not the
> first magistrate of a great nation. [45]

Harper also noted that Jefferson was entirely too Anglophobic
and far too disposed toward the French for the situation at hand.
He also made capital of the interest of the French government in
seeing Jefferson elected, particularly the disastrously brash electioneering of the French minister Pierre Adet. This amounted to
nothing less, Harper said, than undisguised interference in a
purely domestic concern by a foreign power. In a parting shot,
Mr. Jefferson was paid the tribute of being "a sincere friend to
liberty," although Harper definitely thought it was a misguided
friendship.

As to John Adams, whom Harper said he preferred greatly to
Jefferson, his firmness, manly character, integrity, and patriotism
were unquestioned. Harper also expressed a belief that Adams
was also a knowledgeable man and that he possessed a sort of
knowledge better suited to a statesman than his Virginia rival,
especially in the fields of government, politics, and history.
Harper felt that the charges of monarchism so frequently hurled
at Adams were based on either partisanship or a misreading of
the president-elect's literary efforts. Harper said that he too had
read Adams' *Defense of the American Constitution* and found
many passages which in retrospect the author might wish to

modify, but he thought it ridiculously unfair to isolate and lift out of context phrases written over a decade before. The American people had made their choice and while it had not been Harper's choice he expressed his ready acceptance of that decision.[46] To suggest that Harper later broke with Adams and became an inveterate presidential critic, within Federalist circles of course, is partially correct. However, it overlooks the fact that Harper was not and never had been an "Adams Federalist" but rather a Pinckney or southern Federalist.

The description of the third presidential inauguration which Harper wrote for the edification of those at home displayed his nearly worshipful feelings for the retiring Washington. "A great concourse of people assembled to see Mr. Adams take the oath, and General Washington appeared among them as a private citizen. He probably never appeared greater; and certainly his appearance never excited more sensibility or more admiration."[47] But Harper also grasped and explained for his readers the much grander meaning of the event, the spectacle of a president stepping down voluntarily and joining with his fellow citizens in the elevation of his successor.

> To see this change made without commotion, without a murmur, without even the appearance of discontent; and to see the two distinguished citizens who lately were rival candidates . . . cheerfully submit to the decision of the majority. . . . These circumstances form the highest encomium on republican government . . . and they furnish . . . confidence, that our constitution will disappoint, by its durability and happy effects, the predictions of its enemies, and the fears of its friends.[48]

Harper recorded no reaction to the brief address delivered by the new president to the audience gathered in the House chamber, but like nearly everyone else probably judged it a fair address that pledged the new administration to respect the interests of all sections of the nation and to seek commerce and honest friendship with all foreign powers. Adams disavowed any hereditary office or body in the national government and declared his respect for and faith in democratic governments, and firmly stated his opinion that any changes in the Constitution were to be instituted by the people themselves, not the executive.[49] Robert Goodloe Harper had absolutely no reason for disagreeing with the speech or the principles contained therein, and he felt no need to comment upon such a moderate and commendable policy statement. Many of the High-Federalists were slightly disappointed that a "firmer" French position had not been taken, but the South Carolinian did not yet agree with the more extreme element in his party.

John Adams was not the only person whose election had included surprises. Having switched party affiliation, deserted the cause of Republicanism for the "Monocrats," and flaunted the will of his constituents, Robert Goodloe Harper had also been elected to federal office. He was reelected, if these Republican charges were correct, in what was to be one of the greatest upset victories in the history of South Carolina politics. The charges were less than accurate but the upset still stands as a vindication of both Harper's explanation of his early career and his willingness to openly bare his conduct to the people he represented, trusting to their fairness. His victory was overwhelming, for Harper defeated his nearest rival in Ninety Six by a margin of better than two to one.[50]

The Jay gamble and his record to date paid handsome dividends not merely for Harper but for the position of his party in the Congress. The number of Federalists in the six-man South Carolina congressional delegation in the next Congress increased to three with the election of John Rutledge, Jr.[51] Harper's popularity among the voters could not but have helped other Federalist congressional candidates in South Carolina, although it must be admitted that with the name John Rutledge this particular candidate probably did not need anyone's assistance. The Federalists and Republicans continued to claim one South Carolina senator a piece with the Republican John Hunter having been elected to the seat vacated by Pierce Butler. Harper was now clearly elected as a South Carolina Federalist with no doubts, either his own or his constituents, as to his political leanings, and with the resignation of the senior Federalist congressman William Loughton Smith in July of 1797 the way was open for Harper's rise to national prominence as the leading South Carolinian in Congress.[52]

NOTES

1. "Atticus," in the *Alexandria Gazette,* reprinted in the *Virginia Herald* and *Fredericksburg Advertiser,* August 11, 1795, quoted in De Conde, p. 115.
2. White, pp. 190-195. The point being that there was considerable precedent for any move to expand the foreign affairs duties of the House of Representatives. The contemporary Federalist charge that such a step constituted serious departure from past practice was ill-founded.
3. See Bemis, pp. 363-365; De Conde, pp. 114-120. The Fauchet-Randolph affair involved some intemperate remarks by Secretary of State Randolph to Joseph Fauchet, the French Minister, concerning the suppression of the Whiskey Rebellion and the fact that several "key" men in the government were pro-British due to British financial obligations. Randolph reportedly remarked that they might be weaned away from British influence by French loans. The Fauchet dispatch containing Randolph's remarks fell into British hands, giving the British a grand opportunity to rid themselves of the pro-French secretary of state and at the same time secure American ratification of the Jay Treaty. Irving Brant, "Edmund Randolph, Not Guilty," *William and Mary Quarterly*, 3rd Series, Vol. VII (April 1950), offers a convincing defense of Randolph's conduct.
4. Fraser, pp. 45-46.
5. John M. Barry, *Mr Rutledge of South Carolina* (New York: Duell, Sloan and Pearce, 1942), p. 356. The writer believes that the Rutledge affair was of considerable importance in dividing northern and southern Federalist leadership. The northern reaction to this assault upon the treaty by a hitherto loyal Federalist who had just been rewarded with the best judicial appointment the national government had to offer was disbelief which quickly turned to vindictive rage. The desperate attempts by southern Federalists to secure confirmation of the Rutledge appointment proved futile. It seems certain that the affair did much to diminish the bonds which bound northern and southern Federalists together. The election of 1796 saw southern Federalists prove independent of the wing of the party north of Mason and Dixon's line. One student of South Carolina in this era stated that "many South Carolina Federalists must have come to

distrust the leadership of a party, even though they called it their own, that could force upon them a treaty . . . injurious to their interests and in addition refuse to confirm the nomination of a man whom they knew and respected." Wolfe, p. 92.

6. De Conde, p. 128, quoting "Speech of Charles Pinckney," Charleston, July 22, 1795.

7. August 19, 1795, reprinted in *City Gazette* Charleston, October 26, 1795; *City Gazette*, July 14, 1795. The treaty was "degrading to the national honor, dangerous to the political existences and destructive to the agricultural, commercial, and shipping interests of the people of the United States.—" from the *Gazette* quoted in Ulrich B. Phillips, "South Carolina Federalist Correspondence," p. 735.

8. Ibid., October 27, 1795.

9. Ibid., October 28, 1795.

10. *South Carolina House Journal*, December 11, 1795.

11. Fraser, p. 45; William L. Smith Papers, L.C. dated 1794.

12. Rogers, pp. 284-285.

13. RGH to his Constituents, December 17, 1795, printed in the *South Carolina State Gazette*, March 16, 1796. Robert Goodloe Harper, *Select Works of Robert Goodloe Harper, Consisting of Speeches on Political and Forensic Subjects* (Baltimore: O. H. Neilson, 1814), beginning on p. 2.

14. RGH, *Works*, pp. 2 ff.

15. Wolfe, pp. 87-88. The meeting was held April 2, 1796, and is reported in *South Carolina State Gazette*, May 16, 1796.

16. It must be noted, however, that daring as RGH's technique was in this instance, he did not allow his own rhetoric to run away with him nor was he himself without doubts about the treaty. When the Federalists in the House tried to ram through an extremely overdone complimentary response to the president's address RGH voted against the resolution and the House response was returned to committee. *Annals*, 4C1S, December 15, 1795, pp. 144-145. On the subject of impressment, for instance, the Republicans were adamantly demanding action from the American government and RGH thought their anger justified. While he opposed a rash reaction to British unwillingness to relinquish the right, he was convinced that something had to be done for the relief of the distressed. Ibid., pp. 811-812. The reactions of Harper and the Republican Livingston were quite similar. Ibid., pp. 381-383.

17. See Bemis; Joseph Charles, *The Origins of the American Party System* (Williamsburg: Institute of Early American History and Culture, 1956); De Conde; Wilfred E. Binkley, *American Political Parties Their Natural History* (New York: Alfred A. Knopf, 1964).

18. *Annals*, 4C1S, pp. 400-401.

19. Ibid., pp. 426-783, 939-1291.

20. Alexander Hamilton to William Loughton Smith, March 10, 1796, Henry Cabot Lodge (ed.), *The Works of Alexander Hamilton* (New York: G. P. Putnam's Sons, 1903), X, 147-148. A search of the Hamilton MSS in the Library of Congress revealed little mention of the South Carolinian.

21. *Annals*, 4C1S, p. 463.

22. Madison estimated on April 18, 1796, that the defeat of the treaty could be accomplished by a majority of twenty-one votes. Irving Brant, *James Madison: Father of the Constitution* (New York: Bobbs-Merrill Co., 1941), pp. 438-439.

23. RGH quoting Albert Gallatin, *Annals*, 4C1S, p. 747; pp. 757-758.

24. Ibid., 4C1S, p. 765. To wit: "the President may have attributed to the majority [the Republicans] motives which they were not willing to avow."

25. Samuel Smith to Jonathan Dayton, Philadelphia, April 11. 1796. William Patterson Papers, Maryland Historical Society. Smith went on to say, "I believe this letter had better be with yourself only—you must be sensible that much Caution is necessary at the present moment." This was particularly true since he was writing to the Federalist Speaker of the House.

26. *Annals*, 4C1S, pp. 1280, 1282-1292, April 29 and 30, 1796.

27. Letters to His Constituents, April 10, 1796, Bayard Papers, pp. 17-18.

28. Ibid, May 2, 1796, pp. 20-22. There are sufficient grounds for questioning this "peace or war" alternative. No one questions the shrewdness of this Federalist tactic but it is possible to doubt its validity. Great Britain's interests required a neutral not a hostile United States and it seems unlikely that if the American government, Federalist and friendly, had requested some modification of the treaty in the interest of placating hostile public opinion, that the British would have been so foolish to belligerently deny the request. Such action was certain to throw the Americans into waiting French arms. Charles, pp. 118-122, and De Conde, p. 138, both suggest this interpretation.

29. RGH to Constituents, March 9, 1796, Bayard Papers. There are marginal notations in Harper's handwriting to strike out all of this letter. He was possibly preparing materials for Volume II of his *Works* [only Volume I ever appeared] circa 1814 and no doubt he might have been embarrassed by the remarks in light of the fact that he had had something to do with the American alien and sedition legislation.

30. *Annals*, 4C1S, p. 969, April 1796.

31. John Jay to RGH, January 19, 1796. Henry P. Johnston (ed.), *The Correspondence and Public Papers of John Jay* (New York: G. P. Putnam's Sons, 1893), IV, 198-203.

32. Chauncey Goodrich to Oliver Wolcott, Senior, June 1, 1796, Gibbs, I, 343.
33. Autobiography, Harper-Pennington Papers, Maryland Historical Society.
34. Ibid. This was not the last time Harper very nearly quit his success-fully launched political career. He was reelected in 1796 and then for a time planned to retire in the summer of 1797 but again changed his mind. Indeed, his career was marked by this restlessness and his early life is a continuous progression of such moves. He maintained later in life that he remained in the House out of a sense of loyalty to those who had elected him and a deep responsibility to the country due to the impending French crisis of 1798.
35. Phillips, "South Carolina Federalist Correspondence," II, 736-737.
36. Wolfe, pp. 96-97. Also see RGH to Ralph Izard, November 4, 1796, Phillips, "South Carolina Federalist Correspondence," pp. 782-784.
37. See Henry McGilbert Wagstaff (ed.), *Federalism in North Carolina* (The James Sprunt Historical Publications, Vol. IX, No. 2; Chapel Hill: University of North Carolina 1910). Even after the results of the election of 1796 were known, Federalists in North Carolina and elsewhere in the South did not "as yet voice . . . the great dread of Jefferson that was so common among Federalists elsewhere." On the other hand, neither were southern Republicans as bitter toward the retiring Washington as their counterparts in the northern states; p. 28. William Loughton Smith to Ralph Izard, November 8, 1796. Smith wrote "another cause which I hope will damn Jeffn. in the Southern States operated strongly with many of the Quakers; that is, his wishes for *emancipation*." Phillips, "South Carolina Federalist Correspon-dence," p. 785.
38. RGH to Ralph Izard, November 4, 1796; Phillips, "South Carolina Federalist Correspondence," p. 782.
39. Ibid. Dr. Ramsay was that ideal sort of candidate who could pick up support in both geographical sections of the state and he would have served, Harper thought, to undermine the chances of Ephraim Ramsay, one of the most prominent "Antis." David Duncan Wallace quotes RGH as calling Ephraim Ramsay "the ablest, the most artful and most dangerous of all the supporters of antifederalism in South Carolina." However, Wallace does not mention his source. Wallace, pp. 348-349.
40. RGH to Ralph Izard, November 4, 1796.
41. For the details of the plot as John Adams understood it see John Adams to Abigail Adams, December 12, 1796, Adams Incoming Correspondence, Reel 382 L.C. "I am not enough of an Englishman nor little enough of a Frenchman for some people," Adams told his wife.
42. See footnote 38.

43. South Carolina House Journal, December 6, 1796; Wolfe, p. 98. Also the national breakdown of the electoral college in William Nesbit Chambers, *Political Parties in a New Nation. The American Experience, 1776-1809* (New York: Oxford University Press, 1963), p. 127.
44. RGH to Constituents, January 5, 1797, Bayard Papers, pp. 24-27.
45. Ibid. It would be difficult to find a finer example of the classic American attitude toward the intellectual in politics. Harper clearly found Thomas Jefferson wanting in those qualities required of the authentic American leader-symbol. The emphasis on "manly conduct" may or may not have been a reference to Jefferson's record as a war governor in Virginia when to satisfy many Federalists he would have needed to allow himself to be captured by the British, and probably hanged.
46. Ibid. In the Bayard Papers containing this letter there is a curious notation in Harper's handwriting in the margin. "As in the original publication of the letter in the Gazettes, the parts crossed were directed to be omitted, they are now struck out, and must not be inserted. RGH." Bayard Papers, p. 27. All of the material in footnotes 43 through 45 was so crossed out but published anyway.
47. RGH to His Constituents, March 13, 1797, Bayard Papers, p. 29.
48. Ibid., pp. 29-30.
49. James D. Richardson (ed.), *Messages and Papers of the President* (New York: Bureau of National Literature, 1897), I, 218-222.
50. William C. Rogers, Jr., William L. Smith's biographer, calls Harper's victory "tremendous," pp. 288-289. The actual vote in Ninety Six saw Harper win by 1618 votes to 774 for his closest opponent. The election results were reported in the Charleston *City Gazette and Daily Advertiser*, October 25, 1796. The South Carolina state records include a copy of Harper's commission as the representative to Congress from Ninety Six but there is no official election return recorded. Volume A, Miscellaneous Records, South Carolina Archives, p. 300.
51. Rutledge was originally elected as a Republican and had been a Jefferson elector in the contest of 1796 but quickly became a warm Federalist following the French rebuff of Charles Cotesworth Pinckney. Wolfe, p. 103.
52. William Loughton Smith is not to be confused with a William Smith elected as a Republican from Pinckney District in 1796. To avoid confusion the former Smith began using his middle name about this time to identify himself. He resigned his House seat in order to accept appointment as minister to Portugal and later to Spain. He did not return to the United States until 1801. He remained a staunch Federalist until 1808, when he broke with the extremists in his party over the Chesapeake-Leopard Affair. One might expect to find evidence of an extensive "Smith-Harper Correspondence" due to their

close affiliation in the House. It would also seem likely that Smith
supplied Harper with European news during 1797-1801, and that
they corresponded during the Republican era after both had left
office. However, no such correspondence survives and one may doubt
whether it ever existed. The suspicion is that perhaps relations between the two men were less than amicable since they were after all
rivals for Carolina Federalist affections. Smith was the darling of the
down country planter class, and married exceptionally well and corresponded regularly with the great men in the northern wing of the
party. Robert Goodloe Harper, being human, must have been at least
slightly envious if not outright jealous of his associate's position and
successes.

7
Working Congressman

By far the most controversial aspect of Robert Goodloe Harper's political career was the Franco-American diplomatic crisis and the undeclared naval war of 1798, which saw Harper veer sharply to the right. It is the segment of his political career that has attracted the attention and most of the scorn. There was, however, another side to his congressional years that is usually neglected. His record as a working congressman has never been examined, and he did work more diligently than many at the day-to-day business of representing the Ninety Six District in Congress. Of concern are his views on the operation of government, his conception of good administration, sound finance, the military establishment, federal-state relations, and the like. There is considerably more to a congressman's place in history than his foreign policy position, his feelings about this or that foreign country, or the way in which he reacted to a wartime situation.

In terms of his approach to the problems of administering the central government Harper was as thorough a Federalist as there was in the Congress. Yet his administrative Federalism was sound, moderate and quite responsible. He was in this instance what one student of the era has called an "Adams Federalist," as distinct from a High-Federalist or an extreme Federalist of the Fisher Ames variety.[1] Similarly, as Harper's Federalist administrative views were moderate, so too were the attitudes of his Republican counterparts in the House, Albert Gallatin and James Madison, when compared to the more doctrinaire in their party. On occasion, when the subject of debate was some question of general administrative principle, Harper and Madison found that they had more in common with each other than either did with elements in their own political camps.

Nevertheless, there did exist between Federalist and Republican a basic cleavage of attitudes regarding the central government, and the most constantly divisive subject was executive responsibility and autonomy. It concerned how one felt about not simply the chief magistrate but his department heads and administrative assistants as well, and what their relationship was

85

to be to the legislature. From the early 1790s Federalist and "Anti" alike had rather consistently advocated either a positive or a negative attitude toward the executive. Republicans generally believed that department heads were officers largely independent of the president and responsible instead to Congress, that the executive branch itself was to be regarded as the ministerial agent of Congress, that legislative control of the purse was crucial, and that specific appropriations, rather than lump sum grants, was the best check on a too powerful executive branch of government.[2] Harper and the Federalists disagreed, in part because they were members of the "in" party and were defending the administration as their administration right or wrong, but also because many or most of these individuals were strong executive men in principle as well.[3]

In general terms the South Carolina representative's ideas about government in the United States suggested constructive Federalist administrative principle at its best. For example, he was committed to the necessity of liberal compensation for government officials, in order, Harper said, to attract the better sort of talented, principled men. He retained this attitude long after leaving office when he was no longer personally involved with the problem of miserly government salaries. "If we wish for able and faithful services we must pay their price. This the federal government has never done," Harper declared, and the quality of the government service had at times suffered for it. [4]

He was also one of the most prominent and eloquent advocates of publications, public records, reports, and other materials of interest to the general public. If the discussion on the floor of the House centered around the popular intepretation of a constitutional question Harper could very nearly always be depended upon to introduce a resolution to order the printing and distribution of five thousand copies of the Constitution. Although it may have amused the other congressmen from time to time, this penchant of Harper's for public information stood in sharp contrast to those who feared providing the people with too much information about anything.[5]

Harper was also an expansive Federalist and saw nothing immoral or unconstitutional about using the power of the central government for all kinds of purposes. For instance, he enthusiastically supported a motion to enable the commissioners for the new Federal City to receive funds contributed toward the project of a national university although he did say that he thought the actual establishment of such an institution was not propitious at that particular time.[6] On another occasion, following a terribly destructive fire in Savannah in 1796, Harper backed a proposal to extend federal aid and assistance to the stricken city. He saw such federal activity as sound policy since Savannah was one of the two considerable ports in that part of the United States. "The present case might justly be included under the head of promoting the general welfare of the country . . . ," he explained, but the proposal was defeated by a margin of two to one.[7] Harper believed that legislating for the whole country, as well as city or state, was perfectly within constitutional limitations provided that the direct object in view was constitutional. On several occasions Harper attempted to secure passage of a bill to provide a uniform system of bankruptcy, the problem being that definition and proceedings varied erratically from state to state; but the bill was usually either ignored by a disinterested House or returned to committee.[8]

On another general question, the necessity and wisdom of political parties and their role in government, Robert Goodloe Harper's views were considerably more sophisticated than those of most other Americans of this particular period. In fact, Harper's belief that parties were a "positive good" rather than a "necessary evil" made him almost unique in Federalist circles and probably in advance of the thinking of most Republicans. Indeed, his comprehension of the role of the party system has been so neglected as to justify quotation at some length. "Ambitious statesmen," he said,

> did not wish for office, but power; They did not wish to hold posts themselves, but to direct those who did hold them; to see their own system adopted . . . and the affairs of the country conducted in the way which they approved. While men should continue to think differently . . . there would always be a number of persons who would disapprove the manner in which public affairs . . . were conducted. These persons, in Governments like ours, would gradually form themselves into a party, and their opinions would assume the shape of a political system, different from that actually adopted. These two systems would be in a perpetual state of conflict, and the supporters of that which might happen to be vanquished, would feel mortification and chagrin. These feelings would become more and more violent in proportion as their defeats were more frequent . . . the party which could not rule [would be] prompted to suspect and arraign the motives which actuated the authors of their defeat.[9]

Parties were therefore inevitable, and to thwart their growth one would have to alter human nature, which obviously Robert Goodloe Harper did not believe possible.

As to the merits of political alignment, Harper explained that:

> He not only knew that it must exist while men should be made as they are, but he believed that it ought to exist. While opposite parties in the Government struggled for preeminence, they were like persons engaged in an exhibition before the public, who are obliged to display superior merit and superior excellence in order to gain the prize. The public is the judge, the two parties are the combatants, and that party which possesses power must employ it properly, must conduct the Government wisely, in order to insure public approbation. . . . In this contention, while the two parties draw different ways, a middle course is produced, generally conformable to public good. Party spirit, therefore, and the contentions to which it gave rise, neither alarmed nor displeased him. It might . . . sometimes run into excess, and produce mischief . . . but its general effects, like those of the great elements of nature [wind, fire, etc.], he had no doubt, were beneficial.[10]

This was no empty posturing. Harper believed every word of this speech; although, ironically, in characterizing the origin and behavior of the Republican party during the Federalist period he was also accurately foretelling the history of his own party during the next decade.

Such, in general terms, was the state of Harper's Federalism except for one major qualification to all of his thoughts regarding the central government. No matter how open-minded his understanding of the role of the central government, the question of slavery or some related topic was always important enough to overshadow all other considerations. Harper, who quite often thought in terms of using federal authority or expanding federal responsibility to new areas, fought against the reception by the House of the emancipationist petitions from northern Quaker groups that periodically arrived at the capitol.

For instance, in the fall of 1797, a particularly all-encompassing Quaker petition was received. The communication stated the group's opposition to the slave trade, the reenslavement of freed slaves, horseracing, "shows, plays, & other expensive diversions." Immediately after Gallatin had moved the second reading of the petition, Harper and John Rutledge were on their feet to attack the petition and its authors. This was not the first time the House had received these "inflamatory declarations," Harper pointed out, and they were not only troublesome but tended to stir up "a class of persons to inflict calamities which would be of greater consequences than any evils . . ." the nation had yet encountered. Every legislative body ought to refuse these "remonstrances complaining of what it was utterly impossible to alter." John Rutledge, who by this time had come over to the Federalist side, fully agreed with his fellow South Carolinian and said that redress for injustice, if it had occurred, was to be sought in the courts and not the House of Representatives." This was obviously the one subject which the federal authority inventory of even the most sophisticated and liberal southern Federalist did not include.

Harper, the working representative, when examined in closer detail, emerges even more clearly as a moderate Federalist who had a very respectable grasp of the machinery of American government and its sound administration. His understanding of the perpetual struggle between the executive and legislative branches of that government, touched upon earlier, needs to be further refined, particularly the matter of executive leadership.

Federalists generally thought in terms of an energetic executive branch of government and like most conservatives of their generation they had a great deal of respect for the necessity for power in government. Thus, they were likely to regard any increase in legislative initiative as a weakening of the executive branch and a dilution of the strength of government. They saw no merit whatsoever in the diversification of power theme, the logical end of which was anarchy. Federalists were constantly complaining about the behavior of Congress, its seeming inability to move quickly, or the noticeable unwillingness of its members to accept marching orders from the president or his congressional friends.[12] Alexander Hamilton went so far as to say that the legislative branch had restricted and weakened the authority of the executive to such a degree that capable men would take their talents elsewhere rather than endure the frustrations of government service.[13]

The opposition Republicans strongly disagreed, for they stood in mortal fear of unrestricted power in any form, at any level of government. Suspicious of the executive branch prima facie, they held that the experience of the early 1790s simply confirmed their fears and further strengthened their commitment to the protection of the liberties of individual citizens and the maintenance of representative assemblies as the best practical approach

to government. Ideologically, this ranged all the way from the
Virginia doctrinaires, with their atomization attitude toward all
concentrations of power above the county level, to the much
more moderate Madison and Jefferson who realized the necessity
for such concentration of authority, even at the federal level,
during such emergencies as war. Whereas many Federalists saw
the legislature constantly floundering, forever in need of the
guidance of a strong hand from its partner in government, the
Republicans believed just as ardently that the legislature if given
its head and freedom of discussion could be depended upon to
make its own way. Jefferson, like Hamilton, grasped the significance of the legislative-executive contest, but he was equally
wrong in predicting the outcome when he expressed his belief
that the executive branch would swallow up the legislature.[14]
Both men thought in terms of a great institutional Armageddon
which would forever decide the relationship between the two
branches of the government. Both failed to conceive of the
struggle as perpetual, with defeats and victories for each side.

Harper falls somewhere between the extremes of these two
ideological battle lines and if, in general terms, he must be placed
in the former rather than the latter camp the assignment will,
nevertheless, require some qualification. Far from being contemptuous of the more representative of the two houses of the
American Congress, Harper valued the opportunities offered by
the House of Representatives over executive officeholding. In
most countries, he said, political office conferred power, patronage, and prestige and was sought for those reasons by ambitious
men. In the United States, however, this was not the case since
office conferred none of these advantages. The House of Representatives was the only place in the American government which
held promise for such men.

> There and there alone they had a conspicuous theatre for the display of
> their talents, . . . there alone could they acquire fame, popularity, and
> political importance, . . . there alone could they make a strong impres-
> sion on the country and the Government. . . . There, of course, they
> would desire to remain and not to undertake offices, which though
> respectable, were not brilliant, imposed much labor, but conferred
> neither splendor nor authority.[15]

By the conclusion of the first session of the Fifth Congress,
which had convened in May of 1797, Robert Goodloe Harper
had become a prominent Federalist in the House of Representa-

tives, so much the more so because he was a southern Federalist. He fell heir to the mantle of William Loughton Smith's occasional leadership of the House Federalist forces when that gentleman resigned to assume his diplomatic duties in Portugal in July 1797.[16] This is not to say that Harper became majority floor leader in anything like the modern sense, for indeed under the two Federalist presidents there was no such person who acted for or was recognized as spokesman of the executive branch. Until he resigned, Alexander Hamilton was either his own executive spokesman or acted through another such as William Loughton Smith, but not until the Republican era did a floor spokesman for the president evolve in the House. Harper and several other congressmen shared command of the Federalist forces in the House and most of the time acted pretty much on their own instead of responding to executive direction and suggestion.[17]

/ Since neither of the first two presidents were inclined to interfere directly in the deliberations of the Congress it was that much easier for individuals outside the legislature to influence what transpired inside the chambers of the House and Senate. This goes far to explain much of the frustration of John Adam's presidency and supports the thesis that the second president's difficulties were to a great degree of his own making. During a national crisis he nearly abdicated his place of responsibility for Abigail and Quincy; he declined to attempt to lead the legislature and thus its members looked elsewhere for advice and counsel. Elsewhere meant New York and New England elder statesmen. Robert Goodloe Harper was able to swim in this rough northern political sea because of his prowess in debate, and also because Federalist votes from south of the Potomac could not be lightly dismissed.

While Harper did not share the doubts of many of his friends in Congress about the House of Representatives, he was completely in agreement with their views concerning the necessity for unity within the Federalist administration. Both Washington and Adams came under attack for appointing only Federalists to important executive positions. Harper could never understand why the Republicans were so disturbed by this practice. He asked, "Was this anything so extraordinary? Was it not practiced by every man of common understanding in the management of his own affairs?" That the president should appoint individuals who disagreed with the fundamental principles of the administration was patently ridiculous. This maxim was most important in diplomacy, for foreign affairs, he said, had proved the most divisive issue of all. "The greatest differences of opinion that exist among us, arise from these relations" and common sense required the appointment of men favorable to the program they were to administer."[18] As Harper outlined it, the Republican course was to criticize the government's policies from the outside and then take their arguments to the electorate in an attempt to replace the administration with one of their own choosing at the next national election. Unfortunately, the party in power came increasingly to deny this recourse to the opposition, and before the decade ended, Robert Goodloe Harper led the lamentable attack against Federalism's critics. However, despite any qualifications concerning Harper's understanding of the executive-legislative conflict, he consistently came down on the side which sought to strengthen the authority and autonomy of the executive branch.

Both Federalists and Republicans were aware that the most crucial confrontation in this power struggle involved taxes and appropriations. These eighteenth-century gentlemen were no more capable of forgetting this fact of political life than they were of dismissing their colonial experience. Executive and legislative partisans needed no reminder about the significance of the purse strings. Thus, what was involved here was not so much a partisan or even a sectional division but how individuals reacted to the basic question of granting the executive branch of government a significant degree of fiscal discretion. Then, too, related questions regarding forms of taxation, disbursement, accounting, and fiscal management had to be answered. And of concern here is Robert Goodloe Harper's role in finding and implementing the answers to these questions.

During the Federalist period the central government had an aggregate income of some fifty-four million dollars, with import duties providing all but four million dollars of the total.[19] The domestic expenses of government alone, which included servicing of the debt, placed a great strain upon the national finances, but the defense measures necessitated by the foreign crisis of 1798 made matters far worse. The national executive branch began the decade by garnering to itself almost all of the fiscal initiative and then watched as an increasingly jealous legislature eroded this prerogative and transferred the initiative back to Congress.

When the First Congress convened in 1789 the House created a "Committee on Ways and Means" to prepare a report of probable expenses and estimated revenues for the remainder of that first year of operation. The committee went to work and reported back to the House two months later. However, it really made little difference what this first committee included in its report, for in the meantime Hamilton was appointed secretary of the treasury. All pending business was gratefully turned over to him and the committee dismissed. Since Hamilton, rather than a committee, was to report directly to the Congress on fiscal estimates this meant that the initiative in planning and budget preparation rested with the executive departments not the Congress, and it remained so throughout the decade. Financial problems were automatically referred to the secretary or the head of the particular department in question, and the legislature then reacted to the detailed estimates returned by the executive.[20]

The resurgence of the Ways and Means Committee can be dated from early 1794 when the House asked its own committee of fifteen to report on revenue recommendations. Albert Gallatin and Harper both sat on this committee and both occasionally served as chairman. The Pennsylvanian acted as the spokesman for those who sought to limit executive independence, while Harper defended the fiscal establishment as it already existed. In actuality, the two men were not as far apart fiscally as they were in the area of foreign policy or other aspects of domestic policy. Their feelings about the national debt, for instance, were not really very different. The real enemy of the Bank of the United States was William Branch Giles, not Albert Gallatin. However, unfortunately for Harper, he and Gallatin did clash frequently on the floor of the House and when the subject was finance the gentleman from South Carolina came off badly. His rhetoric might get him by any other time, but in these instances Gallatin had the facts and knew how to use them while Harper was out of his element. The meetings of the Ways and Means Committee must have been anything but dull.[21]

The central government was in need of new revenues even before the French crisis of 1798. Indeed, the Land Act of 1796 had originated as much in a need for revenue as in a desire to settle the western lands. In the spring of 1796 the House debated a direct tax program, and the possibility of having to resort to this expedient troubled many a congressman. The Ways and Means Committee had introduced a series of proposals to provide the House with the necessary alternative programs should such a tax be necessary in the future. Harper's reaction was curious. In

April, he went on record as being in favor of direct taxes, but thought that limits as to amounts ought to be established before the Congress went very much further. However, perhaps because it was an election year, he added that the present taxes and the revenues they produced were sufficient to meet the needs of the national government.[22]   Direct taxes meant, in South Carolina terms, property taxes, which were not at all popular when levied from Columbia, let alone Philadelphia.

By January of the next year Harper was announcing his opposition to a recommendation from the same committee for an implementation of direct land taxation. Instead, he said he favored indirect levies such as raising the duty on tea, wines, foreign spirits, and oddly, considering the district he represented, higher duties on salt and sugar. In addition, he had in mind a stamp duty and window tax. Reliance on indirect taxation, he said, was more equitable to all sections of the country, notably the area away from the coast which he represented. Harper lost, for the land-tax part of the resolution passed the House by a vote of forty-eight to thirty-nine with Federalists and Republicans on both sides of the division.[23]

His up-country predilections were dramatically revealed, when after the House went on record in favor of the land-tax plan with Harper voting against, he then spoke in favor of the accompanying tax on slaves. He was opposed to the direct tax idea per se, but since the House favored the suggestion he thought "it right that a tax on slaves should be introduced with a tax on land . . ." and, since direct taxes had to be apportioned among the states "whether the Southern States paid on slaves, or the Northern states on land, made no difference in effect. . . ."[24]

This southern unwillingness to resort to the direct tax was later modified by revenue needs, but on most occasions Harper still thought along the lines of combining direct and indirect tax programs with the latter carrying most of the revenue load. In February 1797 he explained his tax position again and incidentally, in so doing, described the situation he and many other southerners found themselves in.

A man might possess a great capital, and yet not possess equal means with the man of small capital. A man might possess a great capital in land but it might be in such a situation as not to be saleable, or too far removed from market to be profitable. This kind of property did not enable a man to pay taxes. . . ."[25]

In the 1830s, even after the cotton boom ran the price of new lands up far higher than in Harper's day, most southerners still shared this southern Federalist view of direct taxes. The ease with which a wealthy planter might be forced to become land poor in order to assure future acreage continued to plague the South long after the Federalist party disappeared.

The debate within the legislative chambers of the American government was not restricted to revenue alone but dealt equally with the other side of the fiscal operation, appropriations. Once again the conflict concerned the fundamental question of how much independence of operation to grant the executive branch of government. Republicans sought to place the controls over spending under strict congressional supervision, while the "friends of government" demanded reasonable freedom of action for the heads of the various departments.[26]   In this instance, Harper strongly supported the Federalist interpretation and posited himself as Gallatin's chief adversary both in committee and on the floor of the House.

When Gallatin and the Republicans sought to replace the older lump sum appropriations with specific grants, Harper and the Federalists charged administrative anarchy, but they recognized, as did their opponents, the crucial nature of the real issue at stake here. Under Alexander Hamilton's direction the lump sum appropriation had offered a great deal of flexibility which the secretary had occasionally taken advantage of. The Republicans from 1792 on sought to restrict this potentially dangerous, as they saw it, degree of administrative discretion. This was certainly the case after Gallatin's arrival in the House in 1795, and they were successful in 1797, in 1798, and 1799 in changing the language of the civil appropriations bills to provide for more specific expenditures. However, Republican success at establishing closer congressional controls over spending is easily exaggerated. For the most part, Harper and the Federalists in the House were able to evade a strict usage of the Gallatin fiscal phraseology; the military establishment successfully resisted specific appropriations, and the war in 1798 undid most of the Republican gains in limiting the operating freedom of the administration.

The Franco-American crisis, which strained the government's ability to raise revenues, also tested the machinery by which the administration actually made the expenditures, particularly defense spending. The story of the American government's attempts to provide for its military establishment during the Revolution reeked of abysmal inefficiency and even war profiteering, and the 1790s did not suggest that things had improved very much. Disastrous military reverses in the campaign against the Indians earlier in the decade had exposed the weakness of the system of independent contracting by individual agencies of government. Alexander Hamilton had been able to convince the Congress that the Treasury Department ought to make all military purchases required by federal forces. Accordingly, the office of purveyor of the public supplies had been created to implement the secretary's plan.[27]

Under the tremendous pressure of the defense expenditures of 1798-1799 this new central purchasing approach to procurement broke down. Robert Goodloe Harper was appointed to chair a committee to investigate the entire matter of defense spending and the committee's report damned the system from top to bottom. The secretary of war did not know to which account to charge supplies, and the secretary of the treasury, while aware of proper accounting, did not know what the supplies his department was buying were to be used for. Responsibility was thus hopelessly divided. Under such a system, the committee reported, "the Secretary of War cannot be responsible for the expenditure of the moneys appropriated for his Department . . . [and] the Secretary of the Treasury cannot be responsible for the due execution of the public service. . . ."[28] Following the Harper Committee's report the program of military purchasing reverted to the older form of departmental contract, which while not any more economical was at least less complicated.

The point that Robert Goodloe Harper's Federalism was of the eclectic variety is further illustrated by his views concerning such diverse topics as defense, the Bank of the United States, and the national debt. On the general subject of defense measures he was consistently Federalist; that is, he voted to retain and expand the existing military organization. However, on specifics Harper's independent ways are once again apparent.

He agreed with a proposed reorganization of the militia in 1796 that was intended to create a more efficient organization constituting a compromise part way between the existing state system and a standing establishment, which Harper said "was not wished by any."[29] Like most Federalists he voted for the Provisional Army in 1798 and against any cuts in defense spending.[30] But he was considerably more of a navy advocate than most northern Federalists, who tended to be far more interested in the provisional army. Harper was a "Navy Federalist" long before 1798. He led the fight in the House not only for enlarging the navy but for the building of a federally operated navy yard and the purchase of reserve naval timber lands to meet future needs. The question, as Harper put it to the country, was, "Will you give up commerce or build a Navy to protect it?"[31]

On the subject of the Bank and the standing national debt he was equally undoctrinaire. A defender of the financial institution against the attacks of both Giles and Gallatin, "he thought the Bank was a very valuable connexion for Government, and they ought to retain it." Nevertheless, he was able to adopt a curiously "antifederalist" attitude toward the debt and his views were considerably closer to Gallatin's than Hamilton's. He told the House that "he wished to pay the debt, because it was a continual source of anathema." He would go as high as $2,000,000 in direct taxes earmarked to pay the public debt "because it was [a] subject of discontent, cavail, and invective."[32]

Upon leaving public service in 1801, Harper wrote his last letter to his constituents in which he outlined what he understood the relationship between the state and central governments to be.

> The Federalists considered it as a principle of the utmost importance . . . to render [the central government] . . . as independent as possible of state influence; to give it a movement of its own, . . . power to enforce its own laws . . . and to restrain the state governments within their just and proper bounds.[33]

This statement of principle was considerably more High-Federalist than Harper actually was if this interpretation of his House career is accurate. There is no doubt that Robert Goodloe Harper in case of a conflict between state and central government interests was most likely to settle on the side of federal paramountcy. That is, there is no doubt except when the state in question happened to be South Carolina, or perhaps it only·had to be south of the Potomac. It may have been that the southern nature of the question before the House was enough to cause him to qualify his Federalism.

Robert Goodloe Harper, working congressman, was not an unsocial boor who spent all his leisure time poring over committee reports and preparing for the next day's business. Even to that generation, fortunate enough to serve in Congress before the advent of the mimeograph machine, the weight of materials to be read was troublesome. Harper did his homework and he did it conscientiously, but there was still ample opportunity to enjoy the most delightful and stimulating city in the country, not the least attraction of which was the charm and beauty of its feminine inhabitants.

Once again, the source of information is the loquacious William Sullivan of Boston. It seems that he and Harper had shared each other's company on the occasion of a great many social forays in Philadelphia, and that they, for a time, were competitors for the affections of the same lady. Sullivan had moved to Boston but kept up both the competition and his correspondence with Harper. Most of the letters between the two gentlemen celebrated the "angelic women" of Philadelphia and contained a curious amount of advice to each other on the subject of how best to win the lady in question. Writing to Sullivan in March 1797, Harper told his friendly rival that he was not to consider calling off his amatory campaign simply because Harper was interested as well. "I repeatedly assured you that your pursuing the lady and gaining her, though it would fill me with regret . . . would never excite in my bosom one unpleasant feeling towards you. This perhaps is not a common conduct, but I feel myself capable of it." [34] Of course, Harper was also telling Sullivan that he had no intention of giving up the quest either and he had the advantage of being in Philadelphia.

On one occasion, Sullivan, writing at midnight and recalling the evenings he and Harper had strolled home late together, chided Harper for having just returned from "some fair one on whose tongue dwelleth music—and from whose lips floweth the sweetness of honey."[35] Throughout the spring, summer, and fall of 1797 the two men exchanged notes concerning their progress with the lady, who may possibly have been one of the daughters of the socially prominent Bingham family. In one letter Sullivan referred to a conversation he and Harper had in front of Mr. Bingham's home and then mentioned that he had departed Philadelphia in order to give Harper a clear field with "the lady who controls yr. fate and mine." In the same letter Sullivan promised that he would not return to Philadelphia until he had Harper's permission to appear before "Miss B. or Mrs. Harper."[36]

It would appear that the pact they had agreed to initially had not worked out and Sullivan had withdrawn temporarily to allow

Harper his chance with the lady. While Harper was making the most of the opportunity either foolishly or confidently given him by his competitor, Sullivan kept him entertained with the latest Boston gossip, and on occasion an exceedingly ribald tale.

The most bawdy such story concerned the amorous adventures of one Williamson who must have been a mutual acquaintance. Williamson and Sullivan, while driving one morning, had encountered an extremely buxom lass who could not be lured into the carriage, but who inexplicably quite willingly went off into the forest with Williamson while Sullivan drove on ahead a bit to wait. Sullivan reported that after a while Williamson returned "with an exulting countenance—What luck? [Sullivan asked, to which Williamson replied] I left her panting in the bushes." Harper's friend went on to say that ever since the episode took place, Williamson had been so impressed with his prowess that "a modest woman must have powerful charms to make him frequent her society."[37]

Harper and Sullivan continued to court the fair Miss B. until the winter of 1799. Both urged the other to persevere, each reminding the other that love was an uphill game. Finally, in January 1799 Sullivan confessed to Harper that he had come to regard his efforts as "sheer quixotism" and was on the verge of giving up.[38] Since this is the last letter in this revealing series there is no way of knowing how much longer the two of them continued to labor unrequitedly in this particular vineyard. Probably not long, for each man had married someone other than the mysterious Miss B. within three years of the date of this last letter.

In one of the most delightful letters in the correspondence William Sullivan quoted the following lines from Pindar to Harper, perhaps expressing both his and Harper's outlook on life.

I own I love to laugh & hate to sigh
and think that visibility was giv'n
For human happiness by gracious Heav'n
and that we came not into life to cry.[39]

Judging by the foregoing, they must have both agreed that neither do we come into life merely to labor. Yet, Harper was to have little time in the months ahead for leisure and the ladies. The United States was on the verge of conflict with France and civil crisis at home, troubled years which tested the nation and individuals alike. The nation was to pass the trial but not so Robert Goodloe Harper.

NOTES

1. Manning J. Dauer, *The Adams Federalists* (Baltimore: The Johns Hopkins University Press), 1953.
2. White, p. 94.
3. This was certainly true of Harper, who remained an advocate of executive leadership later in his life when the executive in question most likely was a Republican.
4. RGH, *Works*, pp. 333-335.
5. See Harper's speech to the House February 1, 1796, *Annals* 4C1S, pp. 286-287.
6. Ibid. 4C2S, pp. 1721-1722.
7. Ibid.
8. Ibid., pp. 1739-1740.
9. This excerpt is from an entire speech devoted to political parties delivered on the floor of the House, January 19, 1798; *Annals*, 5C2S, pp. 873-875.
10. Ibid., pp. 873-875, January 19, 1798. This speech drew little comment from Harper's fellow Federalists in the House and his views on this subject were never accepted by even a minority of his own party.
11. Ibid., pp. 658-659. Rutledge was not opposed to recommitting the petition "if he thought the strong censure they [the petitioners] deserved would be the report of the committee . . . a set of men who attempted to seduce the servants of gentlemen travelling to the seat of Government" had to be dealt with quickly and decisively.
12. White, p. 89.
13. Alexander Hamilton to Oliver Wolcott, February 17, 1797; Gibbs, I, 443. Fisher Ames to Oliver Wolcott, April 24, 1797; Gibbs, I, 449. Fisher Ames to Hamilton, January 26, 1797; *Hamilton Works*, VI, 200-201 (Hamilton, ed.). "The efficiency of the government is reduced to its minimum—. . . committees already are the ministers; and while the House indulges a jealousy of encroachment on its functions, which are properly deliberative, it does not perceive that these are impaired and nullified by the monopoly as well as the perversion of information, by these very committees."

14. White, pp. 88-89.
15. *Annals*, 5C3S, January 19, 1798. It must be admitted that Harper's strictures concerning the willingness of the House to enhance legislative authority at the expense of the executive branch did not always square with the congressman's pronouncements about not wishing to leave the House for higher office.
16. Gibbs, I, 556. The first mention of Harper in the Gibbs Federalist narrative referred to July 1797. ' Among those who were conspicuous in the Federal ranks . . . in the House [were] Otis, Sewall, Griswold, Goodrich, Bayard, Sitgreaves, Harper, Rutledge, and Smith."
17. Ralph V. Harlow, *The History of Legislative Methods before 1825* (New Haven: Yale University Press, 1917), p. 177, quoted in George B. Galloway, *History of the House of Representatives* (New York: Thomas Y. Crowell, 1962), p. 98. "This floor leader was not looked upon as the personal representative of the president himself. He was rather an assistant to the speaker." Harlow went on to point out that for the first twenty years the speakers themselves were merely figureheads with little real power comparable to the modern Speaker of the House. L. D. White was probably close to the truth when he pointed out that so much is made of the origins of parties in sectional, class divisions, etc. that a basic, older, and more important power struggle is overlooked—the contest between the executive and the House. White, p. 51. Congressional resistance to executive leadership existed from the very beginning and indeed preceded the convening of the First Congress. This natural unwillingness to be led was only aggravated by Alexander Hamilton's and later Federalist's aggressiveness. Much of the opposition to Hamilton's programs may well have stemmed from this fear of executive interference and growth of influence rather than opposition in principle to all facets of the suggested programs.
18. *Annals*, 5C2S, January 19, 1798, pp. 874-877.
19. *American State Papers: Finance*, I, 665, quoted in White, p. 336.

Tariff and Tonnage Duties	$50,321,525.77
Internal Revenues	3,632,768.93
Postage	280,808.84
Land Sales	100,339.84
Fines	17,078.81

These figures reveal just how completely dependent the Federalist financial system was on a continuation of foreign trade.
20. White, pp. 323-324. The policy of automatic referral ceased with the reactivation of the finance committee in the House and to some extent represents House resistance to Hamilton's strong fiscal leadership during the first few years of the decade.

21. Gallatin left the following description of Harper. He was "as great a bungler as I ever knew, very good hearted, and not deficient in talents, exclusively that of speaking, which he certainly possesses to a high degree; but his vanity destroys him." A. G. to Hannah Gallatin, December 19, 1797, Albert Gallatin Papers, quoted in Walters, pp. 87-88.

22. *Annals*, 4C1S, pp. 849-852.

23. Ibid., 4C2S, January, 1797, pp. 1863-1864, 1933.

24. Ibid., p. 1934.

25. Ibid., p. 2169. Harper recognized that the nature of southern agriculture dictated that only a part of a man's real estate holdings were probably productive and profitable at any given time.

Andrew Jackson represented the newly created state of Tennessee in this session of Congress and while he contributed almost nothing to the debates it is interesting to compare his voting record with Harper's. Jackson voted with the Republicans from the start and obviously he and Harper were most often on opposite sides. But, on what can be called "southern questions," direct taxation being such a question, the voting record of the two congressmen compares favorably.

26. White, pp. 323-324.

27. *Annals*, 3C2S, February 1795, pp. 1227-1229. The purveyor of the public supplies was, as expected, directly responsible to the secretary of the treasury and, in effect, this gave the secretary of the treasury considerable influence within the War Department. The same unsuccessful Indian campaigns also produced the first congressional investigating committee in the nation's history.

28. Ibid., 5C2S, July 1798, pp. 21, 31-32; *American State Papers: Finance*, I, 591; White, pp. 361-364.

29. *Annals*, 4C2S, December 1796, pp. 1677-1678.

30. Ibid., p. 1981.

31. Ibid., pp. 2125-2126, 2130. This navy speech is an excellent example of Harper's oratorical style at its best. He never really modified the approach he had learned in college debating and it proved very effective for him. See also, *Annals*, 5C2S, April 25, 1798, pp. 1550-1551, for his remarks on the establishment of the Navy Department.

32. *Annals*, 4C1S, pp. 1441-1443; 4C2S, p. 1891.

33. RGH, *Works*, pp. 324-325. The letter was dated March 5, 1801, but was not printed in the South Carolina newspapers until some time later, after Harper had left office.

34. William Sullivan to RGH, March 12, 1796, William Sullivan Papers, LC; RGH to Sullivan, March 19, 1797, Sullivan Papers.

35. Sullivan to RGH, May 4, 1797, Sullivan Papers.
36. Sullivan to RGH, October 3, 1797.
37. Sullivan to RGH, June 28, 1797.
38. Sullivan to RGH, January 7, 1799.
39. Sullivan to RGH, May 4, 1797.

8

The French Crisis: Preparedness

John Adams began his administration under the darkened skies of European troubles that plagued him until his last moments in office. Conflict with England had been temporarily resolved by the Jay Treaty and Anglo-American relations were luxuriating in an unaccustomed amicability. However, the very treaty that avoided a war with England threatened to provoke a war with an expansionist France.

The diplomacy of the revolutionary period still bound the United States to France, particularly so in time of conflict involving their old mutual foe. Involved in a life and death struggle with her ancient enemy, France attempted to take full advantage of the agreements respecting the defense of the West Indies and usage of American ports by French warships and privateers. The French government sought to implement these treaty guarantees and Citizen Genêt had proceeded on the assumption that the Americans were more than willing to honor the commitments of the 1778 Alliance.

The Jay Treaty, when finally publicized, produced a great cry of treachery and indignant shouts of betrayal from America's erstwhile ally. Gallic resentment was temporarily lessened by Minister James Monroe's sincere pronouncements that the treaty contained nothing that might impair the 1778 Alliance. Unfortunately Monroe's assurances were based on sincerity rather than accurate information.

During the winter and spring of 1796-1797 the Directory set out on a course intended as an object lesson to the Americans, whose diplomatic crimes were added to by the election of that notorious Anglophile John Adams to the presidency. Beginning in December of 1796 French seizures of American merchantmen and their cargoes showed a marked increase. The French definitions of contraband and "English goods" were broadened to such a degree that a single English handkerchief was sufficient to warrant confiscation by French officials. In March 1797, in the most barbarous statement of the new attitude of the French government, the Directory announced that American citizens who had been impressed into the British navy were to be executed whenever captured, like common pirates.' Judging from the anguished pleas from those unfortunate American seamen cast up on foreign beaches by French prize courts, the squadrons of French privateers were just as efficient at their work as the British navy had been.

American reaction to this vindictive shift in French policy was not immediate in forming, but coalesced slowly over a period of some twelve or thirteen months stretching from January 1797 through the shocking revelations of the XYZ papers in the spring of 1798. Actually, America's response to the new French attitude had begun to take shape during the last months of George Washington's presidency. Charles Cotesworth Pinckney, South Carolina Federalist of impeccable reputation and character, was dispatched by President Washington to Paris to attempt the negotiation of the outstanding differences between the United States and France. The other Mr. Pinckney had been so successful in Spain, perhaps the General hoped that the Pinckneys were blessed with a particular talent for coping with the Latin mind. Regrettably, however, Talleyrand was not Godoy, the French and Spanish situations were not analogous, and Minister Pinckney was unable even to secure permission to remain in France, let alone negotiate a settlement.

While the French were rejecting the new American minister the Fourth Congress was sitting in its final session. As part of the laborious practice begun in 1789, the House was taken up with the task of replying to the president's annual State of the Union message. Both Republicans and Federalists took the business quite seriously, with most congressmen seeing a good deal of symbolic importance involved in the formal reply of the House to the address. During the first several congressional sessions there really had not been very much difficulty drafting a message, but as the 1790s wore on and as party alignments became more rigid, the process of constructing a response became a ridiculous and meaninglessly time-consuming exercise. The nature of the debates was such that grammatical construction and choice of phraseology consumed hours. At times it all became exceedingly farcical; especially since their reply, which generally emerged in a compromised, watered-down form, counted for very little either as an expression of congressional opinion or any sort of check upon the president.

Giles and the Republicans complained that the reply to the

executive was too flattering and that the state of the Union was
not what it should be. Harper rose to make clear that the nation
was prosperous, free, and happy and that all this was owing to
the Federalist system.[2] He and Giles then proceeded to debate
the economic and social state of the country with neither convincing anyone not already committed. Finally, on December 16,
the reply was finished and in this instance it was of some
significance. A Federalist-sponsored resolution calling for a more
bellicose French position, a harder stance than the American
government had taken, was defeated.[3] American sentiment at
this juncture supported negotiation but not much beyond that.

Predictably, Harper spelled out his own thoughts about revolutionary France and the prospects for improving relations between
the Directory and the United States in his letters to his constituents. His attitudes tended to be considerably more Francophobic and hardened more quickly than was the case with
many of his southern colleagues in Congress. Moreover Robert
Goodloe Harper became more violently anti-French with each
new Gallic "insult." Perhaps this is to be explained as the
reaction of a zealot who had been converted to the opposing
cause, the believer who, having rejected the errors of his past,
becomes "the true believer." By way of rationalizing his former
behavior, he seeks to be loudest and most damning in his condemnation of that which he once fervently supported. Perhaps—
except that Harper was never the ardent Jacobin he was supposed
to have been.

Years later, in a series of letters written for a Philadelphia
newspaper and intended as an evaluation of the Federalist period,
Harper reflected upon the American reaction to the French
Revolution and contrasted himself to James Monroe, who was
then retiring from public life and also writing articles for the
newspapers. The opinions, Harper wrote, which different men
had entertained about the French Revolution in its early stages
had depended on the cast of their minds and their personal
temperament rather than their political principles.

> Those of an ardent and sanguine temperament viewed its first workings
> and movements, with hope approaching to confidence, with joy, and
> with exultation. To those of a cooler temperament, a more cautious
> . . . and hesitating character, the opposite view of the picture was
> presented. They had gloomy and fearful forbodings, and viewed the
> scene with apprehension and dread.

Initially, he and Monroe were both of the "sanguine party."[4]

However, no matter how often Harper asserted that he had originally been a warm friend to the French Revolution, there is sufficient reason to doubt his assertions. Harper's explanation of the reasons why he quit the "sanguine party" are unique. He most often dated his disenchantment with the revolution from the post-Jay-Treaty-period and he related it in one way or another to the shift in French policy respecting American shipping and neutral rights. There is not a single instance of Harper's mentioning the Terror, or the fate of Louis XVI, as the turning point in his attitude toward the revolutionary struggle in France. Most Americans who went the Francophobic route did so in the disgust and fear engendered by the reign of Madame Guillotine, and they generally made their decision long before 1797.

Perhaps Robert Goodloe Harper, like many of his countrymen, had simply not been that concerned or involved with the distant revolutionary struggle, and it can be suggested that they reacted only when that revolution posed an immediate problem for the United States. When the anti-Gallic storm erupted in 1798, for most Americans it was essentially a nationalistic knee-jerk response rather than an ideological reaction, as has been so often asserted. How else can one explain the outburst's rapid disappearance once the diplomatic crisis abated in 1800? This interpretation flies in the face of most of the scholarship that emphasizes the pervasive impact of the French Revolution on the origins of American political development. The democratic--republican societies were certainly the nuclear beginnings of the Republican Party, but just as certainly they would have come into being even if the French Revolution had never occurred.

American reaction to the French Revolution in its early stages might well be compared to the civil rights movement of the 1960s. No one suggests that most or all Americans were directly involved on one side or the other in this contemporary struggle; yet, some time hence it may well seem to some future historian that this was the case, because the historical record will be affected largely by those who are participants, not by the great mass of the noninvolved.

At any rate, in January of 1797 Harper detailed the course of European events in a letter to Ninety Six. After recounting Napoleon's successes in Italy, he commented upon the new direction the revolution was taking. As long as the French were fighting for their national independence, he said, every heart supported them. But now the desire for independence had been replaced by the quest for imperial dominion. Liberty, equality, and fraternity for liberated Europeans meant only the exchange of one form of tyranny for another. France was attempting to emulate the Roman conquest of the world under the pretext of making men free, and the protective despotism of the "New Rome," Harper asserted, threatened the "happiness of mankind." [5]

> While they pretended to be our best friends, they plundered us of many millions of dollars, probably more, by one half, than was seized from us by the British. . . . They now, under pretence that we have treated them ill, take all our ships that are alledged to have British property on board, or are bound to or from British ports, and condemn them under the most frivolous and shameful pretexts. [6]

While those in the know in Charleston shipping circles might doubt Harper's figures regarding damages, the folks in his western baliwick could applaud his assessment of this affront to American honor and their response was to elect him again in 1798.

Harper despaired of the prospects for peace as long as France enjoyed military success. Reading a conspiratorial motivation into the decision of revolutionary leadership for the program of war and conquest, Harper said he believed that this foreign war was being continued for domestic reasons. Peace meant civil commotion in France and internal division, as well as economic dislocation once the vast revenues of conquest were halted. The French people were not accustomed to free government and were disposed toward insurrection and revolution; their temperament was violent, fiery, and turbulent and they could be restrained from civil war only by foreign war and the splendor of military victory. The "New Romans" grasped the psychology of the circus just as their imperial predecessors had. Harper thought the only way to bring the French to their senses was to keep their armies home for awhile; the people would very soon tire of war and standing armies and the government would be compelled to make peace. "As to the question of invading them and compelling them to change their government, it is quite out of the question . . ." Their enemies had attempted that approach and were heartily sick of the idea. [7]

In spite of his rather gloomy picture of European prospects, Harper nevertheless, in this same letter, emphatically stressed the necessity for American neutrality. He was desperately afraid of a land tax and had just finished projecting government revenues to

1803 without resorting to the form of taxes so costly to the interests he represented, and particularly to those speculating in western lands. Everything depended upon continued peace for the United States and uninterrupted American commerce. However, if the nation's foreign trade were suddenly disrupted or sharply diminished, the central government's customs duties, which constituted the largest source of federal income, would also decline. This was certain to happen if the United States were drawn into the "Quarrels of Europe" and if that occurred there would be no alternative but to resort to a direct tax. [8]

Harper's reaction to affairs in Europe in the spring of 1797 was still considerably more temperate than that of many of his northern Federalist associates in and out of Congress. The New Englanders were far in advance of Harper at this time in their Francophobia and its political possibilities. Uriah Tracy, Connecticut Federalist, viewed the convening of the Fifth Congress as the most important event in the country's brief history. Tracy thought it would witness either "a stable independence or a separation of the Union." He saw nothing short of wickedness and perhaps worse in the efforts of Gallatin and company to block defense measures. [9] Oliver Wolcott, secretary of the treasury, was equally alarmed. "It is contrary to the System of France that we should remain neutral . . . we must join France, or defend ourselves. . . ." If the American people did not support their government on this occasion, Wolcott declared, "our country is undone." [10]

George Cabot, patriarch of Massachusetts Federalism, was opposed to sending another envoy to France, for fear that "if an envoy is sent and received, the French will completely reestablish their undue influence in this country." [11] He seemed more satisfied with events when he wrote again one month later, applauding the rapidity with which the American people had come "to a right way of thinking on French politics." He was so impressed that he believed that "almost any measures the government may take would be approved, especially if the public danger were stressed." [12]

Harper was every bit as disturbed by the new French maritime policies and if anything he was more concerned, especially about the devastation of the American West Indian commerce that was so important to Charleston. He approved of the determination of the new administration to exhaust all means of amicable settlement even though these diplomatic attempts might fail. He went

on to state that he did not believe they would fail and that he
thought that France did not intend a serious quarrel with the
United States. It was against all her most obvious interests. [13]
Harper expressed his hope that the French government would
not misunderstand the American diplomatic initiative and read
weakness or submission into it because to do so would constitute
a grievous misjudgment. As he saw the matter, America's only
escape from the dilemma depended upon a speedy termination of
the European war before the young nation's commerce was
entirely ruined. If peace came soon to Europe the United States
might take advantage of the opportunity to build a defense
establishment sufficient to command respect for American neutrality and maritime rights when the next inevitable European
struggle erupted. Harper, Cabot, Wolcott, and company were
obviously not of the same mind—not yet.

     Harper had problems much closer to home and most of them
stemmed from the new delegation sent to Congress by the voters
of South Carolina. There were three definite Republican votes in
that delegation, and John Rutledge, Jr., was probably more
Republican than not at the time of his election in 1796. The fact
that the opposition party prevailed in their own delegation would
never do if Harper and Smith were to count for very much in
party caucuses. There was not much chance of weaning Lemuel
Benton of Georgetown District, or Thomas Sumter of Camden
away from Republicanism. But there did seem some likelihood
that Rutledge, who represented Beaufort and Orangeburg, and
William Smith from Washington and Pinckney Districts were only
loosely attached to the opposition, and Harper and William
Loughton Smith went to work on them. [14] They had scant
success with the other Mr. Smith. Several times they invited him
to dinners attended by the right kind of people, such as James A.
Bayard and Harrison Gray Otis, but it was for naught. William
Loughton Smith finally admitted failure. "We tried to infuse
good opinions into him, but he appears to be composed of
materials very unpromising." [15]

     The two proselytizers had better luck with Rutledge, who,
though extremely resistant at first, eventually came over. Rutledge had good reason for his Republicanism in the fact that it
had been a northern Federalist Senate that had refused to confirm his father's appointment as chief justice, and no doubt his
Republican uncle Edward influenced him. Harper and Smith
must have been openly wooing Rutledge, for his uncle wrote to

him in June 1797, warning him away from South Carolina's two "English" congressmen. The younger Rutledge assured his relative that there was nothing to be concerned about. "S & H can make no more impressions upon me than the pressure of my little Daughter's little finger would upon the pillars of Saint Philip's Church—I regard the one as a cold-hearted selfish little angloamerican & the other as a pompous thick-headed Prater." [16] It is difficult to say just how much his opinion of these gentlemen changed, but his voting record showed a marked Federalist orientation thereafter. As Smith's biographer comments, "Smith and Harper, of course, only wanted Rutledge's vote, not his admiration." [17]

By the time the session was fully under way there was an even split in the state's delegation with Harper, William Loughton Smith, and Rutledge on the Federalist side while Sumter, Benton, and William Smith voted with the Republicans. Actually, Rutledge's alliance with the Smith-Harper group was always rather tenuous, which was indicative of the ever-present factionalism within the ranks of South Carolina Federalism. [18]

The spring of 1797 was taken up almost entirely by the deepening Franco-American disagreement. The Congress, which convened at noon on May 16, had its work set out for it. President Adams' address to the Congress was exceedingly temperate, and though firm on the subject of American independence from foreign interference it was at the same time free of anything approaching saber rattling. [19] Once again the time of the House was spent answering the president's address, and that reply turned out to be considerably stronger in its anti-French tone than Adams' position. As a matter of fact, Alexander Hamilton, John Jay, and others outside of Congress thought the reply was too harsh, with too many hard expressions. As Hamilton put it, "*real firmness* is good for everything. *Strut* is good for nothing." [20] Robert Goodloe Harper was in part responsible for much of that "strut."

From the spring of 1797, Harper began to adopt a progressively anti-French attitude, and he served as something of a national barometer reflecting the growing intensity of the French storm. William Loughton Smith was increasingly impressed by Harper's expertise on the floor of the House, and he predicted an important career in politics for his associate. Smith noted happily that as the summer of 1797 drew to a close Harper became decidedly more bitter in his criticism of French policy and he

described Harper as being "fully charged . . . a very bold speaker
. . . and very industrious." [21]

What Smith did not note was that Harper and the president,
whose foreign policy Harper was criticizing, had several things in
common. In addition to a propensity toward rotundity, both
Harper and John Adams were highly receptive to flattery; both
were easily carried away by this exhilarating elixir and the trait
got them both into serious difficulty. Both gentlemen, in the
developing crisis, allowed themselves too great a measure of
public rhetorical license. In so doing, they only encouraged the
extremists to greater jingoistic, nativistic efforts that in the end
spelled disaster for the Federalist party. However, there was a
curious difference between the two men. Harper was far more
"fully charged" in the House debates than in his letters home,
while Adams gushed chauvinistic sentiment responding to petitions of support but held back in his dealings with the Congress.

President Adams proposed the three-man mission to the
French Republic in May of 1797 and while there were those
among the High-Federalists who grumbled opposition, Harper
was not among them. He expressed enthusiasm for the mission
and its chances for success. He hoped, he said, to see America
strengthen the hand of the negotiators by authorizing an ambitious program of defense measures. The first session of the Fifth
Congress saw the Federalists attempt passage of such a program
and the Republicans stage a partially successful delaying action,
which delayed the appearance of a crisis atmosphere and all that
went with it. Some money was appropriated for harbor fortification, and three frigates were ordered completed, and the export of arms and ammunition was prohibited. But the plan to
create an expanded army of fifteen thousand men was
sidetracked by astute Republican maneuvering and by the long-
standing American feeling against such armies. Instead, eighty
thousand militia were ordered held in readiness.

Harper expressed the belief that a great deal more was needed
in the way of defense preparations, but he enjoyed little success
in convincing enough other gentlemen in the House to proceed
further. Additional revenues, he said, were of the utmost importance. "Should we be driven into war, for which a full treasury is
one of the best preparations," new taxes would be necessary,
while if the mission was a success the new revenues could be used
to reduce the public debt and improve the nation's new navy. [22]
Aware that the back-country had never been overly appreciative

of the sort of tax program suggested by stamp and salt levies, he went to some lengths to justify the measures. Possibly to placate frontier opposition to a tax on salt, Harper pointed out that a stamp tax would fall almost entirely on money transactions. New taxes were a distinct possibility, however, and no matter how distasteful stamp and salt duties were in South Carolina the only alternative was land taxation, which, no matter how it was managed, constituted an unequal and unfair burden upon Southerners great and small alike.[23]

In addition to his support of this defense program Harper had several contributions of his own to offer for the consideration of the other members of Congress. Throughout the Fourth and Fifth Congresses he campaigned for an expansion of American naval facilities and introduced many times the proposal that the government establish a navy yard. He was equally persistent in his sponsorship of federal purchase of timber lands, especially live oak, as a reserve for future needs. The point has been made often enough concerning the quality and quantity of such timber tracts in the Georgia claims and the Yazoo region. One is tempted to doubt his professed lack of interest in the contested Yazoo lands and his sundering of all direct connections with the Georgia land speculators.[24] Nevertheless, whatever his motivation, Harper was unsuccessful at securing House approval for his proposals, and the navy yard idea along with the timber land purchase project languished on the table throughout June and July, to be lost in the rush to more important things in the following session.

As the Fifth Congress grew older, Robert Goodloe Harper seemed with the passing days to become more anti-French, more belligerent, and less tolerant of those who disagreed with him. He began referring to something a critical colleague had said in debate as indicative of his "want of sense and good manners," or on one occasion resorting to even stronger terms with which to combat the misguided opposition.[25] The Republicans seemed to Harper to be advocating a ridiculous defense posture consisting of sound, balanced budgets and a paper military establishment which relied on the unpredictable militia. Convinced that an expansionist France only respected complaints which were supported by a military capability, he found it easy to oppose Republican obstructionism bitterly, and also to question the motivation of the opposite party and its leaders.

They simply could not be so blind, he charged, and still be

sincere. As Robert Goodloe Harper viewed the situation, the
French crisis might explode into a cataclysmic struggle so fraught
with danger as to justify the serious repression of those who in
their enthusiasm for the French Revolution had drunk from
poisoned ideological springs. Made myopic by the potion they
had consumed, these individuals constituted a very real threat to
the American republic.

After Gerry and Marshall had departed for France to meet
Pinckney and after the modest defense program had been approved, the spring and summer of 1797 were largely devoted to
that most exasperating of pastimes—waiting. There was really
little else to do. Nothing more could be done until either good or
bad news was returned from Europe, and Federalists and Republicans alike spent their time sniping at one another. Harper
devoted a great deal of time to writing to his constituents and
haranguing the opposition for not seeing the French threat more
clearly. "I think our chance of escaping a war is better now than
it appeared some time ago," he wrote in late July. He thought
that neither France nor England had very much to gain from
continuing the war, and he believed that the war-weariness of the
French people was sufficient deterrent to any western hemi-
spheric ambitions entertained by the Directory. These facts taken
together with the American coupling of negotiation with a firm
stand encouraged him to anticipate peace in Europe and a settlement of the Franco-American disagreement.[26]

It was about this time that William Loughton Smith departed
for his diplomatic post in Portugal, leaving Harper the most
important member of the South Carolina delegation and certainly the most articulate spokesman for southern Federalism in the
House.[27] Much of his time was devoted to fending off Republican attempts to water down defense legislation and to defending the administration against opposition charges that
granting too much discretionary power to the central executive
was dangerous, in that it encouraged Federalist hopes of establishing a government closer to the English model. Harper refused
even to answer the charge respecting Federalist monarchism.

As before, there was no more ardent champion of executive
prerogative in the Congress than the South Carolinian. On one
occasion in June 1797, in reply to Giles' objection to a clause
empowering the executive to use the several frigates recently
provided for, Harper retorted that hobbling limitations upon
presidential freedom of operation were absurd. Certain responsi-

bilities belonged properly to Congress, while others were quite clearly the responsibility of the executive branch. "If we were at war with Great Britain, [Congress] should have no right to say to the President, attack Canada or the Islands" because that power belongs to the president and "if he abuses it, upon his own head would lie the responsibility, and not upon them."[28]

The turn of future events was presaged in these early months of the first and second sessions of the new Congress. Harper began manifesting signs of the ultranationalistic behavior tinged with nativism and domestic reaction which was to erupt one year later. The House was discussing one of the revenue measures under consideration when someone from the Republican side made the peripheral remark that increased taxation would act as a bar to immigration. Harper said that there was no real connection between taxation and immigration and that the Republicans were, as usual, off on the wrong track. He then proceeded to give the House his views on immigration and they were sadly indicative of the direction he was taking. For some years, he lamented, America had encouraged immigration and willingly granted citizenship to all those who came to our shores. Experience and observation had convinced him that this had been completely wrong. He believed, he said, that "no man should become a citizen of this country but by birth . . . he would have all Foreigners freely admitted, and he would admit their children to have a right to citizenship." But he felt it was far too disruptive and dangerous to admit their unassimilated parents to citizenship.[29]

On another occasion he responded to Republican charges that he and other Federalists were anxiously anticipating a war with France. He did not really care what the Republicans thought, but he answered their charges anyway. He thought that France had some justifiable complaints regarding the Jay Treaty, but these could be settled by the negotiation already in progress. However, if France was determined, with or without pretense, to have war with the United States, war she would have. He said that he was not afraid to pronounce the word war. "He was neither afraid of the thing, nor alarmed at the sound; and he could conceive easily of circumstances in which all the interests of this country would call for war.[30] While he did not believe these circumstances presently existed there remained no doubt in the minds of enemies or friends, if there ever had been any, as to Robert Goodloe Harper's pacifism.

As he increased in importance in the House his willingness or ability to tolerate the loyal opposition seems to have decreased proportionately. By the time the second session opened in November he was barely able to sit in respectful silence through a Republican speech. He did not yet openly question the opposition's loyalty, but he felt they were wrong and he corrected them. "Do we not confine lunatics, and keep knives and razors out of the hands of children? Why? Not because we are afraid of their intentions, but of their actions." The Quakers afforded a splendid example, he asserted, of a group of well-intentioned individuals whose abolitionist position necessitated that the community be protected from them, lest they make the United States another Santo Domingo. [31] Harper thought it lamentable that the opposition members of the House were lately falling into this category of well-intentioned fools when they advocated an isolationist stance for the United States or when they opposed necessary military expenditures.

He began lecturing to the House with increasing frequency on the error of Republican thinking on foreign policy, the exposed and inadequate state of American defenses, and the opposition attack upon the executive branch, which Harper saw as the real motive of Republican diatribes. With each new lecture he became more pedantic in tone and more contemptuous of the deluded individuals who were unable to recognize the truth when it was set plainly before them.

The finest example of this sort of speech was one that he delivered on the eve of the arrival of the XYZ news, and while it was not so entitled, it might well be called his "anatomy of a revolution" lecture. There was a remarkably Burkean quality about his remarks in this instance that distinguished this address and its author. No one in this House of Representatives, or indeed any preceding it, was responsible for a more articulate exposition of the eighteenth-century conservative American attitude toward revolutions and revolutionaries. Revolutions were effected, no matter what the country or situation, by three descriptions of men, Harper stated, and the three types were philosophers, Jacobins, and sansculottes. Every country had some of each type and since certain proportions of each were required for internal disorder it was possible to measure the danger of revolution by keeping track of the relative size of the three groups of persons.

After this Delphic opening, Harper went on to elaborate. The "pioneers of revolution" were the philosophers, for they were always in the forefront. They prepared the way for the others by spreading the gospel of infidelity and lessening the respect of the people for the time-tested institutions of their government. They tended to be fanatical, although personally virtuous and probably not without talent: *"Satis eloquentia, parum sapientia—* eloquence enough, but very little sense." These philosophers are so engrossed in their discussions of the perfectability of man and the dignity of his nature that they entirely forget what he is, and declaim perpetually what he should be. "Thus, they allure and seduce the visionary, the superficial, and the unthinking part of mankind." For obvious reasons, Harper said, the philosophers were the most dangerous of the three types of revolutionaries, for it was their responsibility to corrupt the otherwise loyal and right-thinking garrison, and then to open the gates to the army which followed them. "Of these men we, in this country, have enough and more than enough."[32]

The United States had its share of Jacobins too, he warned, more than enough to incite the revolution their ambitions required. They were of that sort of men, daring, talented, possibly courageous, but totally unprincipled, who were for one or another reason unable to obtain power by established means. It was power and power alone that they craved. Principles had very little to do with their quest. Their pattern of behavior was readily predictable—tyranny when in power and demagoguery when out. They used the philosophers to obtain their ends and then liquidated them after they had outlived their usefulness. Without specifically stating it Harper was pointing out the fact that once the old regime had been overthrown there was a tendency in all revolutions for the new power structure to adopt a tight-fisted ultraconservative posture, and even to act in the most brutally repressive way toward the very ideologues who, although once useful, now threatened the newly established order just as they once had the old. The Jacobins were the generals in the armies of revolution, "but both pioneers and generals are useless without an army; and fortunately, the army does not exist in this country."

By the "army," Harper was referring to the sansculottes, whom he identified as "that class of idle, indigent and profligate persons who so greatly abound in the populous countries of Europe, especially in the large towns." These destitute wretches were forever ready to join in toppling an order of things in which

they had no stake. Paid by wealthy Jacobins and influenced by
the fanatical philosophers, such an army had destroyed fourteen
centuries of civilization in France. America's salvation lay in the
absence of such a population except for a sprinkling of the rabble
in a few towns.

The vast majority of Americans, he assured his listeners, resided on their own lands with no knowledge of oppression and
want. Even the minority, the town dwellers, possessed property,
owned their own houses and enjoyed a stable family life. Thus
among such a population as America enjoyed, the sansculottes
phenomena did not yet constitute a threat to order and security.
He concluded by observing that "it is probable that the nature of
our government and the abundance of untilled land in our
country will secure us from them for ages." Neither John
Randolph of Roanoke, nor his more famous cousin could have
found anything the least bit objectionable in this "Jeffersonian"
reliance on agrarianism as the nation's future security. Indeed
there was nothing remarkable at all about such a statement being
made by a southern Federalist.

Robert Goodloe Harper, like most Federalists, identified the
greatest danger to the republic as the rise of a popular demagogue, a sort of combination philosopher-Jacobin. Such demagogues would convince the people that all power and discretion
must be denied the executive and vested in the representative
assembly—all in the name of democracy. Once this had been
achieved, Harper said, the demagogues might openly appear,
obtain control of the assembly and establish their arbitrary rule
in the name of the people. The only dependable bulwark against
such a fate for the American republic was, as Harper saw it, to
preserve the system of government as already established, toler-
ating no incursions of popular power. "Governments like ours
. . . may be compared to the planetary system, whose preservation depends entirely on the exact preservation of its
balance."[33]

Obviously, much of Harper's argument was constructed to
combat Republican strength in the House of Representatives, and
would have been considerably different had the Republicans
controlled the executive branch and Harper's party dominated
the lower house. However, the fact remains that in the late 1790s
partisans of both stripes were troubled by the bugaboo of revolution, the difference between them being that while the Federalists feared the Jacobin and the mob, their counterparts were far

more afraid of the man on a horse. This matter of attitude
toward the military represents one of the most dependable and
accurate measurements of partisan feeling available for the student of the 1790s. For nearly without fail, and despite wavering
on other issues, Republicans and Federalists hewed to strict party
lines where the military was concerned.[34]

The immediate battle in progress in the House, however,
concerned the American diplomatic establishment abroad rather
than demagogues and the threat of revolution at home. The
Republicans were engaged in their annual assault upon the necessity of maintaining the costly diplomatic network in Europe, and
their sentiments were for reducing the number and size of the
American legations abroad. Many Republicans thought that the
missions in London and Paris were more than sufficient to
represent the nation's interests. Their chief arguments were economy and the necessity for retrenchment.

Once again Harper and the Federalists interpreted this position
as merely a ruse to cover the real objects of interfering in the
business of the executive, diminishing of the autonomy of the
executive branch, and the elimination of the diplomatic corps
altogether. He defended the present conduct of American foreign
policy and belittled Republican opposition to the maintenance of
the diplomatic missions as either ignorant isolationism or the
opportunistic posturing of the "friends of France." Harper and
the Federalists were guilty of the very fault they charged the
opposition with, for they were reacting to every Republican
commentary as an attack upon the administration. In this instance Gallatin, Nicholas, and the others had questioned the
necessity of the diplomatic post in Berlin, and their motivation
derived as much from parsimony as partisanship.[35]

However, the underlying issue, at least to Robert Goodloe
Harper, was the question of isolation versus European involvement for the United States. Peripheral discussions notwithstanding, this was the crux of the disagreement. What angered
Harper was the way in which the Republicans had changed their
tune and come full circle since 1794, yet hypocritically denied
that they had altered their principles one iota. To say, as the
Republicans did, that America ought to have no connection with
Europe was almost as wise as saying that a man ought never to
have a fever. No one disagreed with this, although Harper said he
doubted their sincerity.

He read an extensive quote from a speech delivered in early

1796 by that paragon of democratical sentiments William Findley of western Pennsylvania. Findley had expressed his support
for expanding the diplomatic corps and pointed out that the step
was inevitable if the nation sought to increase its stature among
the nations of the world. Why, Harper asked, was Mr. Findley
now opposed to a very small expansion of the corps? In answering his own question the South Carolinian once again clearly
illustrated the direction he was rapidly moving in. The reason for
Findley's change of heart, Harper said, was the fact that in 1796
the American nation had not been involved in a dispute with
France and now it was.

> At that time, the French Government had not declared us to be a
> people divided from our government & now it has. At that time we
> were not on the eve of a conflict . . . now it is feared we are. Can we
> avoid the impression of a concert with those on the other side of the
> water, the impression that gentlemen are playing into the hands of a
> foreign Government?[36]

There it was. He had finally made the charge that was to become
the tragic hallmark of the remainder of the Federalist decade.
Harper was not the first Federalist to train this weapon against
the opposition and neither was he the most extreme of the
Francophobic marksmen, but like many another Federalist he
turned to this tactic with increasing regularity.

When Harper was fully charged, as he apparently was now,
there was almost no way he could be beaten in debate. If a
Republican congressman tried sarcasm Harper either ignored it or
turned the remark around and gave back as good as he got. In
physical appearance and forensic style Robert Goodloe Harper is
reminiscent of the English hunting bulldog: the short heavy neck
carrying the great, impressive head, the excitable temperament,
the absence of that necessary element of wisdom—fear, and the
tenacity with which the quarry is pursued, caught, tormented
and then shaken until lifeless. Once he caught the scent, Harper
hounded his Republican prey until the opposing gentleman was
either silenced or left Congress. Only Albert Gallatin stood toe to
toe with Harper, Harrison Gray Otis, and the rest of the Federalist pack. James Madison and Giles had both retired to the
safety of Virginia by late 1798 and Gallatin was left to lead the
depleted Republican forces in the House alone.

The hunt was made that much more exciting by the developing foreign crisis and the resplendent raiment of patriotism in

which the hunters dressed themselves. There had to be something insincere, perhaps worse, about the facility with which the Republicans could abruptly shift their foreign policy positions.

Why were these men who were so bent on war in 1794 now so disgustingly pacific in what, Harper said, impressed him as a similar situation? The same gentlemen who in 1794 reprobated a single attempt at negotiation as pusillanimous, or the idea of compromise as bargaining with the Devil, now reacted quite differently. What was the explanation for this remarkable change of mind and heart? The answer, Harper assumed, was that the opposing nation in 1794 had been the ancient foe of the Republicans, but now the prospective enemy was France, in whose service the "Domestic Friends of Liberty, Equality, [and] Fraternity" had enthusiastically enlisted. A war against England had held out the possibility of political gain for the Republicans while such a conflict with France could only do their cause harm, and for these base reasons they were willing to surrender American interests to the tender mercy of France.[37] It appeared to Harper that the Republicans had entered the United States into a system of war and alliance on the side of France and, if allowed, they were intent on completing the scheme of unification.

He charged that this idea of joint Franco-American action had been concocted in France and then imported into this country by none other than the new vice-president of the United States, Thomas Jefferson, "the missionary who was to convert us to this new faith."[38] The expected outcome of the scheme was, in all likelihood, the conversion of the United States into another Holland, that is, a subordinate state ruled in effect by the orders of the French minister with Jefferson acting as governor. Harper, who in 1796 had not expressed a very great fear of Jefferson, now saw the Virginian in the most conspiratorial hues possible. The irony of the situation was that Harper's own party had also undergone almost an identical transformation. The doves and hawks of 1794 had exchanged positions, except that neither side was willing or able to admit that this is what had taken place.

Yet Harper was still not quite in step with his northern colleagues in their impatience to get on with the House discussion of the critical state of Franco-American relations. As a matter of fact, as the news of the mission began to trickle into the United States in March 1798, he went on record against continuing the debate until additional information was available. All of the facts were necessary, Harper said, if the debate were to end in greater unanimity in the difficult months ahead. Harrison Gray Otis rose to differ with Mr. Harper's views concerning unity. Otis "did not contemplate any great unanimity with respect to all the measures that would be necessary to be pursued in the present crisis." They had to do their duty and leave the balance to Providence.[39] Unlike Harper, Otis viewed public approbation as something to be obtained after, not before, the representatives of the people acted in the nation's interest.

President Adams reported the mission's failure to Congress on March 13, 1798, and there was an immediate Republican reaction. Smelling a foul, they demanded that the papers of the negotiation be sent to the House. Harper supported that call, he said, not because he questioned the integrity of the President, but because Giles, Gallatin and the other Republicans wished it. He thought that the papers would answer all their questions and possibly save the House a great deal of wasted time.[40] Adams complied with the request and submitted the XYZ papers in early April. In so doing, he removed the last section of the crumbling dam which held back the flood waters of anti-French sentiment. The national reaction was one of outraged indignation at this insult to the national honor which could not be allowed to stand unchallenged.

Robert Goodloe Harper was not outdone by anyone in leading the public outcry. He had prepared the people of South Carolina for any contingency in early March when the first rumors of the mission's failure swept over the capital city. "Every amicable advance on our part, is met by a new outrage on the part of France," he wrote, and the French were treating the Americans as rebellious subjects, not as citizens of a free, independent nation. Quoting from a letter from Charles C. Pinckney, Harper joined the general in urging defense preparations should the negotiations fail. He issued a call for a resurrection of the "Spirit of '76" among his constituents. He recalled that when he was only fifteen he had taken up arms to resist British tyranny. He had resolved "to live free or die" and at thirty-three his determination to continue to do so was still unshakeable. He knew, he said, that the people of the South Carolina back-country were no strangers to war and that they joined him in declaring that the blood which flowed so freely at Cowpens and King's Mountain did not flow in vain. He told them that he had no property to stake on the outcome of the contest, but his life was his country's to command and he vowed that "in the hour of danger they

shall find me by their sides."[41] The response of his readers was
to reelect him in 1798 by an even greater majority than 1796.

Harper's "Live Free or Die" phrase failed to become the
rallying cry of the French War of 1798. That honored distinction
is usually attributed to the slogan, "Millions For Defense But Not
A Cent For Tribute," credited to Charles C. Pinckney. Pinckney
is supposed to have hurled the remark at Talleyrand after the
latter had demanded a bribe for instituting the negotiations. The
French foreign minister, having lost his fortune in the Revolution, had for some time been embarked on a campaign to rebuild
his finances, and the sort of bribe he demanded was not at all
unusual. Actually, Gerry, Marshall, and Pinckney were willing to
pay, but only after the diplomatic arrangements had been attended to, which Talleyrand rejected. Pinckney's actual phrase
was, "Not a sixpence, sir," a somewhat less colorful retort.
However, Pinckney is generally credited with the more famous
remark, which was not his at all but was uttered by none other
than Robert Goodloe Harper. On June 18, 1798, Harper, offering
a toast at a dinner in honor of that other southern Federalist
John Marshall, declared, "Millions For Defense But Not A Cent
For Tribute," which evoked loud shouts of approval from the
patriotic assemblage.[42] But it seems that Pinckney's name carried greater prestige and made the slogan more impressive. Thus,
Harper lost his chance for immortality.

No matter who the author of the slogan was, the nation
responded mightily to the Federalist-led huzza for "Adams, defense, and liberty," and it is difficult to ascertain who reacted
more enthusiastically to this upsurge of nationalistic sentiment,
those leading or those doing the cheering. The incoming correspondence of John Adams abounds with petition after petition
affirming, in the most bellicose language, the loyalty of the
signers and their determination to meet French insult and depre-
dation with force. There is no doubt that the president was
greatly influenced by public opinion and that by answering these
petitions in equally bellicose language John Adams only encouraged the spread of the wartime atmosphere so responsive to the
extremist influence. It is conceivable that under the heady influence of popularity the executive might have over-reacted and, in
effect, did a great deal to worsen an already bad situation. Adams
and the nation were carried away in this flush of exuberant
patriotism and the result was an undeclared war at sea combined
with an administration-sanctioned campaign of xenophobia at

home. Adams recovered his senses in time to win the plaudits of latter-day historians. Robert Goodloe Harper did not similarly recover and his reputation has suffered.

The XYZ news had broken across the country in shock waves, each greater in intensity and creating still others like it. The nationalistic upsurge was quite similar to the reaction that followed Jay's Treaty. However, this time the Federalists found the popular upheaval delightful since it was now in defense of their position. They found themselves being toasted with fine wines and ales instead of over bonfires. Petition after petition arrived in Philadelphia during April and May 1798, and the great bulk of those written after the March revelations were of the extreme patriotic variety. The petitions extolled the virtues of the courageous John Adams, swore resistance to the death in the face of French attack, and heaped praise upon the Federalist saviours of the Republic. They were heady tonic to Federalist throats long parched from the lack of such refreshing drafts of public approbation and praise. For men who quite often scoffed at the antics and opinions of the crowd, when such were against them, they proved strangely and easily intoxicated by the cheers of the people when such accolades came in their support.

Robert Goodloe Harper had been a rather moderate southern Federalist prior to the XYZ crisis, but he, like so many thousands of others, was carried away with the movement to defend America against the dreaded Gallic foe that threatened to mount an invasion of the defiant little republic. He became increasingly militant and chauvinistic as the crisis worsened, but that was the nature of the emerging American nationalism of which he was so splendidly representative. That he emerged as a veritable fountain of xenophobia cannot be denied, but neither is it possible or fair to view Harper as a unique phenomenon and in so doing excuse the rest of the American population. The nation faced, or thought it faced, war with the most militarily successful, expansionist power in recent European history, a nation to be feared not simply for its overwhelming military might but because it represented an ideology which to Federalist minds threatened the foundations of western civilization. For individuals of this persuasion, a possible conflict with France held out all the prospects of a holy war between the forces of light and darkness, and there was no doubt in their minds about which side they were enlisted on. Harper came to be inalterably identified with those who thought along these lines and he shared their political fate.

After the XYZ affair Harper grew even more extreme in his denunciation of those who did not agree with him and contemptuously dismissed their remarks as "silly speeches." In reply to a speech by Edward Livingston in which the New Yorker criticized the proposed massive expansion of the navy, Harper labeled Livingston's remarks as "one of those puffs which were introduced for no other purpose than to round off a period, and he was astonished that any gentleman could get his own consent thus to impose upon himself." [43]

Republicans could handle Federalist scorn and invective well enough, but charges began to fill the air about the existence of not only an external threat to the nation's security but an internal one as well, which in the minds of many was far more despicable and dangerous. As early as the middle of June 1798, having labored for months against the recalcitrant obstructionism of the Republicans and their resistance to what Harper considered the minimum defense program, he flatly charged that such a conspiracy did in fact exist and he intended to expose it. He had heard news of the so-called "Logan Peace Mission," and he was appalled by what he called "a treasonable correspondence carried on by persons in this country with France, of the most criminal nature." This, added to the publication of a letter from Talleyrand in Benjamin Franklin Bache's newspaper before the president had released the government's copy, Harper said, constituted all the proof necessary. "Every means had been made use of to excite resistance to the measures of our government and to raise a spirit of faction in the country Favourable to the views of France," and Harper blamed the Republicans. [44] Under this kind of attack the opposition wilted and the party's stalwarts began retiring, some temporarily, others permanently, from the public arena.

Almost all of those who anticipated the threatened war with France and the possibility of invasion expected the attack to come in the southern states. Harper took this point of view. Geography seemed to support this view. The nearby French West Indian islands could be used as staging bases. But a more compelling reason struck southern imaginations. An invasion of the South would surely be coupled with a French inspired insurrection of the slaves. The large slave population of the southern states was the nation's great strategic weakness in the event of foreign invasion, and this fact was amplified tenfold by the tales of those white refugees fortunate enough to escape the horror of the black revolution in the West Indies in the middle of the decade. Santo Domingo was to the southern mind of the 1790s what Nat Turner's Rebellion and John Brown's Raid were to a later generation—the harbinger of events so terrible that they had to be discussed in whispers. Many southern Federalists of this era were driven by their fears toward reaction and made more willing to accept legislation curbing freedom of the press and speech, because they sincerely believed that a French invasion was likely, and certain to carry the consequences of overlooking the possibility of racial warfare.

The degree of one's fear had little correlation to whether or not the individual owned slaves or was a great plantation owner. Harper was neither. He was not even living in the threatened area, but his reaction was just as extreme and the specter of such a possibility haunted his mind as if he had been ensconced amidst a hundred slaves on the upper Santee. This threat of internal disorder, so far as Harper was concerned, was justification enough for the Provisional as well as the Additional Armies. It was not enough to wait for the sighting of the French warships and then call out the militia. The consequences of being unprepared were too grave. He summed up the southern situation thus:

> We know . . . that Victor Hudues and Toussaint have each of them considerable force . . . sufficient to send against our Southern coast, . . . and if they were to get possession of Savannah or Charleston, they might do immense mischief before they could be dislodged. . . .[45]

The southern people, Harper continued, were alarmed and needed reassurance. The gentlemen from Pennsylvania felt quite safe, but they ought to respect the fears and needs of their southern neighbors. His constituents had been told that there was nothing to fear since the white population of the region was equal to the defense of the country, but, Harper pleaded, if the man who says this "was well acquainted with the seacoast of that country, he would know that the black population [there] is very great . . . and the terrain provided ideal location for guerilla activities. The people in that quarter expect . . . to receive aid [and unless they do] their confidence in the Union will be much weakened."[46]

Harper advocated providing the southern states with all sorts of the necessary military supplies at once, and he thought the emergency justified three or four million dollars in direct taxes to finance the southern armaments program. He saw the South nearly devoid of the means of defending herself, and by this he meant military weapons of a uniform type, not fowling pieces. Harper's willingness to spend large sums of money for this purpose shocked even some other southerners of the Federalist calling. The newly converted John Rutledge, Jr., for example, thought Harper's expenditure proposals were entirely out of line.[47]

However, it seems that the gentleman from Ninety Six had plans for the newly created armies that went beyond repelling an invasion force. As early as late April 1798, Harper was drawing a connection between the Provisional Army and the existence of the "Domestic Menace." The provisional force was necessitated, he remarked, not just by the foreign danger, but equally by the presence of an internal threat. The French Directory had long ago worked out the details of a plan to subvert and subjugate the United States. The French plot depended, according to Harper, upon a "certain class of men, who abound in the Southern parts of this country ... [and] ... gentlemen from the Southern States knew it."[48] These "Southern Jacobins" were, however, as he viewed the matter, not the greatest danger, but together with the possibility of a slave insurrection they had to be taken seriously and dealt with.

What Harper had in mind was an armed force large and powerful enough to smash the foe, in whatever form, whenever and wherever it might show its head. It is possible to question Harper's accuracy or perception, but there was a crisis quality to his pleas for national military assistance to the southern states which makes it difficult to doubt his sincerity. By mid-May he was able in all seriousness to remark in the House that the army collecting in French coastal ports ought to be called the "Army of America" rather than the Army of England, for its destination lay across the ocean, not the channel.[49]

So far as Robert Goodloe Harper was concerned, the nation's situation called for wartime measures even though the war was as yet undeclared. Between January and July 1798, he either introduced or supported a whole series of measures designed to improve America's defense posture as rapidly as possible. From sponsoring a bill to prohibit all trade with France to suggesting that the central government purchase and operate foundries for the manufacture of cannon, he supported every fortification and armaments bill to come before the House. He proposed arms expenditure bills as high as 1,200,000 dollars for additional arms alone, large enough to make Harrison Gray Otis complain.[50]

No one in the House was more navy-minded than this representative of up-country South Carolina, and scarcely any other member of the House surpassed him in defending the rights of American merchantmen on the high seas. An early advocate of arming merchant ships and the convoy system, he denied any inconsistency with the nation's announced neutrality policy and he dismissed Republican ideas about embargoes as reprehensible. To say to the maritime section of the country, "We cannot protect you," was unthinkable. It was also highly dangerous, he thought, since such a policy of inaction would seriously divide the people and possibly even prompt talk of disunion. The maritime interests of the nation could not be abandoned without destroying, Harper said, any semblance of public confidence in the government.[51]

Arming merchantmen might, as the Republicans charged, lead to war with France, but Harper maintained that the perils of not acting were even greater. He was more than ready to proceed faster down the preparedness path than most of his House colleagues, including a sizable number of Federalists.[52] As might be expected he was very prominent in the movement to rebuild the nearly mythical American navy and he was very much involved in the attempt to establish a separate Navy Department.

Harper by no means confined his interest in improved organization to the new navy; he had rather definite ideas about the efficiency of the office of the secretary of war as well. Whether he was party to a plan for replacing the unimpressive James McHenry or whether he brashly acted on his own cannot be determined, but in late April he wrote to Alexander Hamilton begging him to replace McHenry in the War Office in light of the approaching conflict with France. Harper assured the "Colossus of the Federalists" that a war minister was vastly more important than a general. "If Adams understood your willingness to come forward," he told Hamilton, "the arrangements would immediately take place, McHenry would give way and there is no difference of opinion among the Federal party on the absolute necessity of his doing so."[53] One can seriously doubt Harper's credentials and authorization for offering cabinet posts on behalf of President Adams, particularly, since in this case the president and the prospective appointee were not exactly on the best of terms. What probably happened was that Harper, imbued with the urgency of the situation, had been struck by this idea and dashed off to Hamilton a superfluous letter which was never answered by the New Yorker.

It is both unfortunate and strange that no substantial body of "Hamilton-Harper correspondence" has survived, although the author doubts whether there was ever much exchange between them. The two men had a great deal in common, especially in their admiration for the military life. Given the choice between public office and the opportunity for military adventure, either would have chosen quickly. It was this very propensity publicly expressed that did much to give color to Republican fears concerning Federalist militarism. Jefferson was obviously exaggerating when in 1801 he stated his belief that the nation had just been saved from monarchy and militarism, but it was the martial pronouncements of the Hamiltons and Harpers that made the Republican charge credible at all.

It was as much the phraseology as what Harper or Hamilton actually proposed that frightened the democrats. For instance, in early 1798 Harper extolled the virtues of "the military spirit" and emphasized the necessity of inculcating such a spirit in the American people. "He wished to see a military spirit in the country; to have a military school; and a corps constantly existing, in which officers may always be found fit to command troops."[54] One can almost visualize good Republicans cringing at this proof of Federalist misguided notions; all three of Harper's points were anathema to the believing democrat. Still, this was not the real visceral question in the party division over the military establishment. It was not merely a matter of whether we should have an army, but what kind of armed force? At stake here was the present role and future of the militia. The Jeffersonians were committed to the belief that all armies were probably dangerous and distasteful and that the militia system provided the least objectionable solution to the troublesome problem of defense in a democratic republic. The militia was the least military and the most democratic of armies, which per se made it highly acceptable to Republicans and totally objectionable to a Federalist like Robert Goodloe Harper. Reconciling these two positions was impossible. Either one or the other had to prevail. For a time in 1798 the Federalists managed to secure popular approval for their military viewpoint but the approbation did not prove very durable. For the most part the American nation has hewed more closely to the Republican argument, although the militia system has long since been replaced.

Throughout the preparedness debate of 1798 the Republicans attempted unsuccessfully to maintain the traditional reliance on the militia in the event of war. Their arguments were turned aside by the Federalists because of what Harper called military efficiency. He did not question the idea, he said, that the militia constituted the backbone of national defense, but it could not respond quickly enough in an emergency, and this was certainly the case in the South, where a ready defense was most needed. He castigated the Republican opponents of the Additional Army Bill for being mistaken in calling a force enlisted for three years a standing army, and he charged them with being afraid to provide the people with arms.

At this point, Albert Gallatin, coming close to the crux of the division, snapped back that the Republicans "are not afraid of putting arms into the hands of our citizens, but they do not wish to put them into the hands of a few chosen persons, to exclusion of others." [55] The Pennsylvanian recognized, as Harper did, that that the army to be created would be a highly select corps and might have uses other than meeting the French on the beaches. When it came to the final vote on the Provisional Army Bill in May 1798, Harper voted with the majority amending the original plan to state that the army could only be called up in the event of war or actual invasion, an action possibly designed to calm the jittery among his constituents if there were any.

He was not, by any means, finished with the militia, for he had some rather controversial improvements in mind for the existing system and once again his remarks must have aggravated already aroused suspicions among the opposition regarding Robert Goodloe Harper. He said that there existed a fundamental defect in the relationship between the central government and the state militias. That was, of course, that the militia was extremely independent of any controls or direction from the national government, which was quite as democrats intended it to be. Harper complained that no matter how much armament the national government might provide for the defense of the states, it could not be delivered unless the governor of the state requested it.

It was quite possible, he said, that the president might think it necessary to call out the militia when the governor of some particular state might not agree and the result would be that the militia could be denied to the central government. He said that the fact that the president had to wait for the request of the governor before he could act was a grievous defect in the system. Obviously, the democrats could not have been more completely in disagreement with this criticism, and it ought to be noted that on this point Harper was considerably well in advance of many of his fellow Federalists.[56]

There is another possible explanation for this furor over defense and it had very little to do with military needs or efficiency, but was strictly political in nature. It originated in the partisan clash over the fundamental question concerning the relationship between the executive and legislative branches of the government. The Republicans favored a continuation of the existing militia defense system which was already in being, state oriented, and required little if any federal action or participation. On the other hand, the plans advanced by the administration party required direct federal action from the ground up, provided a standing army at the disposal of the central government, and since the new army had to be staffed with officers, the appointive power of the executive branch of the government was greatly expanded. The positions of the two parties might have been considerably different if the administration which was to fill these numerous appointments had been Republican instead of Federalist.

Republican fears on this subject were more than justified since one certain way to insure that a man did not receive a commission in this new army was to pin the label "democrat" on him. Washington's views on the subject left no doubt how he felt about the "loyalty" of his officers.[57] The defense group in the House won out and both the Additional and Provisional Armies were provided for, although the former never really amounted to very much and the latter was not called up after all.[58]

Defense cost money and those who were willing to spend lavishly had to be prepared to tax heavily to provide the necessary revenues. Harper was just as willing to tax as he was to spend, and he was in a position in the House to do both as chairman of the Ways and Means Committee during the Fifth Congress. His significant role in fiscal affairs is evident to anyone who surveys the record of the three sessions of that Congress. On almost every fiscal question Harper either introduced the measure or commented upon it as first speaker, while his chief antagonist, Albert Gallatin, spoke for the minority members of the committee. This emergency tax legislation covered the spectrum from increased import duties, to a stamp tax, to a direct tax in the southern states on slaves, and the opposition minority attempted at every turn to reduce the estimates submitted by the Harper group on the committee. Nevertheless, the difference between the Harper and Gallatin approaches was considerably more complex than simple budget cutting.

In part it was a matter of attitude toward taxation and the question as to when a tax burden became too heavy or was unfairly distributed among sections and classes. Robert Goodloe Harper, who several years before had spoken in defense of the interests of western settlers, seems to have lost or forgotten the western outlook he once had. By the summer of 1798, he maintained that the tax burden on the western section of the country was so light as to be negligible. He even justified the direct tax by saying that these people desired it, for they wanted to pay their share of defending the United States in this emergency. Harper brushed aside complaints from Gallatin and other representatives from that section of the country that money was already scarce on the frontier and that a tax requiring specie payment was doubly oppressive. Harper said he knew the people who lived in those regions and that they would find the means to pay their fair share without complaining half as loudly as some gentlemen he knew in the House.[59]

Judging from his reelection that fall Harper was correct in his assessment of the mood of the people in one small section of the frontier at any rate. However, Harper won reelection to a third term before the tax collector arrived in Ninety Six, which may have had some effect on the outcome of the election. Fortunately for Harper he stood for an up-country seat, for his views on the subject of direct taxation of slave property probably did not win him much support in the low counties of South Carolina. He wanted to set the rate at fifty cents per slave, even though the slaveholders of his state, he said, could properly be called on for a higher tax since slavery was so very profitable and productive in South Carolina. However, there were other slave states where slavery was not nearly so productive and this tax rate was as high as practical for those areas.[60] The large planters of the coastal counties might have appreciated Harper's honesty, but still they must have thought his diplomacy left something to be desired.

The representatives of the people were also in disagreement over the structure and operation of the new revenue programs.

Gallatin and the Republicans fought manfully, but unsuccessfully, to make all revenue laws annual, while Harper and the
Federalists insisted that any taxes necessitated by the "foreign
crisis" had logically to continue in effect until relations with
France improved.[61] One additional question, that of national
loans, illustrated the clash of fiscal philosophies so apparent in
the 1790's. In the event that in addition to all other revenue
sources, the central government had to turn to subscribing a
national loan, the Federalists in the House sought to grant the
executive what amounted to a blank check in terms of the
amounts to be secured.

In this instance Gallatin was able to muster enough votes to
block what the Republicans must have interpreted as but one
more scheme to increase the power of the executive branch at
the expense of the legislature. Predictably, the Republicans also
tried to fix maximum interest rates on any such loan, but the
attempt was beaten off by what was coming to be Harper's most
trustworthy weapon against attacks from across the aisle—a
blood-chilling vision of French armies marching across a defense-
less America, left prostrate because of Republican reluctance
properly to defend the nation. In this situation and for some
time to come this technique worked.[62]

By mid-July 1798, an Additional Army of ten thousand men
and a Provisional Army of fifty thousand had been provided for,
at least on paper; a Navy Department of cabinet rank had been
created, hopefully to provide the necessary ships and men to
defend American commerce, and with the financial means secured by the new tax program Robert Goodloe Harper and the
nation resolutely scanned the eastern horizon for the first
glimpse of the expected foe. Now there was time to deal once
and for all with the enemy within.

NOTES

1. Gardner W. Allen, *Our Naval War with France* (Boston: Houghton
   Mifflin, 1922), pp. 29-30, quoted in Miller, p. 205.
2. *Annals*, 4C2S, pp. 1617-1618.
3. Ibid., pp. 1665-1666. Harper voted for the resolution and consistently for such positions as long as they were coupled with adequate
   defense preparations.

4. The Harper letter appeared in the *National Gazette* (Philadelphia), December 15, 1824. In all there were five such extensive letters. Copies of all five are in the Harper-Pennington Papers, MHS.

5. RGH to Constituents, January 5, 1797, Bayard Papers, pp. 27-28.

6. RGH to Constituents, March 13, 1797, p. 38.

7. Ibid., March 13, 1797.

8. Ibid., p. 34.

9. Uriah Tracy to Theodore Sedgwick, March 29, 1797, Sedgwick Papers, Massachusetts Historical Society.

10. Oliver Wolcott to George Cabot, March 27, 1797, in Henry Cabot Lodge, *Life of George Cabot* (Boston: Little Brown and Co., 1877), p. 118.

11. George Cabot to Wolcott, April 22, 1797, in Gibbs, I, 496-497.

12. Cabot to Wolcott, May 15, 1797, in Lodge, p. 138. Cabot was not, however, eager for war and he stated that his "greatest reliance is that Great Britain will keep the monster at bay, until he destroys himself, or becomes less dangerous to others."

13. RGH to Constituents, March 13, 1797, Bayard Papers, pp. 38-39.

14. The two William Smiths in the South Carolina delegation have caused historians some difficulty, but are easily identified. William Smith the Republican represented the new Washington and Pinckney Districts and he was never of much consequence in the House. However, the other William Smith, and it was about this time that he began using his middle name, represented Charleston and was one of the leading southern Federalists in the House.

15. William Loughton Smith, quoted in Rogers, p. 298.

16. John Rutledge, Jr. to Edward Rutledge, June 27, 1797, Rutledge Papers-Dreer Collection, Pennsylvania Historical Society, quoted in Rogers, pp. 298-298.

17. Rogers, p. 298.

18. Rogers differentiates between what he calls the Smith Federalists and the Rutledge Federalists in South Carolina. "The former always supported funding, banks, and commercial interests, while the latter exhibited strong distaste for moneyed men," p. 302. Harper, according to Rogers, falls into the first category. It seems to this author, however, that the elements which made up Carolina Federalism are not so easily delineated, and that the degree of "factionalism" was more extensive and complex than this. By 1797, the questions which divided South Carolina Federalists were no longer centered around "funding and banks," but rather questions of foreign policy, disenchantment with the northern wing of the party, and local questions with their corresponding rivalries. The best discussion of southern Federalist difficulty in building and holding together a party structure is Lisle Rose, *Prologue to Democracy: The Federalists in the South, 1789-1800* (Lexington: University of Kentucky Press, 1968).

19. Richardson, I, 223-229.
20. Gibbs, I, 543-544. Hamilton to Oliver Wolcott, June 6, 1797. The House reply is in Richardson, I, 232-235.
21. Smith to Ralph Izard, May 23, 1797, Phillips, "South Carolina Federalist Correspondence," pp. 787-788.
22. RGH to Constituents, July 24, 1797, Bayard Papers, pp. 41-42, 42-44.
23. *Annals*, 5C1S, p. 44.
24. Ibid., 4C2S, February 13, 1797, p. 2151; June 17, 1797, p. 333; 5C1S, pp. 461-462.
25. Ibid., June 2, 1797, pp. 222-223.
26. RGH to Constituents, July 24, 1797, pp. 44-45. Harper was always far more moderate and encouraging when writing to the people in South Carolina than he was on the floor of the House. Indeed, there were times when some of his rather rosy expectations for home consumption just did not square with attitudes he had expressed elsewhere. This is not to say that he was untruthful or insincere in his reports to Ninety Six, but that he certainly was not as candid as he had been prior to the Spring of 1797.
27. U. B. Phillips noted that with Smith's resignation, "Federal management in South Carolina passed entirely to a more moderate man, Robert Godloe Harper, who differed greatly from the local Federalist type both in origin and residence, though not in politics." Wallace, p. 348.
28. *Annals*, 5C1S, June 22, 1797, p. 364.
29. Ibid., June 27, 1797, pp. 424-425.
30. Ibid., June 7, 1799, pp. 264-266.
31. *Annals*, 5C2S, pp. 1176-1177.
32. Ibid., pp. 1177-1178. The speech which took up eight pages in the *Annals* is one of the most lengthy Harper delivered while in the House and would appear to have been less extemporaneous than most of his addresses.
33. All of these remarks are contained in the "Anatomy of Revolution" address. *Annals* 5C2S, 1178-1185.
34. Harper's youthful fascination with the military life and his dreams of a soldier's career were never really outgrown. Following the defense of Baltimore in 1814, in which he played an important role, he delighted in being addressed as "General Harper." This military orientation, one is tempted to say fixation, of the Federalist mind has never really been explored.
35. *Annals*, 5C2S, pp. 873-879, 1189-1190.
36. *Annals*, pp. 1190-1192. Harper drew the quotation from Findley's address to the House May 30, 1796.
37. *Annals*, pp. 1194-1195, 1198-1200.
38. Ibid., pp. 1192-1193 and footnote on p. 1192.

39. *Annals*, pp. 1253, 1255.
40. Ibid., pp. 1369-1371. Harper again broke ranks with Otis, Coit, Dana, Goodrich, etc., who voted against calling for the papers; April 2, 1798. Harper may have known, by way of McHenry, the contents of the papers. If so, he was merely allowing the Republicans to hang themselves.
41. RGH to Constituents, March 9, 1798, Bayard Papers, pp. 50-51.
42. Rogers, p. 318; also, *The South Carolina Historical and Genealogical Magazine*, I (1900), 100-103; Albert J. Beveridge, *The Life of John Marshall* (4 vols.; Boston: Houghton Mifflin Co., 1916), II, 348-350; Wallace corroborates this interpretation of the derivation of the slogan, pp. 347-348.
43. *Annals*, 5C2S, April 10, 1798, pp. 1519-1520.
44. *Annals*, 5C2S, pp. 1972-1973.
45. See RGH's speech in the House, April 24, 1798, on the "threat to the Southern States," *Annals*, 5C2S, pp. 1529-1531. Note the many references to "Black Troops" and domestic insurrections. The frightening prospects of such an event also greatly disturbed the man who in all likelihood would be asked to command the American Army if the worst happened. See George Washington to Timothy Pickering, July 11, 1798, Pickering Papers, XXII, 284, Massachusetts Historical Society.
46. *Annals*, 5C2S, May 9, 1798, pp. 1646-1647.
47. Ibid., pp. 1431-1432, 1439.
48. Ibid., p. 1530.
49. Ibid., pp. 1691-1693.
50. Ibid., pp. 1393, 1414, 2178; April 17, 1798, pp. 1427-1429. Harper was in fact calling for near-total mobilization of the nation's resources in light of the gravity of the situation.
51. Ibid., pp. 1449-1450. There was considerable breaking of party ranks on questions which touched sectional interests. For example, on what could be called maritime questions Samuel Smith, Maryland Republican representing maritime Baltimore, voted as consistently "Federalist" as Harper.
52. In early June RGH introduced a resolution which would have empowered such armed vessels to attack any ship which violated American neutral rights, but it was defeated, 47 to 28. *Annals*, 5C2S, pp. 1915-1916.
53. RGH to Alexander Hamilton, April 27, 1798. *Works of Alexander Hamilton*, VI, 282, quoted in Bernard G. Steiner, *The Life and Correspondence of James McHenry* (Cleveland: The Burrows Brothers Co., 1907), pp. 301-302. Steiner found no evidence that Hamilton replied to Harper's letter. Harper wrote to Hamilton on numerous occasions, but the author was unable to find proof that Hamilton ever responded. In this instance, Harper did not claim to be author-

ized to speak for John Adams, but he hinted that there had been "conversations" which had led Harper to take this action.

54. *Annals*, 5C2S, p. 1421.
55. Albert Gallatin, *Annals*, 5C2S, p. 1752. His fears were justified by the conscientious attempt to staff the new army with good, sound Federalists since the military leadership from Washington on down feared that Republicans could not be depended upon in the event of trouble with the French.
56. *Annals*, 5C2S, pp. 1931-1932. Harper put his thoughts on the subject into the form of a motion and it was defeated 42 to 28. At times his ideas regarding the military force being established were remarkably inconsistent. In one instance, he went to great lengths to show that American troops would fly to every part of the continent to defend their country, and then he later voted for a guarantee that the volunteer forces, once excused from militia duty, would not be required to serve at great distances from their homes. Ibid., pp. 1945-1947. What he probably had in mind from the beginning was an improved militia but under direct federal control.
57. Miller, p. 219, quoting from John C. Fitzpatrick (ed.), *The Writings of George Washington* (Washington: Government Printing Office, 1931-1944), XXXVI, 474; XXXVII, 138, 159, 160-161.
58. Dauer, pp. 213-216.
59. *Annals*, 5C2S, June 13, 1798, pp. 1920-1922.
60. Ibid., pp. 1604-1606. The tax rate was finally set at fifty cents per head and since there was not much objection from the representatives of the slave states Harper had obviously been fairly reasonable in setting the rate as he did.
61. Ibid., pp. 2057-2058.
62. Ibid., pp. 2040-2042, 2048. This particular speech was masterful and typical of the oratorical efforts which Harper was capable of on very little notice.

9

Harper at the Zenith: 1798-1800

Few sessions of the American Congress have been more lasting-
ly controversial than the second and third sessions of the Fifth
Congress which ended in March 1799. This was the Congress that
enacted the Alien and Sedition Acts and nearly brought on the
French war which many of its leaders had predicted. Men
emerged from this Congress historically marked; they were destined either for the pantheon of Republican heroes or the troubled repose of the High-Federalist damned. Few individuals were
to fall heir to greater condemnation for their role in these
proceedings than Robert Goodloe Harper.

There has been among historians a nearly universal attempt to
exonerate the president and the so-called Adams Federalists by
emphasizing the significance of the Hamiltonian influence and
the extremists' ability to dominate the proceedings of the legislature. Thus, it is possible to take a highly sympathetic attitude
toward Federalism in abstract terms by differentiating between
"good" as opposed to "bad" Federalists. This is, of course, all
necessitated by the demands of ideological attachments which
require today's liberal historian to be extremely selective in his
eighteenth-century biases. For these reasons it is relatively easy
to alter our standard of evaluation in the case of a "good"
Federalist like John Adams, but utterly impossible to take any
but the narrowest view of the Robert Goodloe Harpers of the
period. Such criticism of the prevailing interpretation is intended
in no way as justification for the Federalist internal security
program, but it is aimed instead at reconsidering the assignment
of responsibility for this questionable legislation and particularly
the part Harper played in the drama.

There is little doubt that the South Carolinian was by the
summer of 1798 one of the most important figures in the
Federalist House alignment. Harper had inherited William Loughton Smith's influence within the South Carolina delegation and
he possessed, by dint of his own initiative, talent, and effort, no
small stature in the party's national leadership circles. Now that
Fisher Ames was gone, the only Federalist who rivaled him as an

orator was Harrison Gray Otis, and judging from the constant barrage of Republican invective which he received, no other House Federalist could claim to have so aroused the ire of the "Antis," which was a mark of honor so far as Harper was concerned.

The publication of a number of his addresses and letters to his constituents in leaflet form had also won him a reputation as the best Federalist pamphleteer in the Congress. William Vans Murray, writing from the Hague, reported that Harper's pamphlet on American-French relations had gone through several editions in England and the proceeds from the sale were going to charity.[1] William Pinkney noted Harper's popularity in London, and William Loughton Smith praised the efficacy of the pamphlet in Spain and Portugal.[2] The demand for his speeches and letters in New England Federalist circles grew to the point of being insatiable, and unfortunately this sort of praise spurred Harper on to greater efforts and greatly aggravated his already blossoming case of Francophobia.[3]

Realizing that much of the preparedness legislation he was advocating in the House involved great expenditure, Harper spent more time than ever explaining the grave necessity for the legislation to the citizens he represented, and for a time they accepted his arguments. The sudden buildup in the armed forces obviously meant a hike in Federal taxation, and in back-country Carolina, as in the uplands everywhere, there was a long and honorable tradition of opposition to direct taxation. The Congressman was fond of resorting to sugarcoating the revenue program with promises that the burden would fall on urban merchants and the great property owners in the coastal counties. Some of these people would pay upwards of one thousand dollars apiece, he estimated. On the other hand, in the district he represented the tax should not amount, he said, to more than fifty cents per person.[4] The two most important themes running through these letters were the indefatigable and unselfish patriotism of the masses of the American people and the impact that this expression together with the preparedness program would have on French ambitions. While he observed that "this is a sort of resistance to which she has not hitherto been accustomed," he pessimistically expressed his belief that the United States still might not escape war with the nation which had once been our sister republic.[5]

As was his custom, he included in his defense of administration policy a detailed resume of the latest intelligence from Europe. The situation in France was so deplorable that friends of liberty and republican government found it unpleasant to discuss. What remained of the revolutionary constitution had been discarded and the legislature reduced to captivity. Free elections were only myths cruelly perpetrated by what was little more than a military despotism controlled by the Directory. This, Harper exclaimed, is what France had fought seven years to obtain, for which two million people died and for which the religion, morals, manners, and culture of much of Europe had been destroyed. France was nearing her apogee and would soon be brought to heel by the rest of Europe, which was squarely faced with the question of fighting France or being devoured by her. For these reasons, Harper said, the course of the United States was to take advantage of this turn of European events. French power was about to decline as spectacularly as it rose, but the United States had to maintain her newly acquired armed might and eternal vigilance until that happy day arrived.

However, there was always the possibility that war between France and the United States might occur before the inevitable Gallic decline and, in what was becoming an increasingly effective "Churchillian" stance, Harper sounded the patriotic call to arms. Even if England fell, which of course was fantastically out of the question, and even if Russia, Prussia, and Austria succumbed and a French invasion of America was imminent, he would still favor resisting tyranny.

> I should be for retiring with the remnant of the nation, beyond the mountains of the Mississippi, and there, . . . opening to ourselves, amidst deserts and their savage inhabitants, an asylum for self-government and national independence. This . . . would be happiness compared with the dominion of a French proconsul . . .

and he knew, he said, that the remainder of South Carolina and the nation agreed with him.[6]

Harper and the Federalists had seen to it that the nation was on the way to being prepared against any such threat of invasion, but there remained the problem presented by the advance force already landed and operating within the United States. Fisher Ames summed it up when he wrote in June 1798 that he "had not seen anytime when I thought the Government stood as strong as at present," with the opposition disorganized, disheartened, and near to rout, but he said, "Congress is yet far behind the people." Now was the time to strike Jacobinism a death blow, now while the public was aroused.⁷ What Mr. Ames did not realize was that Congress was not as far behind the people as he suspected, for within the next month the Alien and Sedition Acts had been rammed through the House and Senate and signed by the president.

The atmosphere in which this legislation passed Congress has been the subject of some confusion. At times one is left with the distinct impression that the Republican opposition was thoroughly put to rout by the overwhelming numerical superiority of the forces of Federalism, while a few heroic, bright figures, most often Gallatin, fought the valiant but doomed rear-guard action against the advancing forces of reaction. There is also the suggestion that the government—cabinet and Congress alike—was responding in Pavlovian fashion to directions from New York. There is little truth to the former interpretation and even less in the case of the latter.

Between 1797 and 1801, that is, from the first session of the Fifth Congress through the last session of the Sixth, the last Federalist Congress, the administration party at no time enjoyed a majority in the House of Representatives larger than nine votes, and this is supposedly the high-water mark of militant Federalism. During the period in question, the last third of the Federalist decade, to say that the House was overwhelmingly Federalist is simply not correct. Similarly, the suggestion that since the High-Federalist wing of the party was in a commanding position, responsibility for the Alien, Sedition and Naturalization Acts belongs to them alone is equally inaccurate. The partisan division in the House was so narrow that the High-Federalists on their own could not have enacted a motion to adjourn, let alone a highly controversial legislative program. To excuse the "Adams Federalists" from responsibility is to ignore the fact that the legislation could not have been enacted without their votes, and indeed, nearly all their votes.

The Republicans, on the other hand, were by no means as disorganized and disrupted as Fisher Ames hopefully thought they were. Compared to later Congresses controlled by lopsided Democratic or Republican majorities the numerical strength of the Jeffersonian Republicans in the House throughout this period was ideal for the party in opposition. They were as powerful as a party can be and still be the minority party. True, they were taken aback by the XYZ shock, but they were never thrown into full retreat. When the Alien Enemies Act passed the House it was by a vote of 46 to 40, and the Sedition Act slipped through on a 44 to 41 division.

The following chart demonstrates how narrow the House division was and how crucial every Federalist vote was if the internal security program was to pass.

Congress	Session	Federalist	Republican
Fifth	I	49	50
Fifth	II	51	48
Fifth	III	50	44
Sixth	I	55	46
Sixth	II	51	52

Note. A member was classed as a party voter if he voted with one or the other party on two-thirds of the occasions involving party questions. The party breakdown data in columns three and four is found in Chambers, p. 138, and Charles, pp. 93-94. Both agree on the two-thirds criterion as the minimal standard of evaluation.

Thus any legislation enacted by any of these Congresses was the recognized offspring of the whole Federalist family and not merely the issue of part of the clan, which could be disavowed later when it became necessary to do so in order to preserve the family's good name. Robert Goodloe Harper was unquestionably a member of the household, but so too was John Adams.

Nevertheless, there was an administration majority in the House during the second and third sessions of the Fifth Congress and in truth it was a Federalist Congress. To those inclined to see the long reach of the former secretary of the treasury in nearly everything the central government did, a Federalist Congress means a Hamiltonian Congress. The New Yorker's influence extended everywhere, touching cabinet members and senators alike. This impression of the period's politics is in need of a new long, hard look. Hamilton's influence with several of the members of the official family is undeniable, with the most dependent secretary being James McHenry, closely followed by Alexander Wolcott.

However, the extent of this Hamiltonian influence in cabinet circles has been too readily and unquestionably transferred to the Congress, where an entirely different set of circumstances existed. Hamilton's influence with McHenry and Wolcott was the result of his expertise and experience in the affairs of their departments and their lack of it. What was directly responsible for his influence with Congress, especially the House, is not nearly as apparent. He no longer possessed patronage or favors; with no political whip to crack, his influence depended upon his stature as elder Federalist statesman, which was certainly considerable but nowhere approached that of George Washington. Actually, Hamilton's great ability to move Congressional mountains had begun to fail even before he departed the Treasury Department and the capital city, and by the time of the disputed election of 1800 the "Colossus of Federalism" was incapable of throwing the election to Thomas Jefferson or anyone else.

Hamilton gradually lost control of the Federalist forces in the House to a newer, younger group of Federalists represented by men such as Harrison Gray Otis, James A. Bayard, John Allen of Connecticut, and Robert Goodloe Harper. These were individuals who had not passed through the crucible of the Convention, the funding and assumption debates, and the Washington years under the guidance of the New Yorker. They now proved far less responsive to his leadership than the older generation of Federalists had been. Ironically, in many ways and instances this newer breed was more "Hamiltonian" than their erstwhile chieftan. That Hamilton feared their hastiness, overexuberance, and extremism has already been noted, and there were situations which saw the former secretary following the House more than he was leading it.

By the late spring of 1798 this newer leadership was clearly calling the Federalist signals in the House of Representatives, and they were becoming, if they were not already, the most vocally anti-French spokesmen in that body. The rest of the Federalist members in the House chose to follow the lead of this cabal willingly since the extremist group was not large enough to compel their allegiance or to retaliate against them for backsliding. They went to political perdition and they went voluntarily.[8]

Several years before Pierce Butler had characterized Robert Goodloe Harper as being "liable to impressions and apt to be hurried away by the feelings of the moment," and 1798 was to offer conclusive proof of that opinion.[9] Had he not been caught up in the war fever of that year Harper would have spent possibly two terms in the House before retiring to establish a law practice in one of the northern cities, and his record would have been that of a fairly moderate southern Federalist congressman. But like a great many other Federalists, Harper gave way to the French hysteria and the chauvinism, nativism, and domestic restrictions upon debate which wartime has always produced in this country.

He and countless others, both in and out of government, sincerely believed that the nation faced the specter of French invasion and slave insurrection. A wartime situation existed and to their minds any and all measures necessary to the nation's defense and preservation were justified. Clearly Harper believed this, and his commitment was to his country's defense first, with the possible opportunity to destroy the opposition party remaining in a subordinate position. The focal point of historiographical dispute regarding the final third of this decade has always been the relationship between the foreign crisis and partisan power politics at home. This association certainly differed from individual to individual, but for Harper the crisis necessitated the domestic defense legislation, not vice versa. His speeches and his letters home all suggested the imminence of invasion and his correspondence with others only reinforced his fears from that quarter. [10]

Secretary of State Timothy Pickering wrote to Harper early in 1799 expressing his own reliance on information he had received concerning a projected French invasion of the United States. The invasion force, Pickering told Harper, was to come from Santo Domingo under a General Hedouville and it was to be preceded by Negro revolutionary agents whose job it was to arm and incite the slaves. [11] As with nearly all of the invasion rumors, this one carried special meaning for a southern Federalist, and in Harper's case this fear of a racial cataclysm was deep-rooted and apparently of long standing. Several decades later Harper became a charter member of the American Colonization Society and energetically labored in that society's efforts to rid the South of its permanent menace, the freed slaves.

His sudden turn in the direction of extremism in the late 1790s is not any more justifiable in the light of these considerations but it is made more intelligible. Like most individuals placed in Harper's situation, taunted by his own fears and suspicions, to partake even slightly of the heady elixir of the counterrevolutionary is to go the whole route of the true believer. It almost had to result in his decision that those who disagreed after being presented with the "truth" were either blindly or willingly of questionable motivation.

During the alien and sedition debates Harper gave full vent to feelings present in every individual and strongest, or most intense, in time of national crisis. "Harper the extremist" was no doubt latent in the man long before 1798, but the crisis was required to remove the last restraints. By the end of the affair in 1801 any resemblance between the High-Federalist and Congressman Harper prior to 1798 was illusory. He was not the same man, and both he and his constituents in the Ninety Six District were aware of the fact that he no longer represented them in quite the way that he had from 1794 through 1797. He was certainly not the only Federalist this happened to. The "Adams Federalists" followed his leadership in the House for a time and they voted for the legislation he helped write. Yet Harper has acted as an historiographical lightning rod to these more "moderate" Federalists, attracting more than his fair share of the criticism.

In all, the Fifth Congress enacted four separate acts designed to safeguard the United States internally, while the new navy and expanded armed forces readied themselves to repel invasion. This program, ranging from the Naturalization Act of June 18 to the Sedition Act of July 14, constituted the minimum guarantee against the forces of subversion and disunion so far as Harper was concerned, and he was instrumental in guiding it through the House. By this time, he and Harrison Gray Otis represented the Federalist leadership of the House of Representatives, and their ability to hold their loosely tied, slim majority together is impressive even from this distance. Indeed, party organization and discipline on both sides had matured greatly since the Jay debates. The Senate was considerably more safe for Harper's party and it is generally thought of as being a special preserve of High-Federalism of the New England variety. However, in the case of three of the four "security" measures enacted by this Congress, Robert Goodloe Harper was far more drastic than the draft bill sent down to the House by the more safely Federalist Senate—an indication of just how far Harper had moved.

In the debate over the Federalist attempt to alter the naturalization requirements Harper went as far as it was possible to go in narrowly defining the qualifications for American citizenship. After much reflection, he said, he had come to the conclusion that in order to preserve the nation from all sorts of evil influences from abroad citizenship ought to be limited to those born in the United States. He did not want to discourage immigration, which of course was very necessary, and he was willing to grant the right to own property, or for that matter, all rights and protection short of participating in the government of their adopted country. He saw no possible constitutional opposition to this complete about-face in the nation's immigration attitudes, although such objections from other members did finally force him to withdraw his suggestion in order to study the matter further. [12]

Harper's phobia concerning the foreign born increasingly became an obsession which had a great deal to do with his role in formulating the Alien Act and the legislation dealing with sedition. [13] Immigrants imported with themselves foreign ideas and ideologies, and Harper thought them to be a constant source of danger particularly in time of conflict with one of the European states. Why, he asked, should they be permitted a voice in government when most of them had not enjoyed that privilege in the lands they came from? Neither Harper nor any other member of the House commented upon what such total prohibition might mean for the Republican Party in northern cities, but surely no one missed the connection. [14] The importance of the slight Federalist majority in the House was dramatically illustrated when enough Federalists joined the opposition to defeat these most extreme proposals.

Ironically, the Naturalization Bill which passed the House in June 1798 and tripled the residence requirement represented a sort of compromise measure far more "moderate" than the legislation suggested by the fast rising, extremist House leadership, which would have been retroactive. [15] This seems at first glance to be rather strange behavior for the son of a Carolina cabinetmaker who had suffered numerous social rebuffs due to his unimpressive rural antecedents, and yet this has so often been the pattern for the evolution of the champions of American nativism. Harper, who was so emotionally concerned with maintaining the exclusiveness of American society, was not quite certain of his own position.

The internal security legislation drafted that summer in Philadelphia did not move through Congress one item at a time but rather through both Houses simultaneously. While the Naturalization Act was still in the works yet another alien bill was taking shape. The Alien Enemies Act preceded the Alien Friends Act in House debate but did not pass the House until after the latter had already become law. Both alien bills dealt with the same problem, as Federalists like Harper understood that problem, which was the presence of dangerous aliens within the United States in time of crisis.

Harper openly admitted his admiration for the British approach to the matter, and he tried his best to convince the other members that the United States faced with a similar situation ought to follow England's lead and take advantage of her experience. Both nations faced possible invasion by the forces of Revolutionary France which had relied upon internal intrigue and sabotage in her former conquests as a means of softening the resistance of the people to be attacked. The French government counted heavily upon "an internal support in each country," Harper said, and the English and American governments had no choice but to act against this internal support. [16]

The defense legislation already enacted by Congress was doomed to failure, Harper said, if the country did not "resist our external enemies and domestic traitors" equally. Harper and Otis had by this time developed what amounted to a standard form for their speeches in defense of Federalist legislation or in their verbal assaults upon the hard-pressed Republicans. The organization of the speech might vary but the two basic elements were always a vivid recounting of the fate of Venice, Holland and Switzerland because they had not recognized the danger in time, together with a horror-filled preview of what a French invasion of the United States held in store, particularly for the southern states. In this instance, Harper concentrated upon the role of this "internal support" in a wartime situation and how best to deal with it. Congressmen Allen, Otis, and Harper saw to it that should war come, the president had the power to deport or confine at will enemy aliens. [17] There was really nothing so terribly unique about this act, since nearly any government feels obligated to protect itself against resident citizens of an enemy power in time of war.

However, the Federalist xenophobes in the House were not quite satisfied that the nation was adequately safeguarded against the machinations of these dangerous alien residents. No protective power came into existence until war was declared and in this instance that might not occur. The High-Federalist reaction to this defense gap was the passage of the Alien Act, commonly called the "Alien Friends Act" on June 25, by the House. This law provided the answer to the question, what to do with the troublesome aliens until the declaration of war occurred, and it did this by empowering the president to do with aliens in peacetime as he had already been instructed to deal with them in case of war. This was, by all odds, a far cry from deporting aliens in time of war and especially so under the terms of the new Naturalization Law of 1798.

Harper and the House "crisis Federalists" justified this sudden shift in alien legislation simply by pointing to the English example for such legislation, the dangers of being unprepared, and the existence of "the plot"—the "monster of sedition" within American boundaries. [18] He found ample support for the alien bills in his conception of the right to national self-preservation as embodied in the common defense and national welfare clauses of the Constitution, and there was no question in Harper's mind as to the action being the immediate responsibility of the central government. To say that "though we see the knife of the traitor held to our throats, we are to wait until the State Governments come and snatch it away," was absolutely ridiculous. [19]

The House leadership did make two humane modifications in the bill before it became law. Harper saw to it that the Senate provision for "life imprisonment at hard labor" for any deported alien willfully returning to the United States was reduced to merely "life imprisonment," which he said could be shortened by the presidential pardoning power. Harrison Gray Otis added another amendment guaranteeing alien property rights, protecting them from arbitrary confiscation, and allowing them to take part of their property with them when they were deported, the remainder to be guaranteed by the American government. Harper agreed, saying that "it never could be good policy for Government to lay its hands arbitrarily upon the property of individuals," and, while he thought the restriction probably unnecessary, he wished to assure the alien community that they had nothing to fear from the American government. [20]

By this point, Albert Gallatin and the Republicans knew exactly where they stood and in which direction the winds of extremism were blowing. They were next and they knew it. The Republicans protested that Alien Friends legislation was certain to lead to similar action against citizens who disagreed with the programs of the central government, a protest which Harper and Otis weakly denied.

Harper had been leading up to a seditious practices act ever since his speech earlier in the session in which he first made direct reference to the domestic menace. The opposition knew this and Harper made no secret of his intentions when he denied that the Alien Friends Act might be turned against American citizens. Citizens were not to be deported, he said, but rather they were to be tried in courts of law. These "internal enemies" and "domestic traitors" would soon be dealt with by means of seditious practices legislation pending before Congress at that moment.

Harper then launched out in a major address pointing up the necessity for such curbs upon the activities of these misguided individuals. In predictable fashion, the crux of the speech dealt with the forthcoming invasion of the southern states, their lack of defense, and the peculiar danger of allowing sedition to go unchecked in fomenting disunion in that region. Harper also took the opportunity to bemoan the appalling state of martial preparedness in this most vulnerable part of the nation and he centered his fire on the overdependence placed upon the militia as the bulwark of defense. Whereas, he said, regular troops were far more desirable.

It was all just a bit too much for South Carolina representative Thomas Sumter, who rose to deliver what amounted to nearly his sole major effort on the floor of the House during his career. He resented Harper's aspersions upon the southern militia and its will and ability to fight. Sumter accused Harper of pointing out to the enemy, time and again, the South's weakness and by so doing "he has exposed our most vulnerable part to their inveteracy, and our wealthiest part to their rapacity."[21] Harper, becoming ever more pompous and supercilious, simply sloughed off Sumter's remarks as being incorrect and went ahead with his lecture to the House.

Citizens, he charged, were more dangerous than aliens because it was much more difficult to restrict their activities due to rights conferred by American citizenship, whereas aliens did not enjoy such a cloak of protection. There existed, exactly as he had asserted earlier, "a domestic—what shall I call it?—a conspiracy, a faction leagued with a foreign Power to effect a revolution or a subjugation of this country," and he hoped "that the projectors, and others concerned in it, may be brought to justice." He went still further and charged that since the Republicans were violently against the enactment of a measure designed to guard the United States from such devious attacks they must be party to the conspiracy itself. No finer example of the logic of the "if you are not for us you must be against us" argument has ever been uttered on the House floor.[22]

On Thursday, July 5, 1798, the House received the Senate's version of the Sedition Bill, which in modern parlance would be called the Lloyd Bill after Senator James Lloyd of Maryland, who was almost entirely responsible for its authorship. Until midway through 1798, it was widely accepted in Federalist circles that the federal government, if it desired, could exercise jurisdiction over any criminal offense which was punishable under the common law. Since the English government's right to proceed against sedition had long been established as deriving from common law there seemed little or no necessity for the Federalist administration to seek authority in an area in which it was already operating by interpretation. However, Justice Samuel Chase of the United States Supreme Court had recently questioned this whole matter of sedition prosecutions unless Congress specifically empowered the executive branch by a statute grant of authority. [23]

For this reason, the High-Federalist Senate had formulated the details of a sedition act that was certain to insure that not a single Jacobin libeler escaped prosecution. The House worked for a time on a combination alien and sedition bill but dropped it in favor of the Senate approach. The Lloyd Bill went far beyond the range of acceptability so far as a sizable portion of the House Federalist membership was concerned. The original bill provided the death penalty for anyone convicted of giving aid and comfort to the French enemy, but this clause did not even win the approval of the Federalist Senate.

The Senate bill defined sedition as any conspiracy or combination with intent to oppose or defeat the operation of any law of the United States, any attempt to threaten any person holding office under the United States with damage, or any attempt to provoke any insurrection, plot, or unlawful assembly. The proposed fine was five thousand dollars and five years imprisonment

Seditious libel was construed to be any attempt to weaken or malign the laws or government of the United States by "inflammatory declarations or expressions tending to induce a belief in the citizens that the government in writing legislation" was motivated by hostility to the Constitution or the liberty and happiness of the people. Also covered were statements tending to justify the hostile conduct of the French government toward the United States or said defamation of the officers of the United States government. [24] The bill as it came from the Senate was simply too repressive to stand a chance of winning enough support to pass the House, the Federalist majority being as narrow as it was, and a compromise was in order.

Whether Robert Goodloe Harper directed the House modification of the Lloyd Bill merely in order to secure the passage of a sedition act or because he sincerely viewed the Senate measure as too extreme we can not say with complete assurance. However, Harper had been quick to rise in defense of the rights of the accused earlier in his career, and the writer would be inclined to believe him when he expressed doubts about several of the bill's most obnoxiously suppressive sections, except that some of his suggested amendments were more objectionable than any aspect of the Senate version.

Such legislation was unfortunately necessitated, Harper said, by the state of national affairs and the licentiousness of a small part of the American public. It was his belief that "it was perfectly within the Constitution to say, that a man shall not do this, or the other, which shall be injurious to the wellbeing of society. . . ." He could see no grounds for believing that the rational freedom of the press would be in any real way restricted by a well-defined law which assured a jury trial for those accused of violating it. The restriction would touch only those who wished to overturn society and any such threatened society had every right to deny conspirators the means by which they sought to accomplish their evil plans. [25]

At first glance it does appear that Harper arranged himself in the role of the moderate by toning down much of the extreme application of the Lloyd Bill. In effect, Harper, James A. Bayard, and Otis rewrote the Senate suggestion almost completely. Harper attempted to turn the much-debated bill back to a select committee and when this failed he offered a series of resolutions on the sedition legislation for the consideration of the House. There were seven resolutions in all, of which only the first was ever made part of the Sedition Act as it emerged from the Congress.

These resolutions, which may well have been the work of all three Federalist leaders although Harper introduced them, altered completely three fundamental aspects of the Senate proposal before the House. Harper's amendments made it the responsibility of the state to prove malice and bad intent, which of course, offered the accused considerably more protection than Lloyd thought was necessary or deserved.

In additon, and of greatest importance, the Harper modifi-

cations departed entirely from common law procedure in allowing proof of the truth of the statement to stand as justification
for what, in terms of the Lloyd Bill and common law, would
have been libel. Under common law, utterance alone had to be
proved to serve as the basis for libel prosecution. Unlike the
ultra-Federalist gentlemen in the Senate, Harper, Bayard, and
Otis apparently had heard of and accepted the principle of the
Peter Zenger Case, or at least they recognized that the American
public had heard of that decision. The third modification was
overshadowed by the first two major changes, but it was nearly
as important in that in all such cases the jury was to be allowed
to determine the meaning of the law as well as the facts of the
particular incident in question.

It would seem that in making these major modifications Harper somewhat contradicted himself. In one instance, he expressed
his belief that the common law doctrine of libels was "as
applicable to the Government of the United States as any other
Government," and then he proceeded to marshal through Congress legislation which significantly altered the American application of that very doctrine. It was surprising that someone from
the Republican side did not call Harper to account, but no one
rose to point out the contradiction. [26]

Harper asserted that he was not as concerned about prose-
cuting seditious editorials in Republican newspapers as he was in
reaching those who by their actions made the calumny in the
press dangerous. He admitted that he was referring to those who
hurled seditious remarks at the president and the government
from the floor of the deliberative chambers of the very government they sought to undermine.

> When he heard a gentleman on the floor of this House, whose character
> and connexions gave him weight with the people, pronouncing an
> invective against the Government, and calling upon the people to rise
> against the law, the business put on a very serious appearance. [Harper
> was referring to Edward Livingstion who had bitterly attacked the
> recently enacted alien legislation.] [27]

Harper was disturbed by the impact such remarks from such a
man might have upon respectable elements in the community
which otherwise would never have been influenced by the rabid
Jacobin newspapers. He recognized that the Constitution allowed
gentlemen to make all the seditious remarks they cared to upon

the floor of either house without fear of reprisal, but he asked whether or not something needed to be done about their spreading this pollution throughout the nation in letters to constituents and printed speeches.

Once again there were the allusions to the threat of insurrection, foreign sponsored but domestically directed, and while, he said, he trusted the good sense of the American people to resist this deceit he nevertheless favored the additional safeguard of a sedition act. The leading student of this sedition episode maintains that Harper's argument represents "a near classic statement of the nip-revolution-in-the-bud philosophy." [28] Harper refused to admit that a sedition law was designed to muzzle Republican opposition in the Congress, but he did say that he hoped to confine its effects to the chambers of the House and Senate.

It was at this juncture that the representative from South Carolina introduced his seven resolutions into the debate. One might make a pretty convincing case for Harper, "the moderating influence" on the basis of his first resolution, which is the only one that matters since it alone was incorporated into the final Sedition Act. The three major alterations in the Lloyd Bill were contained in this first resolution. Yet, there remains the sticky matter of the other six parts of this statement of principle, and the dangerous suggestions they contained demolish any argument in behalf of the "moderate Harper," who by this point no longer existed. Much of what he included in his proposals might easily have come from the pen of the extremist Lloyd or Timothy Pickering.

Liberty of the press, Harper explained, had been all too often misunderstood in the United States, and he defined it "as being no more than that a man shall be at liberty to print what he pleases provided he does not offend against the law, and not that no law shall be passed to regulate this liberty of the press." [29] The remainder of the proposals directed the already stated provisions of the sedition proposals specifically at congressmen writing to constituents, or campaigning, treasonable communication by private citizens with the government of a foreign power, and attendance at meetings the intent of which was to oppose the execution of any law of the United States government.

Harper did not stop with this extension of the central government's new jurisdiction in the field of criminal law. He favored

expanding the coverage of the act to *"any* [italics mine] correspondence with any person or persons whatsoever, with intent to
form any plot [which he never defined] against the peace of the
United States, or to aid any hostile designs of any foreign
nation. . . ." [30] It was obvious that in order to make the en-
forcement of this last proposal even moderately effective it
would be necessary to learn what was contained in the private
letters of the American people. Harper failed to explain the
mechanics of this suggested coverage, but of necessity censors of
the federal mails were required who would pore over the thousands of private communications, just as Timothy Pickering spent
his mornings scanning the newspapers for evidence of sedition.

As the Sedition Law finally came from Congress it constituted
an effort at punishing mere criticism of government officials.
Robert Goodloe Harper's other suggested proposals made that
seem almost permissive by comparison. Had all of Harper's resolutions become law and not merely the first, the nation could
have been immediately turned into a police state governed, in
effect, by the Federalist administration with the assistance of the
Federalist courts and the police powers of the newly provided-for
army. The Federalist Sedition Law of 1798 proved to be one of
the most violently controversial pieces of legislation ever enacted
by Congress. Much is made of the fact that it was this Sedition
Act that called forth the Virginia and Kentucky Resolutions in
the first instance of state juxtaposition between the federal
power structure and the people. By contrast Robert Goodloe
Harper's sedition proposals would have produced a revolution.

As if to compound his error, Harper then attempted, unsuccessfully, to rewrite the enacting clause in the law's preamble to
read as follows: "Provided that nothing in this law shall be
construed to extend to abridge the freedom of speech and the
press as secured by the Constitution. . . ." [31] The tragedy of the
episode lay in the fact that the representative from the South
Carolina back-country sincerely believed that the guarantees of
the First Amendment to the Constitution had not been
weakened.

On July 10 the Sedition Act passed the House of Representatives by a narrow margin of three votes out of a total of one
hundred and five. Only two congressmen from south of the
Potomac River voted with the Federalist majority and, of course,
Harper was one of them. William Wirt, the future attorney
general of the United States, recorded the reaction of a Federalist

acquaintance who applauded the act's passage. "*Wait*, said he till the sedition bill is passed and then we will shew you what we will do—we will begin first with Jefferson and Gallatin, banish them and then we will take the *others*, one by one. [The italics are Wirt's.]" [32] Only one prominent Federalist objected publicly to the law, and even John Marshall's objection was not based upon the law's constitutionality but its inexpediency. [33]

Insofar as John Adams is concerned, his biographers have managed to salvage his reputation by pointing out that he neither asked for nor enthusiastically enforced the legislation, and the High-Federalists have been left to take the full responsibility. On the contrary, the president was just as responsible as Harper or Lloyd. Adams' excessively belligerent response to the petitions of support in the XYZ aftermath had fanned the fires of reaction and suspicion; the fact that he took no stand for or against the legislation while it was in Congress, and his approval of the act by affixing his signature constitutes an abysmal failure of presidential leadership. A president is not responsible simply for selective actions of his administration, or those that meet the approval of later generations, but for the full record for his term of office. [34]

Throughout all of the alien and sedition debates Robert Goodloe Harper was, as always the advocate of the ascendancy of federal power. In this instance his conservative nationalism was evident in his attitudes toward every part of this legislation and especially in the case of the Sedition Act. The reference is not to his six unsuccessful resolutions but rather to the necessity for enacting a federal sedition law in the first place. The fact that all of the states by 1798 had made ample legal provision for the protection of individuals against criminal libel in no way prevented Harper and others of like mind from viewing a national law as absolutely necessary.

Previous state activity had never deterred these proponents of federal authority. Nor was this the first instance in which these nationally minded gentlemen were anxious to push into a new area, not merely in spite of prior state legislation, but also because of it. To individuals of state rights persuasion the Sedition Act was as obnoxious for its extension of the power of the central government as it was for its assault upon the First Amendment. Harper admitted openly that the transfer of jurisdiction from state to federal courts would serve to strengthen the one judicial structure at the expense of the other. He thought this was inevitable and made immediately necessary by the like-lihood that state and local juries were not apt to enforce the new legislation as stringently as the situation required. [35]

As so often happened with the Federalist legislative program, Harper complained, rumor and Republican calumny had so dis-torted the true meaning and intent of the Alien and Sedition Acts that many of the citizens were troubled by misrepre-sentation and misunderstanding. Opposition to these laws had to be based on ignorance of the laws.

True to form, he announced that the solution was the imme-diate printing and distribution of twenty thousand copies of the laws, which the Republicans countered by demanding a like number of copies of the Constitution for purposes of compar-ison. Harper retorted by charging that this was all part of the many "attempts he believed were made in some places to pro-duce an armed opposition to . . ." the laws of the land. [36] The partisan harangue began anew and the public printers published nothing.

Harper stood for election in the fall of 1798, and for the first time since his initial election in 1794 he conducted something of a campaign in a series of letters to his constituents. He had by this time become a national figure, which no doubt helped considerably in securing a third term in the House but which, judging from the following story, was fraught with all sorts of drawbacks as well. The inhabitants of Fredericksburg, Virginia, were supposed to have waited for "an especially hated Federalist Congressman, Harper of South Carolina, to pass through . . . on his way home, . . . with the intention of treating him . . . roughly." [37] There is, however, no indication that the crowd and Mr. Harper ever actually encountered each other, and he went on to win reelection, there being no serious opposition to him.

As a matter of fact, this proved to be the most successful Federalist congressional contest in recent years. For the first time since Harper had entered the House his party won a majority of the South Carolina seats. Of the Republicans, only Thomas Sumter survived the Federalist vote of confidence. William Smith of Pinckney District lost to the Federalist Abraham Nott, and Lemuel Benton went down before Benjamin Huger. [38] Now at last, after all the work had been done, Harper had a Federalist delegation. Such news from the southern states delighted the ears and eyes of New England Federalists, who interpreted the results as both a vindication of past performance and a mandate for the future. Timothy Pickering was ecstatic about the "great changes in the Southern States. . . ." Two Republicans had been defeated in Georgia, all but one in South Carolina, and only three were elected in North Carolina to seats in the House. [39]

In actuality, the Federalist victory in South Carolina was not nearly as impressive nor as permanent as the secretary of state believed it to be. The gains in the federal legislature were more than balanced by the election of a state legislature that was more Republican than Federalist—Edward Rutledge as governor, and the hated Charles Pinckney to John Hunter's Republican Senate seat. [40] South Carolina Federalism appeared far more healthy on paper than it really was in early 1799. The new Federalists in the House, along with Harper's reelection, really stemmed from the extent of the war scare in Carolina. It was the reaction to rumored landings of conspirators from France or the West Indies, the hackle-raising nightmare of insurrection among the Negroes, which Harper had used so effectively, rather than a widespread approval of the legislative record of the Fifth Congress. As 1799 wore on, it became increasingly apparent that this was the case and that Pickering's "great changes" were really quite transitory. The Federalist mandate from the South Carolina voters was eroded rather rapidly by the decline of the war fever and the antidote administered by Jefferson's imaginary physician "Doctor Tax Collector." By late 1799 the political complexion of South Carolina had changed so markedly that it was not by simple coincidence that Robert Goodloe Harper made the decision to quit politics and establish a law practice in Baltimore. [41]

However, that was still very much in the future, and Harper's immediate concern was the final session of the Fifth Congress, which convened in December 1798 with every indication that not all the political sparks had been struck. Armed with the "sword of defense," as Harper had termed the Alien and Sedition Acts, this lame duck session directed its attention to further guaranteeing the national security within as well as without. As it turned out, the first such "threat" to materialize was not covered by any of the existing defense measures, and the Federalist Congress was forced to enact an additional special law to deal with such grave emergencies.

All of the furor was occasioned by the most unlikely source— Doctor George Logan, Philadelphia physician, Quaker, pacifist, and leading Pennsylvania Republican. It is impossible to determine which of these qualities made him more hated by the extreme Federalists, although with Harper it was most likely Logan's Quakerism. In the summer of 1798 Logan had appointed himself envoy extraordinary to the Republic of France in an effort to head off the approaching war. Harper and the Federalists charged that Jefferson had given Logan letters of introduction to the Directory, to Talleyrand, and to Merlin, the temporary head of government, and so far as the High-Federalists were concerned this constituted the "treasonable correspondence" Harper had alluded to earlier during the Sedition Act debates. [42] The Logan alarm was sounded throughout the summer of 1798 and increased to crescendo proportions, under Harper's direction, when the doctor returned to the United States in late November.

In the Federalist view of things, Logan had usurped the treaty-making authority of the executive branch of the government, and legislation to prevent this ever happening again was very much in order. At first, the Federalist leadership in the House sought to label any such correspondence with a foreign government by unauthorized persons as treasonous, but not enough of the "moderate" Federalists could be cajoled into agreement.

John Rutledge, Jr., predicted calamitous results if this sort of spur of the moment diplomacy by amateurs was not nipped in the bud. Imagine the results, he asked, if all of the discontented people decided to negotiate with foreign powers, and he had no doubts about the "discontented" being agents of the French and that they were intent upon overthrowing the government of the United States. If they were suffered to be successful at their game, he said, a French invasion of the American republic would not even be necessary. [43]

Since Logan had not been mentioned by name, the Federalist majority was able to deny the Republican allegation that the suggested legislation was aimed at a particular individual. Harper alone admitted that he had someone special in mind and that he considered the person "as an agent employed and sent by a party in this country." Who could imagine, Harper asked, that such an individual, hardly known outside of Philadelphia, would be able to gain a hearing before a foreign power entirely on his own. [44] Of course this mischievous Quaker could claim that he went to France in that manner, but who would believe him?

As he had pointed out so many times, Harper said, this was only additional evidence of the existence of a "French Party" in the United States. This party had been established by the French

for the same reasons similar parties had been fostered in Switzerland and Holland, and he said that he need not tell the House
what those reasons were. This viper clutched to Columbia's
bosom was bent upon so dividing the American people that the
government should be bound hand and foot. If the authors of
this mission said they were counting on an appeal to French
justice they were not telling the truth of the matter, or "they
were downright blockheads." [45]

The "Logan Law" debates deserve attention because of their
indication of the degree to which the High-Federalists had accepted the "internal conspiracy" threat, but also because the
Harperian style is encountered at its pinnacle of perfection.
Harper reconstructed an imaginary conversation between Logan
and the Directory which he facetiously declared to be a true
account. It began, according to Harper's narration, with Logan
correcting the flaws in French policy which were unfortunately
injuring "her party" in the United States: "You overshoot the
mark, and rouse the public indignation . . . disabling your friends
from rendering you any service. . . . Slacken your hand a little
. . . You need not repeal your decrees against our commerce, but
abate a little . . . Talk about calling in privateers; release a few
seamen and a ship or two . . ." This, Logan is to have said to the
French, would assuage American opinion and "leave you at
leisure to prepare your plans for execution at a more favorable
moment. . . . After your war with England is at an end, we may
perhaps . . . show you the way into America, as well as Citizen
Ocks and friends showed you the way into Switzerland. . . ." [46]

Actually, this sort of rhetorical performance was really unnecessary, for try as hard as they might, Gallatin and the Republicans could not possibly block the bill's passage. Gallatin might
very accurately and eloquently illustrate how the Federalists
were using the war scare, what he called the "doctrine of alarm,"
to get their program through Congress; he might charge that the
Federalists sought to alter the fabric of government to suit their
centralizing ideas, but it made little difference. Harper had the
necessary Federalist votes for passage, provided he could hold
them in line. The argument ran on for better than six weeks until
finally in early 1799 the "Logan Law" passed the House of
Representatives, making it a federal crime for a private citizen to
correspond with a foreign power on a matter in dispute with the
United States. The law carried a five thousand dollar fine and
three-year prison term, and although Doctor Logan was never

prosecuted the law is still on the statute books of the United States. [47] It was the final act in the Federalist national defense drama.

At almost the same time the Logan legislation was being debated, news of the resolutions passed by the Kentucky and Virginia legislatures arrived in the national capital. Harper took surprisingly little notice of the resolutions and his reaction was amazingly restrained. In light of all his remarks about the internal threat to the nation's security his colleagues might well have anticipated an "I told you so" speech.

Instead of identifying the resolutions as the traitorous call to arms, the French sponsored rising against the government, Harper very calmly said that public information and education would correct the situation. He did warn that these inflammatory resolutions, coupled with a public misunderstanding of the laws, might lead to another Whiskey Rebellion unless corrected by a liberal dosage of the truth by the government. He knew of at least one public meeting in Virginia, he asserted, where copies of the original Senate bill were distributed to purposely deceive the people in attendance. Since the Republicans traded upon this sort of misunderstanding it was not difficult, he said, to understand their opposition to his suggestion that the government print and distribute fifty thousand copies of the Alien and Sedition Acts. [48]

The states sovereignty resolutions had a much greater impact upon South Carolina than they did upon the state's senior congressman, although Harper was not immediately aware of this discrepancy since the Carolina Senate did not vote on considering the resolutions until December of 1799. [49] By that time Robert Goodloe Harper was well aware that he was no longer in tune with the state's political pulsebeat.

The remainder of the Fifth and the opening session of the Sixth Congresses were somewhat anticlimactic. The great struggle to save the Republic had been won, and little remained to be done except maintain the national vigilance with regards to both the foreign and domestic threat. Harper was not aware until it was too late that the magnificent hand dealt him and his colleagues by the XYZ crisis had been overplayed. The political magic of the war scare began to wane just after the elections of 1798, even in South Carolina. When neither invasions nor insurrections materialized, and after President Adams had deserted the war hawks in late 1799 by dispatching the three new negotiators to France, after the taxation legislation became fully operative, and in light of the vigorous prosecution of the Sedition Act by overzealous administration officials and Federalist judges, the tide began running against the spokesman of the "Spirit of '98."

Harper continued exhorting his constituents to remain at the ready. He wrote to them explaining the Alien and Sedition Acts and the ridiculousness of the Virginia and Kentucky Resolutions, which were based, he said, upon a misinterpretation of the laws which he hoped he had done something to correct. [50] The Federalist defense program had had a great effect upon the French Government, for the Directory had discovered that the United States was not easily frightened into line, and Harper believed that the French would soon become more respectful of American rights and independence. The capital city had heard numerous rumors about French willingness to accept a new envoy and Harper told his constituents that the president intended to keep the door open for an honorable settlement. Nevertheless, it must also have been apparent to his readers that there were those in the Federalist Party, Harper among them, who did not fully approve of the executive's eagerness to negotiate.

Harper told his constituents that there was little reason for alarm, however, since the "Congress, taking warning from the perfidious conduct of France towards other countries, has resolved not to be the dupe of her artifices on this occasion, nor to relax, in any degree, from its measure of defense." He warned that the olive branch had to be balanced by the unsheathed sword, or the United States might yet share the fate of those other nations who were lulled into slavery by French deceit. He continued his support for maintaining the defense establishment and, if anything, he became a more enthusiastic navy booster than before. [51]

Throughout the summer and fall of 1799, and into 1800, much of his time was devoted to a constant stream of these letters home urging the necessity of standing firm against France, warning of false peace overtures and French hypocrisy. He preached the virtues of military and financial stability and praised the successes the administration had enjoyed in both areas, particularly the patriotic manner in which Americans had oversubscribed the 1798 National Loan by nine million dollars. He nearly neglected to mention that the loan carried an interest rate of eight percent, which may have done much to stimulate that patriotic reaction.

Harper had some extremely kind words for Napoleon Bonaparte, which may have disturbed some of his constituents. Harper
applauded the fact that a despotism of madmen and knaves had
at last been replaced by the despotism of one man, but a sensible
man who might not turn out badly. Harper said that he thought
Napoleon was the best thing that had happened to France in ten
years and that the gentleman deserved the thanks of the world.
So far as Robert Goodloe Harper was concerned, he held it to be
"an indisputable truth that whoever, by any means, suppresses an
anarchicial democratical despotism . . . ought to be considered as
a benefactor to mankind." Those who loved "true republicanism" should be particularly grateful to Napoleon, Harper
thought, because he had overthrown a disgraceful imitation of
Republicanism which had soured the thinking part of mankind
on the genuine article. [52]

Throughout the remainder of his term in the House, Harper
was still obsessed by rumors of a landing by West Indian agents in
the United States to foment trouble among the slaves. In late
March 1798 he included a warning to his constituents to keep
their guard up against French double-dealing. He told them that
he had it on the best authority that the previous summer, even
while the Directory was entertaining Mr. Gerry in Paris, "Hedouville was preparing to invade the southern states from St. Domingo, with an army of blacks; which was to be landed with a
large supply of officers, arms and ammunition, to excite an
insurrection among the negroes by means of missionaries previously sent. . . . Hence may we learn to appreciate the professions
of the French government; and the wisdom or honesty of those
counsellors, who perpetually tell us that there is no danger of an
invasion from France, and no need to prepare for such an
event." [53] Robert Goodloe Harper's much-predicted insurrection
finally materialized in early 1799, but it occurred in eastern
Pennsylvania rather than Carolina, and it was purely domestic in
origin and leadership.

Not even Harper was able to make a case for Jacob Fries'
"rebellion" being French inspired or prompted by West Indian
agents. It must have been doubly distressing, not only because
the insurrection did not follow the Federalist script but equally
so since it took place in what had been respectable administration territory, and it involved not the volatile Whiskey Rebellion Scotch-Irish but the solid elements of eastern Pennsylvania
burgher society. The precipitating incidents had involved oppo-

sition among these heretofore solidly Federalist farmers to the new program of land taxation to finance the war effort. As was the case with every hint of overt resistance to the central government or its policies, the High-Federalists in Congress and the cabinet grossly overexaggerated the rebel force and greatly overreacted. Fries' rebellion was even smaller than the Whiskey Rebellion and never involved more than a few hundred men, many of whom were probably spectators. However, to some Federalists, driven nearly to paranoia by their own fears of invasion, it was even possible to see the hand of the dreaded Society of Illuminati among these good Pennsylvania yeomen who had probably never even heard of the society and who would have been appalled by the association. [54]

Harper wrote several times to the secretary of war offering his unsolicited advice as to how best to proceed against the rebels. He harped on the necessity of using an adequate military force, preferably considerably larger than would ever be necessary. The rebels were "ignorant, biggotted, numerous & united [and] their leaders . . . are committed to the full length of treason." [55]

As Harper saw it, the only way to deal with such people was to completely overwhelm them by the size and power of your own forces, and if this was done the rabble would quickly surrender—they always did. He thought it was best to call up "the whole of the Volunteers and the requisite cavalry" and then march the whole lot into Bethlehem immediately. Sending too small a force was an invitation to the rebels to continue resistance and might well lead to disaster. Perhaps in order to press his suggestions, Harper went along as a volunteer aide to one of the staff officers in the expedition against the insurrection. He apparently had a grand time and greatly impressed the military men with his enthusiasm if not his experience. The old dream of a military career, a sword, a prancing charger, and ten thousand men, frustrated by the end of the Revolution, had come alive once more, only to be dashed again. [56]

Fries was captured and marched off to Philadelphia to be tried for treason, and the rebellion, such as it was, ended. No doubt though, the incident added incentive to Harper's opposition to the series of Republican attempts during 1799 and 1800 to reduce the size of the army, which had never been brought up to full strength as it was. As his "invasion and insurrection is imminent" arguments began to lose their sting, Harper was forced to resort to appeals based on the necessity of strengthening the position of the new American negotiating team dispatched to France in November of 1799 by John Adams. [57]

Privately, Harper expressed ever more bitter comments about the president and the whole business of a new mission, which he thought "an ill-judged & unlucky measure" that probably had to be gone through with since it was already instituted. What seemed to rankle him most was that Adams by his precipitous action had pushed the party far out on a limb that the Republicans might saw off. If the government found it necessary to break off the negotiations the "French party" could be counted on to hurl the charge of insincerity and hypocrisy at the Federalists. Such a charge was difficult to disprove and might wreak havoc with public opinion, which was already showing dangerous signs of flagging.

Harper, not alone among his associates in the House, began laying the blame for the increasingly apparent decline in public confidence in the Federalist administration entirely at the feet of John Adams. [58] By the time the election of 1800 approached, Harper and company had, in a masterly stroke of self-deception, succeeded, at least in their own minds, in exonerating themselves of all responsibility for the tragedy of Federalist leadership. Adams was equally adept at shifting the responsibility from himself to the "Juntomen," and historians have chosen to accept his point of view.

During the remainder of 1799 Robert Goodloe Harper spent most of his time attempting to reconcile two problems which were of great concern to him. At nearly the same time as he decided to quit politics and South Carolina and move northward, establishing a law practice in Philadelphia or Baltimore, he also set out on an attempt to secure a commission for himself in the Additional Army, which he seems to have believed was to be permanent. The latter objective was probably the more sought after, if only to satisfy his old dream of military glory. Harper was never prone to underestimate his own worth, and he devised two alternate plans for his military career. Most desirable was the chance for an appointment to Washington's staff as an aide, with the rank of lieutenant colonel or brigadier general. If that was not possible, Harper had in mind a brigadier's rank in command of a "Legionary Brigade" which he planned to raise in the back-country of South Carolina should war occur. [59]

He coaxed McHenry into writing a number of letters of recommendation to Washington, and when that fell through, to the governor of North Carolina and General Charles C. Pinckney in South Carolina. Washington, who had discussed the matter with his chief lieutenant, Alexander Hamilton, was very courteously and diplomatically resistant to McHenry's efforts in Harper's behalf. Hamilton had written to the general recommending Harper for an appointment, but a somewhat offhanded compliment probably had some influence on Washington's decision. Hamilton pointed out Harper's virtues, most notably his exemplary Federalism, but then the New Yorker commented that the "only shade to his useful qualities was his vanity"; nevertheless, Hamilton concluded, "the good much outweighs the ill."[60]

From Mount Vernon in February 1799 Washington wrote McHenry saying that he did not wish to commit himself, and at any rate, he thought he should maintain his established military family. By way of smoothing Harper's feelings, Washington expressed his belief that in time of crisis Harper might be of greater service where he was, in the legislature.[61]

McHenry did not give up that easily and he wrote again to the general, and on this occasion he received a far less diplomatic reply. McHenry and Harper had unfortunately not recognized a firm, but subtle, Virginia "no" when they first heard it. Washington, losing patience under a flood of such requests, tersely spelled matters out for the two gentlemen. Harper had talents, Washington said, he did not deny them, "but there is too much of something else accompanying them, which must not render [him] the most pleasing character in a family. . . ." McHenry had emphasized the probability that Harper's feelings would be injured by a refusal and this brought an obviously angry blast from Mount Vernon. "Why should *he* be more hurt by my circumspect conduct than [the other candidates]? Is it not an evidence that the same cause or similar would produce the same effect to the disquietitude of harmony among the persons about me?" the general asked.[62] The Harper personality, defects as well as virtues, had never been better summed up than by the two southerners Pierce Butler and George Washington. Needless to say, Harper never again disturbed General Washington.

The summer of 1799 saw Harper and McHenry turn elsewhere in their quest for a commission. They wrote first to C. C. Pinckney in June and July, and after Pinckney informed Harper that all available positions which Harper thought suitable were filled, the supplicants turned in desperation to Governor Davie of North Carolina, who also turned them down.[63] In each instance

Harper could easily have secured an appointment at the rank of captain or possibly even major, but his vanity proved to be the obstacle, as it always is for those who wish to start at the top. Possibly, the changed nature of southern politics and Harper's ever more awkward position as a southern Federalist was in part responsible for the chilly response.

As late as the fall of 1799, even after he had decided to give up politics, indeed, after he had already opened a law office in Baltimore, Harper would have thrown it all over if James McHenry had been able to come up with the right appointment. The military orientation, the martial ambitions, the dream of expansion and foreign conquest, significantly present in the Federalist mind, were denied again by circumstance to the erstwhile commander of a "Legionary Brigade" in the old Southwest. Years afterward, during a foreign war that did materialize, Robert Goodloe Harper finally became a general. [64]

NOTES

1. William Vans Murray to James McHenry, April 12, 1798, Steiner, p. 301.
2. William Pinkney to James McHenry, February 26, 1798, ibid., p. 298; William L. Smith to Oliver Wolcott, Lisbon, August 14, 1798, Gibbs, II, 119-120.
3. Chauncey Goodrich to Oliver Wolcott, August 12, 1798, Gibbs, II, 105, and George Cabot to Wolcott, April 25, 1798, ibid., p. 48.
4. RGH to Constituents, March 9, 1798, Bayard Papers, p. 52. Reports received in South Carolina were not very encouraging. See Charles C. Pinckney, from Paris, to John Rutledge, Jr., January 25, 1798. "There is not the least hope of an accomodation with this government." Pinckney urged the South Carolinians to guard their coasts and "prepare for every event." John Rutledge Papers, Southern Historical Collection, University of North Carolina Library.
5. Ibid., July 23, 1798, Bayard Papers, pp. 58-59.
6. Ibid., pp. 60-69. Years later, when he edited the original letters for publication in the *Works of RGH*, Harper made the following note in reference to his expectations of a decline in French power. "Note— All these predictions were approaching fast to their fulfillment, when the usurpation of Buonaparte, and the able, vigorous and systematic administration which he introduced again changed the face of affairs." Ibid., p. 68.

7. Ames to Timothy Pickering, June 4, 1798, Pickering Papers, XXII, 189, Massachusetts Historical Society.

8. This competition for influence in the House may well have been the reason for the absence or scarcity of correspondence between Hamilton and some of these "Young Turks."

9. Pierce Butler to James Madison, January 23, 1795. Chapter IV, fn. 1.

10. Letter to Constituents, July 23, 1798, pp. 68-69. The best recent study of the relationship between the foreign crisis and domestic politics is Alexander DeConde, *The Quasi War: The Politics and Diplomacy of the Undeclared War with France, 1797-1801* (New York: Charles Scribner's Sons, 1966).

11. Timothy Pickering to RGH, March 21, 1799, Pickering Papers, X, 502, Massachusetts Historical Society. Also quoted in Samuel E. Morrison, *Life and Letters of Harrison Gray Otis* (2 vols.; Boston: Houghton Mifflin, 1913), p. 68.

12. *Annals*, 5C2S, pp. 1567-1570.

13. Wolfe, p. 117.

14. *Annals*, 5C2S, pp. 1567-1571.

15. The details of the internal security program are developed in James M. Smith, *Freedom's Fetters, The Alien and Sedition Laws and American Civil Liberties* (Ithaca: Cornell University Press, 1956). Smith comments upon the fact that Samuel Sewell, the chairman of the House Defense Committee, who introduced the first bill was eventually brought around to Harper's more extreme position on naturalization. Mr. Smith also suggests that the younger element in the House took the leadership away from Sewell and the older Federalists in the midst of these debates. Smith, pp. 30-36. As a matter of fact, Massachusetts and Connecticut had proposed an amendment to the Constitution which would have made citizens naturalized since the Declaration of Independence ineligible for election to either house of Congress or the presidency. John C. Miller, *Crisis in Freedom: The Alien and Sedition Acts* (Boston: Little, Brown and Co., 1951), pp. 48-49.

16. *Annals*, 5C2S, pp. 1996-1997. Rumors concerning French invasion plans were discussed everywhere. John Rutledge wrote home to his father, April 1, 1798, that unless remarkable changes occurred "*war will be inevitable.*" "We have strong reasons for believing that a project is now carrying on, by the French, to take Canada and the Floridas and to revolutionize a great portion of our western Country." John Rutledge Papers, Southern Historical Collection.

17. Ibid. The Aliens Enemies Act is still on the statute books. In 1948, the Supreme Court in a five to four decision in *Ludecke v. Watkins* held it to be constitutional. Justice Felix Frankfurter wrote the opinion upholding the application of the 1798 Act. Alfred H. Kelly and Winfred A. Harbison, *The American Constitution* (New York: W. W. Norton and Co., 1955, rev. ed.), p. 885.

18. This is from a Livingston speech which attributed the phraseology to Harper. *Annals*, 5C2S, p. 2007, also quoted in Smith, pp. 67-68.
19. *Annals*, pp. 1965-1967, 1990. Smith maintains that it was over this bill that the extremist group captured the leadership of the Federalist membership in the House, while this author is inclined to feel that in effect they were in control earlier in the session.
20. Ibid., pp. 1973-1983, 1998-1999.
21. *Annals*, p. 1692. Harper was able to dominate the delegation, and the Republican members scarcely ever challenged Harper in open debate.
22. Ibid., pp. 1992, 2024-2026.
23. Miller, pp. 65-67.
24. Ibid., pp. 66-67. Miller incorrectly refers to Jonathan Sewell as Chairman of the House Defense and Commerce Committee. The Chairman was Samuel Sewell of Massachusetts.
25. *Annals*, 5C2S, pp. 2101, 2121-2122.
26. *Annals*, p. 2141. An excellent discussion of the English background for the American sedition proceedings is contained in Kelly and Harbison, pp. 196-199.
27. *Annals*, pp. 2103-2104.
28. Smith, pp. 121-122.
29. *Annals*, 5C2S, p. 2104.
30. Ibid., pp. 2115-2116.
31. Ibid., p. 2134.
32. William Wirt Papers, Box 1, Maryland Historical Society.
33. Albert J. Beveridge, *The Life of John Marshall* (4 vols.; Boston: Houghton Mifflin Co., 1916), II, 390-394. Marshall was bitterly censured by New England Federalists for his mild criticism of the Sedition Law, so much so that Pickering and George Cabot found it necessary to defend the Virginian in the Massachusetts newspapers. Of interest are: John Marshall to Pickering, August 11, 1798, Pickering Papers, XXIII, 33, Massachusetts Historical Society, and George Cabot to Pickering, October 26, 1798, XXIII, 265.
34. Adams expressed the following opinion of the Sedition Act to Pickering in October 1798. "The Alien Law, the Sedition Law and the appropriations of money for defense, have been the subjects of continued clamour and complaint. Livingston's and Gallatin's speeches . . . have been circulated, and many poor deluded beings led to believe, that because Congress have passed a law for the removal of *traitorous* and *seditious aliens* . . . the liberties of the people are destroyed—and that by the Act for punishing False scandalous and malicious libels upon the government, the liberties of the people is anihilated. Here then we may clearly see that the liberty which these _____ contend for; is treason and sedition, and their Liberty of the Press is Slander & Licentiousness." Adams Papers, Outgoing Correspondence, Reel 119, L.C.

35. *Annals* 5C2S, p. 2124.
36. *Annals* 5C3S, December 11, 12, 19, 1798, pp. 2224-2227, 2428-2430. Later in the session he compromised by asking for the printing of five thousand copies of the statutes of the previous session with appended copies of the Constitution, which was accepted. Ibid., p. 2462.
37. Beveridge, II, quoting from Carey's *U. S. Recorder*, August 16, 1798.
38. South Carolina Records, A, 351.
39. Pickering to Rufus King, December 14, 1798, Pickering Papers, XXXVII, 370.
40. Just why the Republican Pinckney was so despised by South Carolina Federalists remains something of a mystery. Rather than one particular action or event it probably derived from the fact that he had been born a Pinckney and then turned Republican, which in South Carolina Federalist circles amounted to betraying not only his party but his social class as well. The question is handled very ably in Wallace, p. 358 fn.
41. Lisle Rose, *Prologue to Democracy* makes the point quite convincingly that the great failure of the southern Federalist party lay in its never really building an organization. The great triumph of 1798 was of remarkably brief duration. There are several revealing letters in the John Rutledge Papers, Southern Historical Collection, University of North Carolina Library, from various prominent South Carolina Federalists, which document how immature, in an institutional sense, Federalist political development was in that state. As late as 1800 they were still doing business in the style of 1792.
42. Frederick B. Tolles, *George Logan of Philadelphia* (New York: Oxford University Press, 1953), pp. 156-160. See also, the Sedition debates as quoted earlier in this chapter. Bache had published in the *Aurora*, June 16, 1798, a letter from Talleyrand to the American envoys which Harper also included under the heading "treasonable Correspondence." Dumas Malone denies that any proof exists of Jefferson's having given Logan letters of introduction. Malone maintains that Jefferson had been more than scrupulous in limiting his transatlantic correspondence after the Mazzei episode. Dumas Malone, *Jefferson and the Ordeal of Liberty* (Boston: Little, Brown and Co., 1962), pp. 430-434. However, there is a letter from William Vans Murray, at the Hague, to the secretary of state, August 6, 1798, in the Pickering Papers, XXIII, 10, which informed Pickering that Logan had arrived in Rotterdam bearing letters from Jefferson and that Logan was attempting to contact Elbridge Gerry. Murray claimed that he had successfully sent an agent, posing as a Republican sympathizer, to contact and pump Logan. The doctor is supposed to have acknowledged what a war would do to American Republicanism, and that a French invasion would be met with unanimous American

resistance. Murray did not see the letters and he was trying to have Logan arrested so that he could seize them. Murray to Timothy Pickering, August 7, 1798, Pickering Papers, XXXIII, 14. William Vans Murray would have had almost no way of knowing about the "treasonable correspondence" unless Logan had made it known that he did indeed possess letters from Jefferson, which may make uncertain the wisdom of Professor Malone's acceptance of the Virginian's denial.

43. *Annals* , 5C3S, December, 1798, pp. 2493-2494.
44. *Annals*, 5C3S, pp. 2502-2503.
45. Ibid., p. 2507.
46. Ibid., pp. 2507-2508.
47. Samuel F. Bemis, *Diplomatic History of the American People* (New York: Henry Holt and Co., 1936), pp. 121-122. De Conde, *The Quasi War*, pp. 155-157, 171-172. It is difficult not to take the Republican view of the Logan Act—that it made it a federal crime to interfere in foreign negotiation if one's purpose was peace while remaining silent on the matter of private citizens who by their actions provoke a war.
48. *Annals*, 5C3S, December 12, 1798, pp. 2429-2431.
49. South Carolina Senate Journal, December 20, 1799, quoted in Wolfe, p. 128 fn. The vote was very close—14 to 11 against considering the resolution.
50. RGH to Constituents, February 10, 1799, Bayard Papers, pp. 75-76.
51. Ibid., pp. 77-79. See also the letter of March 20, 1798.
52. RGH to Constituents, April 7, 1800. p. 82.
53. General Hedouville had been dispatched by the Directory with orders to check Toussaint's rise to complete power, until French troops could be sent to Santo Domingo in greater numbers. He was unable to contain L'Ouverture's revolution, let alone invade the United States. C. L. R. James, *The Black Jacobins* (New York: Alfred A. Knopf, 1963), p. 201.
54. J. C. Miller, *Crisis in Freedom*, p. 145, quoting Jedidiah Morse to Oliver Wolcott, April 22, 1799, Wolcott MSS, Connecticut Historical Society. The Society of the Illuminati was supposed to be a highly secret international conspiracy intent upon bringing down the pillars of society represented by organized religion and existing governments.
55. RGH to James McHenry, March 22, 1799, McHenry MSS, 2nd Series, L.C.
56. Ibid. Harper estimated that the force in the counties in revolt could run as high as three thousand men. See also a letter from James McHenry to Governor Davie of North Carolina, August 6, 1799, in the RGH Papers, L.C.
57. *Annals*, 6C1S, pp. 22-24, 326-351, 389-393, 404.
58. RGH to James McHenry, August 2, 1799, Steiner, pp. 407-408. See

John Rutledge, Jr., to Bishop Robert Smith of Charleston, February 27, 1799, for another Federalist view on the new French initiative, and the impact of the President's response on the party. John Adams' actions were "highly displeasing to his best friends. . . ." Rutledge noted that they wanted Cabot and Hamilton linked with Vans Murray, "however, with the obstinacy manifested by the President there is no altering this business and his nomination will be confirmed." John Rutledge Papers, Southern Historical Collection.

59. RGH to C. C. Pinckney, July 26, 1799, McHenry Papers, Series I, L. C. Pinckney was to be ranking commander in the Southern Theater in the newly created army.

60. Hamilton to Washington, *Works of Hamilton*, VI, 334-338, quoted in Wolfe, p. 116.

61. Washington to McHenry, February 26, 1799, McHenry Papers, L.C.

62. Washington to McHenry, March 5, 1799, McHenry Papers, 2nd Series, L.C.

63. C. C. Pinckney to RGH, June 13, 1799, Harper Papers, L.C., RGH to C. C. Pinckney, July 26, 1799, McHenry Papers, Series One; McHenry to Governor Davie, August 6, 1799, Harper Papers, L.C.; McHenry to RGH Harper Papers, August 7, 1799.

64. During the attack on Baltimore in 1814 Harper commanded part of the makeshift defense force and thereafter took great pleasure in being at last "General Harper."

10

Jefferson and Defeat

Harper's decision to retire from the House when his term expired in 1800 was irrevocably made in the early part of 1799. Having long complained that men of moderate means could not afford national office, Harper, who had nearly quit in 1797, announced his intentions by moving his residence to Maryland and opening a law office in Baltimore in the summer of 1799. He had no way of knowing that the elections in South Carolina would turn out to be extremely close and that perhaps there was still a chance of reelection, but it would have made little difference to him. He served out his final session as the congressman from South Carolina's Ninety Six after the move to Maryland and there was no shirking of responsibilities which he faithfully met until the day his term expired.

The reasons for his choice of the Old Line State over New York or Pennsylvania are unclear, but geography must have had a great deal to do with the decision. His final term was divided between Philadelphia and the new capital city on the banks of the Potomac, making a law practice in Baltimore, half-way between, eminently logical. Then too, Baltimore was rapidly becoming the most "northern" of southern cities, which made it the best of both worlds for someone of Harper's tastes and background. It was as far north as he could go and still feel comfortable as a southerner, and Maryland was, by this time, the most solidly Federalist of the southern states. But there were other, purely personal reasons that figured in the choice. In the fall of 1798, as he journeyed home to campaign for reelection Harper had been extremely fortunate in being introduced to one of the South's leading families, the Carrolls of Carrollton.'

Charles Carroll, signer of the Declaration of Independence, was beyond doubt one of the wealthiest men in America. His position, estates, and financial interests placed him with Washington in the company of the very highest level of the southern squirearchy. Like Washington, Carroll had seen the signs of the economic future, diversified his holdings, and was successfully making the transition into the nineteenth century. Unlike

Washington, however, Charles Carroll was quite taken by the impressive political career of the thirty-three year old Harper, and unlike the general, Mr. Carroll had a daughter both attractive and unmarried. This is not to say that Harper moved to Baltimore because of Kitty Carroll, but then, men have undergone far greater inconveniences for considerably lesser prizes.

At the time, Harper's friendship with Secretary of War McHenry, and the latter's business and social connections in Baltimore, were probably more significant in influencing the congressman than the possibility of a future entente with Miss Carroll. McHenry had urged Harper on several occasions to settle in Baltimore and he obviously considered the prospective citizen as an asset to the community. The secretary's arguments eventually carried the day and Harper decided to make the move.

By late July, ensconced in his newly rented law office in Baltimore, Robert Goodloe Harper waited for clients, mulled over his choice of cities and his future prospects, and confided in McHenry, who along with Justice Samuel Chase of the Supreme Court attempted to assist the establishment of the new arrival's law practice.[2] Chase had suggested to Harper that a better location might have been in Annapolis since the state's government, offices, and courts were situated there, but Baltimore, Harper had decided, was to be his center of operation.

The attempt to secure a military commission was not yet dead and Harper mailed McHenry a copy of the answer he had received from C. C. Pinckney. He asked McHenry to inform President Adams that he was definitely still interested in military service, and if all other positions were filled he would not refuse a regiment of cavalry.

Nevertheless, the situation was changing so quickly in Europe that there would probably, Harper thought, not be commissions for anyone. He exclaimed to McHenry, "progress has infinitely lessened the probability of an attack upon us . . . ," in which case, they would all have to wait for another war in order to "seek occasions for acquiring military glory. . . . What a pity that so many Buonapartes in embryo, should be chilled into mere Lawyers Planters & merchants by the cold breath of Peace." He instructed McHenry not to let the "Democrats" see the letter, "for they will take it literaly & say that I wished for war, in order to gain an opportunity of acquiring glory in the field."[3] Harper knew quite as well as McHenry that the Republicans had already come to that conclusion.

James McHenry was delighted when he learned that Harper had definitely decided upon Baltimore, and he again promised to do his best to get the lawyer off to a good start. Nevertheless, there were matters, unrelated to either the law or Harper's military career, which deserved the immediate concern of both men.

There was the question of the new mission to France, about which Harper had expressed doubts earlier, and Harper had received disturbing reports from McHenry and other correspondents regarding the mission. Talleyrand, McHenry had told him, was toying with William Vans Murray, using his favorite weapons of unclear declarations and silence upon several of the important conditions established by John Adams for reopening the negotiations. It seems evident that McHenry read new French deceit into Talleyrand's enigmatic communications, and the secretary of war wished to break off the proceedings. There was, however, the question of the president, who was off again at Quincy. And there amidst his orchards and fields who could predict what Adams would do?[4]

From Baltimore Harper answered with a slightly more optimistic interpretation of French intentions. At any rate, Harper said, the Adams administration had committed itself, and there was no alternative to going through with the attempt at reopening negotiations. Any sign of unwillingness to negotiate, for less than excellent reasons, could be depended upon to evoke a Republican blast which had to be avoided if at all possible. The Federalists were caught in a dilemma which was the making of a president of their own party, something which constituted political stupidity, with national elections only one year away. Harper was not convinced that the Directory had good intentions of fairly and honestly settling the dispute which had provoked a major undeclared naval war in the West Indies, but there was really no other choice but to carry through with the diplomatic initiative and leave it to the Directory to fish or cut bait.[5]

While Robert Goodloe Harper's time was divided between these exchanges with McHenry and others, his law practice, and his duties in the House, he did not neglect his correspondence with his constituents. For the most part he concentrated upon vindicating the final acts of the Federalist Sixth Congress and delivering his parting blasts at the French Revolution.

It was in so many ways sadly ironic, he wrote, that after a decade of upheaval, anarchy, murder and bloody wars, that the

French Revolution, a struggle begun in the name of Liberty, Fraternity, and Equality, had to end with Napoleon. Regardless of his belief that the Corsican would be good for France, Harper declared that Bonaparte was nonetheless a military usurper invested with more absolute power than Louis ever enjoyed. What road the new dictator would take, Harper did not know, but he was impressed by the fact that Napoleon had the power to make peace and end the European war, if only he would choose to do so. However, Harper informed his constituents that events in Europe required American maintenance of the present defense posture, and he still opposed any attempts to reduce the size of the army and navy.[6]

Harper continued as chairman of the Ways and Means Committee until the end of the session, defending the Federalist tax program until the end, and he even managed to introduce new legislation ranging all the way from a new uniform bankruptcy law to an expansion of the information-gathering function of the federal census. With the latter item, Harper had in mind the accumulation of data in order to assist the government in making decisions regarding matters such as taxation and programs fostering the progress of manufacturing.[7] He was an early advocate of the suggested overhaul of the federal judicial system, and he supported both an increase in the number of circuit courts and the appointment of a distinct set of federal judges to preside over them.[8]

Unfortunately Harper also clung to the 1798 preparedness measures long after many of his colleagues were ready to desert the abortive legislation, which had neither expelled the undesirable aliens nor in any way curtailed "sedition," but instead made "traitors" out of formerly respectable—meaning Federalist—Pennsylvania farmers.

Several Republican attacks on the Alien and Sedition Laws, the most serious in early 1799, had been thwarted by party discipline and the High-Federalist's use of the patriotic whip to bring the recalcitrant into line. At that time, Harper had written to his constituents that the Sedition Law could be allowed to expire since the offenses it was designed to deal with might as well be handled under the common law, which allowed no defense based upon the truth. No such subtle justification for the continuation of the Alien Law was necessary as far as Harper was concerned. He merely expressed his belief that the law afforded the United States a very valuable protection against inundation by the least desirable of immigrants. This was particularly true of the situation in which the nation was probably going to find itself for some time to come, that is to say, aligned against France. In the case of an enemy known for intrigue, aliens constituted a serious internal threat even during peace time.[9]

Even as the Federalist era drew to a close in 1801, the last Federalist Congress attempted to secure renewal of the hated 1798 legislation. Harper and Otis tried to convince the other members of the House that the basis for an effective, honest political opposition rested on having in effect the sort of sedition legislation enacted in 1798; a law designed, they said, to offer protection to both accuser and accused, with the truth inevitably triumphant in the end. [10] The sad aspect of this last desperate attempt to save the Sedition Law was that Otis and Harper, and many other Federalists, had stumped for this argument for so long and so passionately that they sincerely believed what they said. With Robert Goodloe Harper there must also have been a strong personal involvement with this legislation he had done so much to enact, and which, if it stood, represented a sort of personal monument. Although not as he would have wished it, these laws long expired or repealed do constitute precisely that—a negative tribute to the Robert Goodloe Harpers of the period.

The arguments of the Harper-Otis element were to little avail, except for the Judiciary Act of 1801 which attracted the votes of the more moderate Federalists because it could be defended to constituents as constructive legislation. The expansion of the judiciary was in marked contrast to the attempt to reenact a bitterly controversial political albatross, which is what the Sedition Law had become. [11] Contrary to an extremely persistent myth, the Judiciary Act of 1801 was not enacted in the eleventh hour of the Federalist period in the wake of Jefferson's election merely to provide a haven for Federalist political ideology. The House had been very much involved in debating proposed reforms in the judicial branch of the government as early as the spring of 1800, during the first session of the last Federalist congress. Harper wrote to his constituents in May in support of the expansion proposal. It was only after the November election results became conclusive that the judicial legislation took on this added significance.

The reaction from the opposition, soon to be the majority party, to this court reform bill was inveterate opposition even before the election results were known, and of course, the events of November only hardened Republican opposition to the plan to pack the courts with the worst of the "Anglo-men." Unable to overcome the bitterness of '98, the Jeffersonians, understandably but lamentably, threw the baby out with the bath when the Judiciary Law was repealed in early 1802. In so doing, they acted to the disservice of the national judicial welfare and the discomfort and inconvenience of the federal judges who were forced to continue to ride circuit.

Not until after the Civil War was the federal court system brought into line with the realities of national growth and judicial needs. Harper and the thinking members of the congressional company formulated and enacted a court reform plan that would have served the nation's needs quite adequately, but the president and his advisors made blatantly political usage of the opportunity for partisan appointment, and the new Republican administration could not possibly have accepted the measure.

For Harper all this must have been terribly frustrating. It simply did not seem possible that a political party could be at the zenith of power in one instant and then, almost in the next, be fighting for its life, and yet this had happened. This agony of the political leader deserted by his followers was certainly difficult enough for Harper to accept, but it was not nearly as demoralizing as it might have been had he not already decided to depart the national political arena, as well as Ninety Six.

The withdrawal from South Carolina was total and not simply a transfer of center of operation. He cut all financial ties and disposed of every acre of land he could sell in an effort to get out from under the heaviest of his debts. The South Carolina land records for the late 1790s and early 1800s show Harper selling his holdings as rapidly as he could. The deed book for Laurens County alone contains between three and four dozen entries recording sales by Harper. Almost all of these sales were for small lots, although several large blocks of 175 or 185 acres were disposed of. There was no doubt more profit from the sale of land in small parcels, which indicates some development activity. Most of the sales, in this instance, were in the vicinity of the Laurens County Court House, which would seem to support the assumption that Harper had bought the land counting on the growth of the area to provide his profit. [12]

No doubt he realized some income from the sale of his holdings but not nearly what might have been expected had

Harper remained in Carolina and disposed of the property ten
years or so later. However, he could not wait another decade, and
the decision to liquidate his holdings having been made and the
process begun, there was no likelihood of his reversing the
process. Robert Goodloe Harper had several times in his life
packed up, completely severed all ties, and moved off to another
part of the nation to begin anew. Perhaps it was the heritage of
frontier birth that made the uprooting easy for him, but this was
the last time. Baltimore was the terminal destination of nearly
twenty years of movement that had begun when he joined
Greene's revolutionary forces and touched every state south of
New York at one time or another.

While Harper was clearing the books in Carolina, the nation
prepared for the most hotly contested national election in its
brief history, and the real estate entrepeneur had to neglect both
land sales and the Baltimore law practice as the last session of the
Sixth Congress showed signs of becoming the most explosive and
important of his congressional career. Now wearing three political hats—congressman, South Carolina political figure, and Maryland Federalist as well—he was kept extremely busy throughout
the election period, which was abnormally extended because of
the Jefferson-Burr problem.

U. B. Phillips contended that the election of 1800 to a large
degree depended upon how South Carolina voted, and certainly
the Federalists entertained high hopes for their ticket in the
Palmetto state. Phillips also thought that the party's failure in
1800 was largely the result of allowing the election to go by
default in that the party was leaderless, having lost Harper,
Smith, Ralph Izard and others. [13] The author had no quarrel with
Phillips' assessment of the importance of the state's electoral
votes in the outcome of the election, but it is necessary to revise
his causal explanation of the Federalist defeat.

The party had been in trouble in South Carolina on the local
level for several years. The point was made earlier that the
Federalist congressional successes in 1798 belied the serious state
of the party's local health. Federalism had always enjoyed that
dangerous luxury of majority parties in power—the tendency
toward factionalism. The Republicans, on the other hand, were
hard pressed after 1797 and they were forced to perfect their
organization, party discipline, and most importantly, to sub-
merge those provincial or personal quarrels which a party on the
outside simply cannot afford if it hopes to succeed. After the

successful election the party motto may well be "no holds barred" as the fruits of victory are distributed, but it has to be "united we stand," at least until after the votes are counted.

The Federalist party in South Carolina, and indeed across the nation, had sorely neglected its organization at the grass-roots level and this, as much as anything else, defeated it. The Republican party, on the other hand, was born at the local level certainly as much as in the early opposition of Madision and Jefferson to the Hamiltonian program. The anti-Jay explosion occurred at the local level and carried upward to the Congress.

The XYZ fever marked the only instance in which the Federalist party took advantage of an expression of a grass-roots political sentiment, molding it to the party's advantage, and even this one success backfired. In South Carolina the Republicans had been hard at work since 1796, even in the midst of the 1798 war scare. By the time of the 1800 elections the Jeffersonian Republicans were in a position to capture the state legislature with a workable majority, and if they could do that, both United States senators would be Republicans and the state's electoral vote would be Thomas Jefferson's. [14]

Harper was in Baltimore and took no actual role in the South Carolina elections except as the state's leading Federalist correspondent. He was actively writing to friends in Carolina and to some of the leading spokesmen for the northern wing of the troubled party. Much of his party's problem stemmed from its inability to profit by past mistakes, or so the elections of 1800 suggest. In 1796 the High-Federalist element had attempted to push Thomas Pinckney ahead of John Adams. It had all depended upon a very complicated maneuver involving a campaign to have the New England and middle states electors vote equally for Adams and Pinckney. The latter's overwhelming strength in South Carolina was sure, or at least this was the plotters' assumption, to move Pinckney into the presidency.

The results were nearly disastrous, and the plan was doomed from the beginning by Adams' popularity in New England, and the intricacy of the plan which assumed a level of political sophistication and organization that neither party possessed at the time. Pinckney was left out completely and Thomas Jefferson, who had not figured in the plan at all, was elected vice-president. The impact of the Pinckney loss only added to South Carolina Federalist doubts about the sincerity of their northern brethren, and this, coupled with the Rutledge confirmation embarrassment, did very little for party unity. However, the 1800 contest produced not one but several schemes within the Federalist party involving once again South Carolina's electoral votes and the Pinckneys, and—this time—it was Charles Cotesworth.

Robert Goodloe Harper, operating from Maryland, was very much involved in this 1800 scheme. The plot was similar to the 1796 variety, the only difference being that the schemers had agreed upon the necessity of electing Charles Cotesworth Pinckney even before John Adams was nominated. The 1796 attempt was, by this time, quite common knowledge, which goes far to explain why the 1800 venture failed. Neither the Adams Federalists nor the "Hamiltonians" trusted the other side, but both pledged to support Adams and Pinckney equally.

There is no question about Harper's candidate. He supported Pinckney from the beginning, although a letter to Hamilton in June 1800 suggests that his method for dropping Adams differed from both the 1796 and 1800 approaches. In both of these schemes, Adams was to be superseded at the earliest stage in the choice of electors. If each state chose an equal number of Adams and Pinckney electors, then South Carolina could select a slate pledged to Pinckney and the trap would be sprung. Harper was extremely afraid that precipitate action might be their undoing. He feared that a noisy rattling of the trap might again frighten off the game.

He informed Hamilton that South Carolina and his newly adopted Maryland could be counted on for a Federalist slate and that most of the people he had talked with favored Pinckney over Adams. However, he was worried about what a direct move to bypass the New Englander might do to what remained of party unity. Therefore Harper advised Hamilton that the best course of action lay in supporting both men equally throughout the election; then, when the electoral college gathered to cast its ballots, "let those who think Mr. Adams unfit to be president drop him silently." Harper said that he knew some men were going to do this anyway and he vowed that he would do it himself if he were an elector. He was, he said, so thoroughly disgusted and disappointed by Mr. Adams' administration, by his weakness and vacillation, that "men of sense & principle" could not support him, and Harper swore that he "could never, under any circumstances give him my vote." [15]

Harper wrote again to Hamilton in August expressing the same sentiments and stressing once more his own approach to electing Pinckney. He assured Hamilton that the Maryland and Carolina electors were resolved to support Adams and Pinckney equally until such time as Adams might be safely dropped. [16]

Throughout the spring and into the fall, Harper, writing from his new vantage point, continued to work for Pinckney's election, and his exertions in that gentleman's behalf leave him open to charges of questionable behavior, if not downright dishonesty. He was privy to the anti-Adams scheme and in complete agreement with its objectives, if not its mode of operation. Yet he continued to press the Adams people for equal support for Adams and Pinckney, telling them that southern support for the president could be counted on, particularly in Maryland and South Carolina.

This is the crux of the argument he reiterated on several occasions to Harrison Gray Otis, who was thought to have access to John Adams and thus to his supporters. Harper assured Otis, supposedly his friend, that there was no doubt about the Adams votes in South Carolina, but he warned that the rumors out of New England about Adams electors discriminating against Pinckney because of the suspicion of a repetition of the 1796 plot, would, if not corrected immediately, wreck Federalist hopes in the South. Should the South Carolina Federalists hear any of these rumblings they might simply stop their efforts altogether, or, even worse, vote for Thomas Jefferson. [17] Harper admitted to Otis that he personally favored Pinckney for the presidency. This had nothing to do with personal friendship since he and the general had never been on anything but "ill terms." It was merely that he believed that Pinckney was more qualified for the office. Nevertheless, in this instance he thought that the dangerous nature of the international and national situation demanded the reelection of John Adams. Harper told Otis that he and the other South Carolina Federalists had been assiduously working toward that end, but unless the anti-Pinckney rumors were quashed, the Adams cause in South Carolina was doomed.

It already looked bad for the president there due to the fact that the presidential electors were chosen by the state legislature. If the choice were left to the people directly, Harper said, the party might get four-fifths of the electors. This was the first time Robert Goodloe Harper had ever complained about the method of choosing electors in South Carolina. It may well have had something to do with the possibility that for the first time the

Republicans stood a good chance of controlling the legislature when the electors were chosen. [18]

At the same time that Harper was up to his ears in the Pinckney business, he was able to express horror, in this letter to Otis, at the rumored prospects of the appearance of a third party based upon some sort of rapprochement or compromise between the Adams men and the Democrats. Harper could not, he said, bring himself to believe that a man of Adams' character and stature would be willing to be on the same ticket with Jefferson, but this rumor had been circulating in Baltimore and probably in Charleston as well, which could seriously damage the Federalist cause in both areas. [19]

The so-called Constitutionalist movement never really materialized, except perhaps in the mind of Robert Goodloe Harper, and there was never any chance for this sort of Jefferson-Adams political rapprochement, not in 1796, when it was first rumored, and certainly not in 1800. The Constitutionalist "party" was part of a vain attempt by the Adams people at disassociating their candidate from the onus of the Federalist label, and it was as unsuccessful as it was unrealistic. [20] The point is that through Otis, Harper hoped to hold the Adams people to their promise of equal support, and also to take advantage of that fulfilled pledge when the time came to dump John Adams. On at least one occasion Harper assured Otis that all was well in South Carolina and that no one there had any idea of bringing Pinckney forward for the top position. [21] At nearly the same time, he was corresponding with Hamilton, George Cabot, and James Mc-Henry in a plan which, even if it had succeeded, would have destroyed the already divided party. Hamilton was assured that Maryland would go for Pinckney and Adams, but Harper warned that Pinckney was, he had learned, very much against the election scheme and would have to be persuaded after the victory was won. [22]

James McHenry, who knew Maryland politics considerably better than his friend, was much more cautious in his assessment of the mood of the state's Federalist voters. He agreed with Harper that there were many Federalists in the state who were interested in seeing Pinckney elected over Adams. However, even these Pinckney men were unwilling to defy the national caucus and the pledge of equal support. If several of the larger eastern states went for Pinckney, McHenry thought that Maryland might go along, but even that possibility was not certain. In any case,

Maryland could not and would not take the lead in any drop-
Adams movement. With respect to Harper, McHenry told Oliver
Wolcott that the congressman was definitely for Pinckney but
that he did not know "whether this will produce any
effect . . . ," referring to Harper's electioneering in Maryland for
his fellow South Carolinian. [23]

It seems that Harper was ex officio advisor to nearly anyone
who would listen and that he was very much involved in every
facet of the campaign. For instance, Alexander Hamilton is
generally credited with breaking the party wide open with his
pamphlet criticizing John Adams' conduct of his office. The
political impact of the pamphlet was unquestionable; however,
there were those, Harper among them, who advised Hamilton
against such tactics. Both Harper and George Cabot, to whom he
had written, expressed concern that this kind of pamphleteering,
signed by Hamilton, might well blow up in their faces if by some
turn of events they had to end up supporting Adams in
Philadelphia when the electoral votes were cast. Cabot and Fisher
Ames agreed that even if such a pamphlet were published
Hamilton ought not to sign it. There was something about
Hamilton's appearing in any election contest that could always
be depended upon to produce more "Jacobin scribblers" than
good Federalists.

The former secretary was not to be dissuaded by Harper, or
even Cabot and Ames, and the pamphlet entitled the "Letter
from Alexander Hamilton concerning the Public Conduct and
Character of John Adams" was printed privately for limited
circulation among Hamilton's close associates. As so often happened, a copy of the tome escaped and found its way into the
Aurora of October 22, in the form of extracts, with the result
that the party in the northern and middle states was left even
more confused and divided than before. [24] If anything, Hamilton's letter worked against the Pinckney scheme, for it only
stiffened the determination of the Adams men to insure more
votes for their candidates than the South Carolinian received,
caucus pledge or not.

While all this was happening in New York and New England,
Federalism was having its troubles in Maryland as well, and, true
to form, the new arrival was very much involved. The trouble
with Maryland, as the Federalists saw it, was the city of
Baltimore. The city, which became increasingly Republican after
1790, threatened to outstrip the counties in population, wealth,

and influence and to gain control of the legislature, which had always been the personal preserve of the rural areas. The counties recognized that reapportionment once done would be difficult to undo, and there was no great haste to surrender their possession of the state government.

The Federalist organization in the state drew its major support from these outlying rural counties and the rural aristocracy. The counties tended to be dominated by a small group of select families, with the Carrolls personifying this Maryland version of aristocratic stewardship. Carl Brent Swisher said of the association between this rural aristocracy and Federalism that young men born into these families accepted without question the tradition of wealth, slaveholding, political noblesse oblige, and membership in the Federalist party which went with the accident of birth. [25] Robert Goodloe Harper had no difficulty whatever in visualizing a future, political as well as social, for himself in this kind of environment much more readily than in either New York or Philadelphia.

The 1800 elections in Maryland involved the explosive local question of the suffrage as well as the choice between the candidates of the two national parties. This in itself was almost the normal political situation in Maryland, for the suffrage question had disrupted the state's political life since the colonial period. The extension of the franchise complicated Maryland politics well into the Jeffersonian Era, and indeed, as late as 1810 Maryland still wrestled with the question. It was not so much a class division, although that was certainly present and had at one time involved a religious issue, but to a larger degree, the problem was one of balancing the economic interests of urban, mercantile, commercial Baltimore against the agrarian, slaveholding, sparsely populated counties.

In the 1800 contest the already existing dichotomy between the two areas was doubly accented by the existence of an electoral system which might for the first time favor the Republicans. As long as the state went Federalist in national elections the "friends of government" had little quarrel with the Maryland practice of choosing electors by popular vote in the state's several electoral districts. The existing district law had worked reasonably well in the past, but it came under increasingly hostile fire as the first election of the new century neared. The criticism came almost entirely from the spokesmen of the state Federalist organization and took the form of an "electoral reform" campaign in which Harper participated.

The objective of the campaign was a new electoral law that would do away with the older district popular elections and replace them with the choice of electors by the state assembly, which by an odd coincidence happened to be Federalist. Those who defended the "reform" did so by arguing that the district system no longer insured a balance of interests between Baltimore and the counties and that to continue under the existing arrangement meant that the counties would eventually be left without adequate voice in federal elections. This was the gist of the pamphlet Harper wrote: that balance of section and protection of varying interests was essential to harmony within the state and that regional animosity was to be avoided at all costs. This was the same argument he had employed in another reapportionment struggle earlier in the decade in another southern state. [26]

It is impossible to estimate accurately the effect this broadside had upon the contest in Maryland, although one suspects that, coming from a brand new citizen as it did, its impact was probably less than spectacular. In any case, it appears that very few people were fooled by the shallow camouflage of the proponent's intentions. This reform movement, like the South Carolina reapportionment movement, was not quite what it purported to be, the difference being that in Maryland this was apparent long before the climax of the struggle.

James McHenry suggested a more honest interpretation of the Maryland electoral problem in a letter to Oliver Wolcott. "Were the votes to be given *now*, by electors chosen by the General Assembly," McHenry thought that Adams and Pinckney were sure to receive all of the state's electoral votes. However, if the "electors [were] to be chosen by the people, each would have three or four votes less, but perhaps an equal number."[27] This was the Maryland dilemma, and it would seem that everyone, those who wrote the articles and pamphlets and those who read them, knew exactly what the real issues were.

There was a considerable amount of interest in the outcome of the Maryland contest, since it might be indicative of the outcome in the other southern states, but there still existed among northern Federalists a certain amount of unfamiliarity, or uncertainty, with respect to southern Federalism. It was as if the members of the northern wing of the party, while appreciative of any electoral support to be had from the other side of Mason and Dixon's line, were never quite sure they really understood or approved of their southern brethren. There exists in the Wolcott papers a marvelous letter which Secretary of the Treasury Wolcott wrote to Fisher Ames during the summer of 1800 in which Wolcott tried to explain what was occurring in Maryland. It is not merely what Wolcott had to say, but the manner, or the tone, of the explanation which is so revealing. The style suggests a lecturer holding forth to the uninitiated upon the subject of some strange and exotic land which, though distant, might affect them, and thus they needed to know something about it.

The character of Maryland, Wolcott wrote, was influenced by the habits of the state's slaveowners, with most of the large property owners being sound Federalists. One of the most distinctive things about the state was the disparity between the very rich and the poor, and this too had marked Maryland politics. "It has been an ancient usage of the aristocrats to pay respect to the sovereign people, by obsequious attentions whenever their suffrages have been requested." At election time candidates of both parties travel through the election districts seeking the support of men with whom they associate on no other occasion. "Men of the first consideration condescend to collect dissolute and ignorant mobs of hundreds of individuals, to whom they make long speeches in the open air." He told Ames that these speeches were unlike anything either of them had ever heard in New England, with the orators knowing no bounds to what he politely termed "eloquence." The speakers promised everything and swore to anything that pleased the crowd or served to advance the cause. All this was irritating to the sensibilities of these two New Englanders with their quite definite opinion on the subject of demagoguery, which is clearly what they regarded the southern style of oratory.

The contest in Maryland was more than a ploy to pack the legislature, repeal an election law, and frustrate the popular will, because it also involved the question of the suffrage, which was, Wolcott affirmed, a highly explosive issue in that state. Repeal of the existing district law was interpreted there as an attack upon the sovereign right of popular suffrage, which in Maryland was considered invaluable for some unusual reasons. Wolcott declared

that the suffrage in Maryland served as a leveler of the distinctions of a society of great extremes. It also acted as something of
a social safety valve in that it "gratifies vulgar curiosity, indulges
the plebeian taste for slander, and furnishes the means of riotous
indulgence, without expense [to the community]." Wolcott did
not approve of the repeal scheme, for in an atmosphere such as
existed in Maryland, it could only increase party spirit and injure
the Federalists in the estimation of the state's citizens. Nevertheless, Oliver Wolcott thought that the repealers were going to be
successful. [28]

Wolcott's prediction was inaccurate, and the forces of repeal
were defeated in Maryland, as the Republicans with some
moderate Federalist votes defeated the plan to overhaul the
state's electoral machinery to suit the Federalist leadership. The
hypocrisy of the entire reform was apparent to anyone who was
aware of Robert Goodloe Harper's position and pronouncements
upon the same subject, the electoral process, in South Carolina,
where he favored popular elections in place of the existing
method of legislative choice of electors, because in that state the
legislature was certain to be Republican. [29]

Actually, in this game of partisan "election rigging" the
Republicans enjoyed greater success than their opponents, although the Federalists have received most of the opprobrium for
attempting to frustrate the popular will by crafty manipulation
of the machinery. In Virginia in 1799, for example, a Republican
legislature enacted a "reform" election law which did away with
the district system in order to eliminate the possibility that half a
dozen districts might choose Federalist electors. The plan
worked, for in the general election in 1800 Virginia gave all
twenty-one of her electoral votes to Jefferson and Burr. [30]

Wolcott was extremely pessimistic about the fall elections,
and, as they approached, he had about given up any hopes of
victory for the party. Instead, he thought the Federalists had to
stand with their principles and not allow the nation to believe
that both parties were activated by sinister and personal motives.
This was their only chance if they hoped to return to power after
the people had a taste of the Republicans. [31]

Harper, on the other hand, grew more confident as the
elections neared, regardless of the failure of the Maryland repeal
plan, the divisive Hamilton letter, the news from Carolina, and

signs that an Adams Federalist counterplot was underway in Maryland to insure the president the first position by throwing away several Pinckney votes on a favorite son.[32]

James McHenry shared Wolcott's pessimism and, as expected, he laid most of the blame for Federalism's difficulties at Adams' chair. McHenry bemoaned the lack of spirit among party members in his state, and he concluded that most of them had pretty much given up hope, with many sincerely believing that one of the Federalist candidates was unfit to hold the chief magistracy.[33]

Even Charles Carroll, Harper's future father-in-law, who was as conservative and loyal a Federalist as there ever was, confided to McHenry that everything was lost and that personally given a choice between Jefferson's "whimsies" and Adams' "weakness, unrully passions, antipathies, & jealousy" he saw less danger for the nation if Jefferson were elected.[34]

As it turned out, Harper's optimism, both with respect to Maryland and the national outcome, was for the most part misplaced. In Maryland the repeal issue had no doubt worked to lash Republicans to new efforts, and the state's electoral votes were evenly divided, with five for Adams and Pinckney and five for Jefferson and Burr. Thus, in the tallying of the votes in the electoral college Maryland's Federalist and Republican electors effectively canceled each other out. Maryland's contingent of Federalist representatives in the Seventh Congress was reduced to one congressman, and South Carolina sent an evenly divided delegation. South Carolina was even more destructive to Harper's bright hope for Pinckney. The Republicans swept the legislature and elected a complete set of Jefferson and Burr electors by an average of nineteen votes in the state assembly.[35]

If the 1800 Pinckney plotters hoped to throw the election into the House of Representatives they succeeded, but in their desire to eliminate John Adams from the running they lost Charles Cotesworth Pinckney as well.[36]   The House of Represenatives was, after all, going to have the final decision as to the chief magistrate, but contrary to plan the choice was to be between Thomas Jefferson and Aaron Burr.

In actual fact, John Adams ran well ahead of many candidates of his party, and his sixty-five electoral votes, to Jefferson's winning seventy-three, constitute an extremely impressive showing, considering the divided state of Adams' party. Given a reasonably united party, some respectable local organization, and John Adams, with the grateful popular appreciation for his securing the Peace of 1800, could conceivably have walked off with the election. This did not occur, and Mr. Adams retired to his farm in Quincy. ´

Many of those who sat in the House, ready to decide between Jefferson and Burr, were themselves about to retire to other pursuits, for this was the last of the Federalist congresses, the final session of the Sixth Congress, which convened on November 17, 1800. So much misunderstanding surrounds this deadlocked election and the role of the House in the final decision that separating rumor from fact becomes extremely difficult. It was, in truth, a Federalist House, elected in the very successful elections of 1798, and at one time the Federalists had been capable of fielding fifty-five votes on a party question to the Republican's forty-six. However, that was two years earlier, and by early February 1801 that power discrepancy had been considerably reduced. Nevertheless, the outgoing party still held a numerical majority. This last fact has always provided the basis for misunderstanding.

By the terms of Article II, Section One of the Constitution, the House had to adhere to a balloting process that further reduced the Federalist strength in the House. The selection of the new president was to be accomplished by each state casting only one vote, which was determined by a polling of the state's House delegation. While the Federalists had a majority of the total House membership, they did not control a majority of the state delegations. Indeed, they could depend on only six states, while the Republicans were able to hold eight delegations in line. The other two state delegations, Maryland and Vermont, were evenly divided, and on the first thirty-five ballots they did not even count.

This odd situation, in which the majority party did not control a majority of the state delegations, is quite easily explained. The actual numerical difference between Republicans and Federalists in the House had always been slight, and the "Spirit of '98" had returned, if only temporarily, a number of Federalist congressmen from states with preponderantly Republican contingents in the House. These replacements swelled the Federalist majority but did not affect the partisan complexion of state delegations. The House was then Federalist in terms of enacting legislation but Republican in the matter of the deadlocked election. Thus, the Federalist majority was incapable of selecting a president on its own but had the votes to block the choice of any other candidate.

There were four possibilities open to the Federalists in the House after the Senate, on February 11, 1801, formally deposited the matter in the House's care. In order of likelihood, or probability of success, the following choices presented themselves. The most daring, or desperate, plan amounted to disregarding the results of the election altogether and choosing one of their own, possibly John Marshall, the new secretary of state, or the president pro tem of the Senate as interim president. This could possibly, but not necessarily, be coupled with the promise of new elections to be held as soon as practicable. There may have been some support for such a plan among those who thought that any Republican victory meant the Illuminati at the gates and the guillotine in the marketplace, but such a step had absolutely no chance for success and received little credibility outside of the minds of the Republicans, who were prepared to believe nearly anything about their opponents.

The second strategem was largely the progeny of Alexander Hamilton, whose distaste for things Virginian was mollified considerably by the rumors he had heard regarding Federalist support for Aaron Burr. [37] The only course of action, as Hamilton saw it, was to hold the Federalist strength in the House together, veto any quick decision of the contest and negotiate with Jefferson, who was vastly preferable to Burr, "the American Catiline." Hamilton thought that Burr might well be the means of extracting important concessions from the Virginians regarding the Federalist fiscal structure, the armed forces, and Federalist appointed government officials. [38] This alternative too received remarkably little support considering the fact that Hamilton was supposedly capable of determining the outcome of the election.

Actually, the idea failed to garner much support among the diehards in the House because, to their way of thinking, promises from Jefferson were like ropes of sand, and a far more intriguing prospect had occurred to them. Thomas Jefferson could be excluded entirely, and they might hope to retain considerable political power, which in the final analysis, was their main concern.

There also existed a fourth possibility, that of recognizing that the intention of the Republican electors and the American people had been the election of Jefferson to the presidency and Burr to the second position, but of all the choices this was the least desirable and the alternative to be avoided if at all possible.[39]

By the time the House began balloting on February 11, the Federalist caucus had already decided to back Aaron Burr, and Robert Goodloe Harper, having thrown all moderation to the winds, was hard at work in his old acquaintance's behalf. When Hamilton pressed his plan to extract concessions from Jefferson, Harper was not one of his correspondents, for the simple reason that Hamilton knew his efforts were lost on the former South Carolinian. Aaron Burr offered all sorts of possibilities to the congressional Federalists. He was, as they put it politely, more amenable to direction, their direction. This would certainly, they reasoned, be the case if Burr could be made president through their efforts. If he accepted the presidency, and he never explicitly said he would not do so if Jefferson failed of election, the Republican organization stood a good chance of breaking up, which could only accrue to the advantage of the Federalists.

As early as December 24, 1800, Harper wrote to Burr and offered his advice as to how best to go about becoming president with the help of the Federalists. All Burr had to do, according to Harper, was to sit back and quietly wait the situation out. "I advise you to take no step whatever by which the choice of the House . . . can be impeded or embarrased. Keep the game perfectly in your own hands, but do not answer this letter, or any other that may be written to you by a Federal man, nor write to any of that party," was Harper's advice to the man he hoped to assist in making president.[40]

At the same time he was instructing Aaron Burr, Robert Goodloe Harper exerted himself in lining up support, within and without the House, for the attempt at president-making. He visited Gouverneur Morris, by this time an important Federalist senator whom Harper may have viewed as a possible means of counterbalancing Hamilton's influence among New York Federalists, and discussed Burr at great length. Harper told Morris that there was certainly no reason to fear Burr or suspect that he would betray his Federalist friends after the election, and in general, Harper painted his candidate in very flattering tones. He thought that Burr should not be pressed for commitments regarding the years ahead. As Morris remembered the conversation, Harper said that the House ought to elect Burr

> . . . without asking or expecting any assurance or explanation regarding his future administration. He thinks Burr's temper and disposition gave an ample security for a conduct hostile to the democratic spirit which Mr. Harper considers as dangerous to our country, while Mr. Jefferson, he thinks, is so deeply imbued with false principles of government, and has so far committed himself in support of them, that nothing good can be expected from them.[41]

Harper seemed more than willing to accept Burr on his own terms rather than endure Thomas Jefferson for four years in the new White House.

Through thirty-five ballots the Federalist spoilers held firm, while the date for the inauguration moved six days nearer, and the strain of the crisis worsened as rumors, which never amounted to more than that, of armed men in Pennsylvania and Virginia troubled the country village on the banks of the Potomac. Regardless of what the Burr apologists have had to say about the famous "open letter" to Senator Samuel Smith, of Maryland, in which Burr denied any pretensions to the presidency, "the American Catiline" really did nothing to effectively discourage the Harpers and Otises in the House. The Federalist response to Burr's rather weak public statement was expressed in a letter from James McHenry to a friend, in which he said, "it [is] extremely doubtful upon whom the choice of the House of Representatives will fall, for President. Mr. Burr's letter to Genl. Smith is not considered as committing him, not to accept the office if elected."[42]

The prompt end of the crisis could have been achieved very easily, if that is what Burr desired, by an appearance in Washington, before the House if necessary, in which he could have abjured all such schemes and plans. All that was required was an "I will not serve if elected" speech from Aaron Burr. The fact that he did not do so speaks for itself, which is precisely the interpretation Thomas Jefferson applied to the affair.

It was left to James A. Bayard, Delaware's lone congressman, to conclude that the national interest dictated that partisanship had gone quite as far as could be tolerated. He announced, after the thirty-fifth unsuccessful ballot, that he intended to change his vote from Burr to Jefferson and that he could not be dissuaded from such a course. The reaction from his Federalist colleagues was bitter, but they knew they were beaten, since Bayard alone cast Delaware's vote and Jefferson was only one state short of the nine necessary for election. [43] When it became apparent that Bayard was intransigent, a face-saving plan was devised whereby not a single Federalist needed to embarrass himself by voting for Jefferson. On the thirty-sixth ballot, Bayard and the South Carolinians, Harper among them, cast blank ballots, while the Maryland and Vermont Federalists abstained, allowing their Republican counterparts to vote those two states for Jefferson. Thus, Jefferson was elected solely by Republican ballots. It was sadly appropriate that Robert Goodloe Harper's last important act as a Federalist congressman had to be a negative one. [44]

Fifteen days later, in a very plain ceremony, Thomas Jefferson was sworn into office by his second cousin, and with this event an era came to an end. Unlike the outgoing president, Harper remained to see the archdemocrat installed in office, before departing the federal city. His initial reaction to the new president was surprisingly mild in light of his earlier inveterate hostility and his energetic efforts in Burr's behalf. In fact, few Federalists, in or out of Congress, publicly expressed a more friendly response to Jefferson's address than Harper. As a retiring congressman who had changed his place of residence, he had nothing to gain, particularly since he wrote these remarks for the benefit of his former constituents in Ninety Six, who would never see him again, let alone have the opportunity to vote against him.

Here was a perfect opportunity for Harper to vent his political spleen at Jefferson's expense, the obvious platform from which to preach to the errant people of South Carolina on the error of their political unrighteousness. No doubt this was the topic of countless Federalist sermons, secular as well as religious, preached in New England during the spring of 1801. Jefferson's presidency was likened to some sort of divine visitation of displeasure with the American people, and there were High-Federalists who might even have considered the Jefferson years as a necessary, albeit obnoxious, purgative that in time would teach a harsh lesson and perhaps be good for the nation's corporate soul. Such a reaction from Harper would not have been the least bit unexpected, and, indeed, it would fit in very nicely with the "decline and fall" approach set forth here, but he failed to oblige.

With the exception of one small, carping opening comment about the electoral crisis just ended, Harper was reasonably objective toward Jefferson and the new administration. This consisted of an understandable attempt to shift the blame for the election deadlock to the Republicans. According to Harper, it had been their unwillingness to bend, their determination "to risk the Constitution and the Union" rather than compromise on Jefferson that had brought the nation to the recent critical state of affairs. In effect, Harper was claiming that the Federalists had, out of patriotism, sensibility, and principle, decided to sacrifice their own political interest to the cause of the Constitution and national unity. [45] It sounded grand, but it is doubtful if very many of his readers accepted his interesting interpretation of the recent events in the nation's capital.

The new executive's address to the Congress was applauded for its moderation, and Harper expressed the hope that Jefferson had meant what he said about no recriminations and everyone being Federalists as well as Republicans. There really was nothing to fear with respect to the new administration, since, as Harper expressed it, the Federalists had laid a splendid foundation and had for a dozen years illuminated the way for all subsequent administrations. No danger need be apprehended as long as the Republicans did not stray too far from that tested pathway and conducted the government "on national principles, and with steadiness, vigor and prudence."

In this concluding act of his public life, he thought it necessary to reaffirm what he understood the major principles of Federalism to be. Most important, he believed, was the preservation of the national government as independent as possible of state influence and interference, with the necessary authority to enforce its decisions and act effectively within its own jurisdiction. With respect to administrative principles, the Federalists had always stood for the execution of the laws of the land with energy, yet balanced with mildness, knowing that if a government is strong it may pardon without diminishing its stature. Another great maxim of the Federalist system was to "support the executive power, against the encroachments of ambition and the superior strength of the popular branch," and he had always defended executive autonomy. Finally, he said, his party had labored mightily to preserve the nation's economic stability within and guarantee her a neutral, but respectable, station among the rest of the nations.

As if to suit the tastes of his readers, Harper constructed an agricultural analogy to make his point. Everything had been done for the new tenants in Washington. "All that is required of them is to preserve things in their present state, to keep up the fences which have been made on the farm, to prevent the buildings which have been erected from falling down through want of repair, [and] to keep the fields from being overrun by briars and weeds." If the Virginia farmer but followed the successful and beneficial habits of his predecessors, "his elevation will prove a public blessing." Harper pleaded for an honest consideration of his party's attainments and asked that they be judged by what they had done for the nation. He then thanked those he had represented for six years for the confidence they had bestowed upon him, and he bade them "a last and affectionate adieu." [46]

No one could disagree very seriously with most of the principles of Federalism that Harper had mentioned in this assessment of political accomplishment, no more than one could possibly deny the validity of Hamilton's definition of freedom of the press, which he expounded in 1804, consisting of the "right to publish, with impunity, truth, with good motives, for justifiable ends though reflecting on government, magistracy, or individuals." [47] Unfortunately, in both cases, the statements were made after the fact, and the actions of the two gentlemen during the critical years between 1797 and 1801 seriously qualified the acceptance of the remarks by their contemporaries as well as subsequent generations of Americans.

With this last letter to his constituents, Robert Goodloe Harper ended a chapter in his life and in the life of the republic. He could look back upon a successful South Carolina political career which had begun in 1785 when he arrived in Charleston as a hopeful, but poor, Princeton graduate. The impact of his career upon South Carolina political life was no doubt lessened by his move to Maryland, since it divorced him completely from the state and people he had represented. Had he returned to South Carolina, it would have been to Charleston rather than Ninety Six, and this time his assault upon that city's legal and business community would have been considerably more successful than his first attempt to establish himself. This, of course, did not take place for personal reasons and for readily apparent political reasons. Yet, there remained in southern Federalism something of the political legacy bequeathed by Washington, the Pinckneys, John Marshall, and Robert Goodloe Harper long after 1801.

In the years ahead, northern Federalism underwent a long and tortuous process of constitutional acrobatics. The northern wing of the party became strict constructionist and espoused the very provincialism and narrow localism of state rights it had condemned as disruptive, if not treasonous, in 1798. Southern Federalism tended to continue, as it always had, to be less violently partisan, probably because Madison, Jefferson, and Monroe were, after all, southerners as well as Republicans. When the Republican administrations, under the pressure of events and the responsibilities of power, found it necessary to adopt and even expand the older Federalist measures of centralization and interpretation of the limits of federal authority, southern Federalists, unlike their northern counterparts, did not reverse their doctrinal positions simply for the sake of opposition. [48] Instead, they became ardent admirers of the administration of James Monroe and the oddly Federalist legislation of 1816.

However, so far as the immediate lasting effect of Harper's career on up-country South Carolina, the legacy was somewhat different and not nearly so attractive. A traveler through the up-country regions in 1805 made the following observations on the subject. He was commenting upon the public career of a Captain Livingston, of Cambridge, and, in particular, that gentleman's term in the state assembly during the 1790s.

> I suppose he was one of those influential citizens who were attached to Robert G. Harper, and who did not afterwards join in the public denunciations against him. All who did not thus join were considered Federalists incorrigible—and to this day, in all electioneering campaigns through the old District of Ninety Six ... there is no weapon with which a candidate can be more successfully annoyed by his opponent, than the public exhibition of him as 'one of Harper's men.' A mere Federalist is a *harmless creature* compared with a Harperian Federalist.[49]

Perhaps it was just as well that Robert Goodloe Harper decided not to return home to South Carolina.

NOTES

1. Harper-Pennington Papers, January 10, 1801, Maryland Historical Society. Harper was actively courting Miss Carroll as early as July of 1799. A letter from a Captain Burrows, Philadelphia, to John Rutledge at Newport, July 16, 1799, notes that "Harper is gone to court Miss Carroll." John Rutledge Papers, Southern Historical Collection.
2. RGH to McHenry, Baltimore, July 29, 1799, McHenry Papers, 2nd Series, L.C. Harper had promised McHenry that if he failed to get a start in Baltimore it would be through no fault of his own, and he did work at establishing his practice. Considering the fact that he was absent for more than six months of the period between July 1799 and January 1801, he reported to his future father-in-law that he had earned approximately $3,200 and was owed upwards of $1,000 more. RGH to Charles Carroll, January 10, 1801, Harper-Pennington Papers.
3. RGH to McHenry, July 29, 1799, McHenry Papers.
4. McHenry to RGH, August 1, 1799, Harper Papers, L.C. McHenry was concerned about whether or not an audience with the Directory had been assured. He seemed to think that perhaps the foreign minister was holding the Americans off as he had done in 1797.
5. RGH to McHenry, August 2, 1799, Harper Papers, L.C.
6. RGH to Constituents, April 7, 1800, *Works.*
7. Gibbs, II, 308; *Annals*, pp. 2467-2492.
8. RGH to Constituents, May 15, 1800, Bayard Papers.
9. RGH to Constituents, March 20, 1799, Bayard Papers, pp. 85-86. Harper concluded his argument by pointing out that if it was necessary to restore the common law coverage of seditious libels "to its ancient rigour, the [Sedition] act must be suffered to expire."
10. *Annals*, 6C2S, pp. 939-940, 957-958.
11. RGH to Constituents, May 15, 1800, Bayard Papers, pp. 102-103.
12. Laurens County, South Carolina, Index to Deeds 1785-1900, South Carolina Archives. The index is all that is available. Most of the listings are for *Book G* and it has not survived.
13. Phillips, "South Carolina Federalist Correspondence," p. 741.
14. See Rose, *Prologue to Democracy*, and Rogers, *William Loughton Smith*, for more recent interpretations of the state of the party on the eve of 1800.
    A letter from Thomas Pinckney to John Rutledge, Jr., September 23, 1800, supports the view that South Carolina Federalists really hadn't progressed much beyond the "politics of 1792." Pinckney

further stated that distinctions between political parties in the state
had "been marked by a very faint line." This had been changing and
South Carolina would probably "arrive at the acme of political
rancour and malevolence which the Pennsylvanians seem to have first
reached."

Also Henry W. DeSaussure, Charleston, to Rutledge, August 14,
1800, in a lengthy letter complained that the Federalist effort in
South Carolina was not well coordinated and that they were not as
industrious as the opposition. John Rutledge Papers, Southern Historical Collection, University of North Carolina Library.

15. RGH to Alexander Hamilton, June 5, 1800, Steiner, pp. 458-459.
16. RGH to Alexander Hamilton, August 9, 1800, ibid., p. 464.
17. That South Carolina Federalists were not completely satisfied with
    the assurances of their northern counterparts for equal support for
    Adams and Pinckney is beyond question. Thomas Pinckney may have
    been articulating these suspicions when he wrote to Rutledge in
    September of 1800. He had heard rumors of federal trouble at the
    "eastward" but said that he and his friends would hold off making
    any decision about a change "unless we should receive such unde-
    niable proofs of . . . foul play . . . ." They regarded Rutledge as their
    lookout and urged him not to let them be surprised "in their camp."
    John Rutledge Papers, Southern Historical Collection.
18. RGH to Harrison Gray Otis, August 28, 1800, Morrison, I, 193. This
    last statement becomes even more damning when compared with his
    literary efforts in behalf of the "Electoral Reform Plan" in Maryland
    in 1800, which sought to take the choice of electors out of the hands
    of the people, where it reposed according to state law, and transfer
    the decision to the legislature, which in this instance happened to be
    ardently and staunchly Federalist. The hypocrisy was obviously due
    to partisanship and it came about as close as Harper ever did to
    openly advocating an ends-justify-the-means stand.
19. Ibid. Harper's concern over this rumored new coalition was, I think,
    not feigned at all but quite sincere. For a man plagued by rumors of
    invasion and slave insurrections, being seriously worried about a
    rumored third party required very little effort.
20. Miller, The Federalist Era, p. 264; Dauer, p. 310.
21. RGH to Otis, August 28, 1800, Morrison, I, 192. It is only fair to
    note that the South Carolina Federalists were also receiving reports
    from Massachusetts which stressed how hard New England Federalists
    were laboring for Pinckney. Fisher Ames to John Rutledge, Jr.,
    October 16, 1800; George Cabot to Rutledge, Brookline, October 22,
    1800. On the basis of their reports Pinckney appeared to have an
    outside   chance.   John   Rutledge   Papers,   Southern   Historical
    Collection.
22. RGH to Hamilton, June 5, 1800. Steiner, pp. 458-459. As it turned

out Charles Cotesworth Pinckney himself scotched the scheme in South Carolina by stating that he was pledged not to accept any votes from electors not committed to the president. Marvin R. Zahniser, *Charles Cotesworth Pinckney: Founding Father* (Chapel Hill: University of North Carolina Press, 1967), pp. 221-222.

23. McHenry to Oliver Wolcott (private), July 22, 1800, Gibbs, II, 385-386.

24. Malone, *Ordeal of Liberty*, p. 488.

25. Carl Brent Swisher, *Roger B. Taney* (New York: Macmillan Co., 1935), p. 49.

26. *Legislative Choice of Electors in Maryland, Bystander* (Baltimore: no publisher, 1800). The pamphlet is in the collection of the Peabody Institute, Baltimore.

27. McHenry to Oliver Wolcott, July 22, 1800, Gibbs, II, 385-386.

28. Oliver Wolcott to Fisher Ames, Washington, August 10, 1800, Gibbs, II, 404. In the same letter he had some equally unkind things to say about the paltry influence of General John Marshall in Virginia, the "crude and unsettled politics of North Carolina," the uncertainty of South Carolina, and the "Jacobin" nature of Georgia, Tennessee and Kentucky.

See also RGH to John Rutledge, Jr., from Baltimore, September 4 1800, for Harper's last minute assessment of the election. His "hopes for South Carolina were greatly strengthened . . ." by the recent accounts from there. "Our business in the great measure of the legislative choice in Maryland has again become very doubtful. The Jacobins [raise] a most loud and vehement cry against it, and . . . many of the Federalists, contrary to my expectations have been weak enough to be shaken. We can, however, secure Pinckney without this measure provided Massachusetts will act right. . . . I confess to you that I support Adams as a means of getting Pinckney. In no other view would I turn a [?] to insure his election, this again is mum." John Rutledge Papers, Southern Historical Collection, University of North Carolina Library.

29. See fn. 16 of this chapter, also Wallace, pp. 349-350.

30. Chambers, p. 161, also Kate Mason Rowland, *Life and Correspondence of Charles Carroll of Carrollton* (New York: G. P. Putnam's Sons, 1898), II, 234-235.

31. Oliver Wolcott to Fisher Ames, August 10, 1800, Gibbs, II, 404-405. See also, Wolcott to McHenry, August 26, 1800, ibid., p. 410.

32. Gibbs, II, 421-422, 430-432.

33. McHenry to Wolcott, Baltimore, November 9, 1800, Gibbs, II, 445. Fisher Ames adopted a much more stoic attitude toward the Federalist efforts at salvaging the party. Most important was the absolute necessity of holding the party together. Something had to be done to "soothe the Federalists who have been made angry and to satisfy

those who are puzzled with the complexity and obscurity of the reasons on which we acted." The party might still have to save the country, possibly from a British war. Ames to Rutledge, December 15, 1800, John Rutledge Papers, Southern Historical Collection.

34. Charles Carroll to McHenry, November 4, 1800, Ellen Hart Smith, *Charles Carroll of Carrollton* (Cambridge: Harvard University Press, 1942), p. 281.

35. Wallace, pp. 349-350, also Wolfe, p. 158, and Phillips, "Southern Federalist Correspondence," pp. 120, 127-129. Henry W. DeSaussure, reflecting on the results in South Carolina, although disturbed that Federalism had not been successful, remarked that he was "satisfied that we did right in refusing a compromise and I rejoice that you and our federal friends concur so fully in the propriety of it. I am now more completely satisfied as I find that Rhode Island Electors threw away one vote from Gen. P. so that he would have had but 72 votes if we had compromised, and that Jefferson would have had 73. General P. could have been V.P. only which was not worth a compromise . . ." To John Rutledge, Jr., January 12, 1801, Southern Historical Collection. The election went badly for the Federalists locally in the Maryland elections. One of the promising Federalist candidates for the assembly who lost was Roger Brooke Taney from Frederick. Taney was later to become Harper's bitter enemy. Swisher, pp. 40-41.

36. Dauer, pp. 256-258. There were any number of Federalists who hoped to throw the election into the House, which was safely Federalist. In a letter to Hamilton, dated October 2, 1800, Wolcott discussed the possibility, but he specifically mentioned that his ideas did not include Thomas Jefferson. Gibbs, II, 430-432.

37. See the series of Hamilton letters to Wolcott, Otis, Theodore Sedgwick, Gouverneur Morris, James A. Bayard, John Rutledge, Jr., and John Marshall, in J. C. Hamilton, *Works of Alexander Hamilton*, VI, 486-500.

38. Malone, pp. 500-502.

39. Nathan Schachner, *Aaron Burr* (New York: Frederick H. Stokes Co., 1937). Chapter XIV deals with the election of 1800, and while the treatment is entirely too favorable, the essential story of the New Yorker's conduct is accurate.

40. RGH to Aaron Burr, December 24, 1800, ibid., p. 192.

41. Anne C. Morris (ed.), *The Diary and Letters of Gouverneur Morris* (2 vols.; New York: Charles Scribner's Sons, 1888), II, 397, quoted in Schachner, p. 193. It seems clear that Harper was not acting for the South Carolina delegation. Rutledge and South Carolina Federalists had already exchanged doubts they had about Burr. See. H. W. DeSaussure to Rutledge, January 12, and February ?, 1801. Rutledge Papers, Southern Historical Collection.

42. James McHenry to John Bleakley, January 6, 1801, McHenry Papers, Maryland Historical Society.

43. Morton Borden, *The Federalism of James A. Bayard* (New York: Columbia University Press, 1955), pp. 85-101. There is a letter from Benjamin Stoddert to John Rutledge, Jr., dated February 1801, which declared that Bayard had been influenced by a "Burr letter" shown him in which Burr is supposed to have threatened to destroy the army and navy and the funding system as well. The letter has an Albany postmark but Stoddert thinks it could be a fake. "Could not it be compared with some he has written to Dayton or Harper?" Rutledge Papers, Southern Historical Collection.

44. The House balloting is reported in the *Annals*, 6C2S, pp. 1020-1030.

45. RGH to Constituents, March 5, 1801, *Works*, p. 324.

46. Ibid., pp. 324-328, 333, 338-350. James Gunn, writing to John Rutledge, Jr., March 16, 1801, castigated "the *Trimmers* among the Federalists, who here to a man [are] willing to cut in with the new administration . . ." who were given great pleasure by Jefferson's speech. Rutledge Papers, Southern Historical Collection.

47. Hamilton, *Works*, Lodge edition, VIII, 383-384, quoted in John C. Miller, *Alexander Hamilton, Portrait in Paradox* (New York: Harper and Brothers, 1959), p. 556.

48. Ulrich B. Phillips makes this distinction very ably in *The Course of the South to Secession*, ed. E. M. Coulter (Gloucester: Peter Smith, 1958), p. 75.

49. "Diary of Edward Hooker," May 23, 1805, pp. 888-890.

11

Baltimore, The Carrolls,
And the Future

From late July 1799 on, Robert Goodloe Harper was no longer a South Carolinian but a Marylander, and his new home seemed to suit him perfectly. Compared to his arrival in Charleston in the middle 1780s and the prospects he had faced then, Baltimore must have seemed worlds apart. It goes without saying that part of the difference, a considerable part, derived from the fact that in the latter instance he was not R. G. Harper recent graduate, but, in Federalist circles, an eminently respectable former congressman, a man of influence and importance during his years in the House. There is no question that his political reputation boosted his legal career, and he came to Baltimore with as much fanfare as his friends McHenry and Justice Samuel Chase could arrange. Then too, he had already met the Carrolls of Doughoregan Manor, which helped socially.

In addition there was also the contrasting state of Baltimore's economy in the late '90s, as opposed to the troubled nature of South Carolina affairs in the middle 1780s. Whereas Charleston had been facing a serious recession in the wake of the war, Baltimore had exploded economically and was growing faster than any other city in the United States as a result of the Revolution. On the eve of independence, Baltimore had been a small, inconsequential port, located where the Patapsco River emptied into the Chesapeake Bay, and exporting, for the most part, foodstuffs, lumber, tobacco, and locally milled flour. The war had made the port in a matter of a few years a serious rival to Philadelphia, heretofore the greatest port in all the colonies.

The fabulous expansion of the port and city that was built was due in great measure to the geography of the region. Situated as it was at the head of the largest and finest bay in the British colonies, Baltimore was, in time of war, a ship captain's dream. The length of the bay, from Baltimore to the Virginia capes, afforded protection not only against Atlantic storms but against the greater threat of British attack. The Chesapeake was a forbidding theater of operations for any enemy daring enough to sail straight in. No finer geographical trap existed anywhere in the

New World, a fact which would have been especially apparent to the masters of sailing vessels. It was small wonder, therefore, that such a port became a center of privateering activity during the war, and, indeed, Baltimore became almost synonymous with piracy so far as the British were concerned. Nonetheless there were also peaceful foundations for the prosperity of Harper's Baltimore which were, in the long run, much more important to the city's continued growth.

Once again the explanation rests upon geography, but, in this instance, of the interior not the coastline. Located as it was, Baltimore was in an excellent position to draw to itself not only the inland commerce of western Maryland but the trade of that part of Pennsylvania south of the Susquehanna River, and the western parts of Virginia as well. Nature insured that the commerce of this great hinterland would drain to Baltimore so long as Georgetown was closed to deep draught shipping and Philadelphia lacked easy, cheap access to the West. By the middle 1780s, Baltimore was nipping at the commercial heels of her rival to the north, and flour had replaced letters of marque as the city's major export.

Without exaggeration, it was grain, brought to Baltimore from the rich western farmland and ground into flour on the banks of the numerous streams emptying into the Patapsco and the bay, that became the peacetime basis of Baltimore's prosperity. This white gold was sold at immense profit in Europe, and the demand and prices increased tremendously when England and France resumed the military aspect of their long-standing rivalry in 1793. Exported legally where possible and distributed clandestinely elsewhere, flour carried by the famous fleet of Baltimore clippers, low, sleek, and able to outsail anything afloat, became the city's most important export to the West Indies. As early as 1789 a foreign visitor was able to count fifty vessels at anchor at Fell's Point alone. The traveler also remarked that at points around the harbor land might bring as high as a guinea a square foot in annual rent.[1]

During the years between the end of the war and the adoption of the Constitution, the city continued to grow and by 1787 it contained some 1,100 shops and 1,900 houses, chiefly of the brick to which Baltimoreans are still passionately attached, and at least one street was paved, that being Market Street, which later became Baltimore Street.[2] In the early 1790s a French refugee, who had escaped from Le Havre just ahead of the order for his arrest, was quite impressed by Maryland's leading metropolis and called the cuisine at the Indian Queen Hotel, at the corner of Hanover and Market streets, excellent. If his estimate is correct, the city had grown to some three thousand houses, mostly of the two-story, narrow-front townhouse variety.

Baltimore Street was still the major thoroughfare, handsomely paved and nearly eighty feet wide, while the average street width was nearer to thirty. All of the downtown streets were filled with animals and vehicles of all kinds, which delighted the visitor who was particularly impressed by the quality of the splendid draft horses. North of Baltimore Street were located the city's public buildings, the court house, with a passageway beneath it for carriages, the city jail, and, not far away, a newly erected theater.

In the same area were located the offices of the Bank of the United States and the Bank of Maryland, the latter opening in 1790.[3] There had been no banks at all in Baltimore prior to 1790, and then, within five years the city had three major banks, the Bank of Maryland in 1790 with three hundred thousand dollars initial capital, the branch of the B.U.S. established in 1792 with a board of directors interlocking the board of the Bank of Maryland, and the Bank of Baltimore chartered in 1795 and quickly subscribed to its maximum capitalization of 1.2 million dollars.[4] No better measurement of the economic heartbeat of the city existed than the suddenness with which Baltimore became a banking town, with capital to invest and the daring to spend it on such futuristic notions as a western railroad.

The city's population doubled between the first and second census and reached 26,114 by 1800, with slaves constituting 1,255 of the total. Property values were rising even faster and increased from 699,519 dollars in 1798 to 2,522,870 dollars in taxable property within ten years.[5] Baltimore was the closest thing the East, in this period, ever had to a real boom town, and Harper, who had found Charleston enchanting, must have been exhilarated by the atmosphere of his new home. Indeed, this, as much as a number of other factors, is probably what attracted him to Baltimore in the first place, for as long as he lived the old "get rich quick" spark of the speculator never really died. He never made that one great financial coup, but Baltimore, with its hustling, marketplace atmosphere added to by the visible presence of fortunes made in shipping, was an ideal location for the man who had to continue trying.

If Harper's Baltimore appealed to that part of him interested in finance and profits, then the political complexion of the state as a whole must also have held out attractions for him. Here was a believing Federalist who needed to keep his hand in and for whom political isolation would have been intolerable. This, too, must have influenced him in choosing his new location. Maryland was as far south as one might go, and he as Southern as one might be and still enjoy the advantages of the prosperity and opportunity afforded by the northern commercial and business economy. At the same time, it was the only state, except possibly Delaware, south of New England, in which a retired Federalist congressman might hope to enjoy some degree of political success, and possibly even run for office again.

The Federalist organization in Maryland had problems, to be sure, and it was to divide into warring factions in the next decade, but it managed to survive into the Era of Good Feelings as a viable, in some ways quite progressive, political party. This was true of Maryland Federalism long after the reactionary, provincial New England elements of the party had been destroyed by the stigma of the Hartford Convention. In fact, Harper was elected to the United States Senate in 1816 as a Maryland Federalist, and having retired from the law, he was preparing to campaign again for public office when he died in 1825. There was hardly another state in the Union where Harper, standing as a Federalist, could have possibly enjoyed the political success and longevity that were his in Maryland.

Harper's adopted state was unique among the original southern states, its only possible rival being South Carolina, in that it incorporated at once three distinct sections representative of the larger sectional division of the nation. Baltimore was, as a commercial, small-manufacturing center, quite northern, at least in economic interest and outlook. Southern Maryland and the Eastern Shore, the oldest part of the state, was by all odds the most southern section. This was plantation Maryland and the part of the state most tied to the colonial past with its gentry, county court politics, great estates, tobacco economy and slavery. The state's capital belonged in this region, scarcely thirty miles away from the city but obviously a part of the state quite separate from Baltimore. To the west, a third section existed which was quite unlike the other two. In 1800, Maryland west of Frederick was as much frontier as it had been at the close of the colonial period, and the war whoops of the former inhabitants had not ceased to ring through the wilderness so long ago that no one remembered how dangerous life there could be. For the most part, small family farming was the rule, although there were significant exceptions, with the common cash crops being cereals and livestock.

That this section of the state was out of step with the other two areas was demonstrated quite colorfully when the Maryland west staged its own abortive "Whiskey Insurrection" during the summer of 1794, which the east rose with a rush to put down. Following the example of their counterparts across the line in Pennsylvania, and possibly with some imported leadership, the frontier counties of Maryland began manifesting the same danger signals which disturbed Pennsylvania that summer and ended in President Washington's call for fifteen thousand troops to put down the "rebellion."

Maryland's insurrection never got much beyond the raucous talk and liberty pole stage, but it frightened the more settled sections of the state and the state government every bit as much as if an armed column really had marched on the arsenal at Frederick, as it was rumored in Annapolis, Baltimore and Philadelphia.[6] The governor issued a call for three hundred troops, and after a brief address from the commanding general exhorting the men to go as volunteers rather than be drafted, the *Maryland Gazette* reported that nearly nine hundred men stepped forth as an affirmation of their patriotism and support of the government.[7] The expedition marched west and encountered just about the same resistance met in Pennsylvania, much to the disappointment of countless young tidewater patriots eager to disperse the western rabble.

In different degrees, all three sections, with their different economic interests and even different populations, were represented in the same state legislature, which insured that peaceful sessions were rare. By coincidence, Harper had chosen to settle in a state agitated by many of the same issues which had divided South Carolina in the 1780s and a state that was even more sectionally divided. Reapportionment in Maryland had been a troublesome question, but not nearly so disturbing as the ancient struggle over the suffrage issue that dated well back into the colonial past. It had not been simply a question of property qualifications but had involved a religious restriction as well. The highly touted Maryland Toleration Act of 1649 had applied only to Christians and was repealed less than ten years afterward by a Protestant assembly. Until the Revolution, Catholicism disqualified a Marylander from full participation in government, regardless of his wealth, with the Carrolls being probably the most famous example of this kind of disqualification.

These religious restrictions went by the boards in 1776 but not so the matter of property requirements for voting. For most of the colonial period, suffrage had been limited to those meeting the fifty-acre freehold and forty-pound-sterling qualification. The democratic upheaval represented by the Revolution brought this older requirement under attack, particularly from the younger and poorer elements. A crisis resulted in mid-1776, when there was a great deal of agitation for extension of the suffrage to all adult male taxables who bore arms, with the implicit suggestion from some of the younger men that if they could not vote they did not intend to fight. The constitution drafted in that year granted the vote to all freemen over twenty years of age with a fifty-acre freehold or forty pounds visible property. This in no way satisfied the demands of the reformers, but they were finally pacified by the promise of the state's leaders to discuss the matter further after independence had been won. True to their word, they discussed the matter until 1801, when a second generation of electoral reformers captured the legislature and rammed the reform bill through.[8]

Even after the mild lowering of the suffrage bars in 1776, Maryland government was, as it always had been, a matter of aristocratic stewardship of the Chases, Pacas, Lloyds, and now the Carrolls. It was not that they had governed badly, but they were accustomed to governing and were reluctant to diminish their own political power by broadening the franchise. Reformers as well as conservatives were, however, in agreement upon one essential point, that the foreign born ought to be excluded from full citizenship, with which Harper was very much in agreement.[9] The decade of the 1790s added to the already simmering Maryland political kettle, and in terms of domestic tranquility Maryland ranked near the bottom of the list of states.

When Harper waded into the electoral fray of 1800, he chose to begin his Maryland political activity by touching the most sensitive of the state's political nerve ends. He had risen to prominence by attaching himself to the most explosive issue of the late 1780s in South Carolina. With that same ability to sniff out the significant questions, Robert Goodloe Harper found himself once again immersed in state politics, and Maryland offered ample opportunity for dabbling.

The highly volatile nature of the political theater he had chosen, and for that matter of the man himself, was never more aptly illustrated than by the Harper duel that never was. As was the case with so many southern duels, the supposed insult originated during the height of an election when one gentleman politician believed himself maligned by something another had written in the public prints or uttered in a moment of oratorical indulgence.

In this particular instance, the would be duelists were Robert Goodloe Harper and the Maryland Republican leader, John Francis Mercer, who was a candidate for the House of Delegates. Mercer, who had been born a Virginian and had risen to the rank of colonel on General Charles Lee's staff during the war, had moved to Anne Arundel County in 1785 and had served ever since in one or another public capacity, including the legislature and the Second and Third Congresses. Mercer had resigned from the Congress in 1794, just as Harper arrived, and in the 1800 contest he was seeking reelection to the House of Delegates. It may be that the two gentlemen had exchanged verbal broadsides before the fall of 1800, but the precipitating event involved an exchange of letters to the Baltimore newspapers in October 1800 that evoked challenges from both men.

When Mercer moved to Maryland he did not dispose of his large holdings in Stafford County, Virginia. The Federalists took advantage of this to label Mercer a Virginia squire who sought political influence in both states, implying that he really did not understand or properly represent his Maryland constituents. As early as September 1, 1800, Harper received from Virginia "documents relative to the assessment of Col. Mercer's estate in Stafford County." He had not intended to publish the information but merely exhibit it privately, until Mercer published his version of the Virginia holdings story, which Harper considered inaccurate.

At this point, he said, he felt obligated to place his documents before the people and allow them to draw their own conclusions. According to Harper, the printer ran the entire letter containing the documents as well as some rather uncomplimentary remarks about Colonel Mercer by Harper's Virginia correspondent.[10]

Mercer interpreted this as a slur and an implied accusation of dishonesty. He replied to Harper in a letter in the *Federal Gazette* of October 15, in which Harper's conduct was termed ungentlemanly. He had concluded that the unkind remarks by Harper's correspondent were in reality from Harper himself, since it was known that the "Civis" who signed the published letter was Harper.[11]

Mercer told John Eager Howard, Harper's representative, that he very much intended the remarks about Harper but could not press the matter just then, for he had to leave immediately for Virginia. Howard replied that Mercer might "hear from Mr. Harper in Virginia," and then he returned to Baltimore to inform his friend of the results of the exchange. Between October 24 and October 30, Harper tried to locate Mercer and pin down exactly what his remarks had meant and whether he intended to stand by them.[12]

Finally, through Colonel John Ross Key, Harper caught up with the elusive Mercer and demanded a straightforward reply, but once again Mercer stalled, and Key had a very difficult time even arranging a meeting. After a long delay, Mercer blaming it on his wife's delicate condition, the colonel affirmed his earlier remarks and said that he had told Howard that he was ready to "receive Mr. Harpers commands in Virginia." He said he had gone there and spent one day waiting for a response from Harper. At any rate he was willing to pursue the matter after his return to West River, Anne Arundel County.[13]

Matters worsened when Mercer's friends in Baltimore and Annapolis began spreading the story that the Colonel had waited forty-eight hours in Georgetown for Harper either to arrive or send a formal statement of his intentions. Harper was furious at this implication of cowardice, and at this point, must have decided to demand satisfaction from the slippery Republican.[14] Throughout November, Harper and Mercer exchanged angry notes, both throwing down the gauntlet but neither very eager to set a definite date for the reckoning. Mercer went off to Virginia again, and Harper demanded to be informed where and when he was planning to be in Virginia, so that there might be no misunderstanding about any appointment they might make.[15]

Finally, after another month of this comic opera posturing, the two men worked out the dispute through intermediaries, with Harper explaining that the original insulting remarks were really not his, and Mercer then exclaiming that if he had only

known this in time he would never have made those terrible
remarks about Harper in October. [16] By the end of December,
both men took advantage of the opportunity to extricate themselves gracefully from what probably would eventually have
resulted in a duel that neither really ever desired, but which if
pushed far enough they would have been forced to fight.

In late December, perhaps in the spirit of the season, Harper
wrote to Mercer and signalled the formal end of the feud by
telling Mercer that he would be happy to meet him in the future
"on the terms usual between gentlemen in society." [17] Harper
had come upon the Maryland scene with a flourish, perhaps with
a bit too much dash and bravado, but that was the nature of the
man and, after all, the duel had been avoided honorably. Be that
as it may, Robert Goodloe Harper had far more important
matters demanding his attention, not the least important of
which was the courting of Catherine Carroll.

The Mercer affair seemed simple by comparison, for this was
no ordinary young lady but the daughter of Carroll the Signer,
and the old gentleman was rather rough on his daughter's suitors.
Having lost his wife when his children were all young, Carroll had
tried to be both father and mother to them and he had not been
entirely successful. One of his biographers writes that "he loved
them [more as young adults than as children], but he still did
not enjoy their company or find coping with them any less of a
problem." [18] It was not really until they had grown and produced grandchildren that he was at last at peace with them, and
no father ever had more reason to be troubled.

The eldest child, Mary, announced at age seventeen that she
intended to marry Richard Caton, a young man from England
about whom the family knew little except that he was hopelessly
in debt. The family was further upset because Mary was infor-
mally intended for a cousin, Daniel Carroll, of Duddington.
Caton, however, went into business and paid off his debts with
absolutely no help from Carroll, and the marriage was finally
allowed.

Charles, Jr., and Catherine had been sent abroad to study, but
the son came home in 1792 not much improved. His father had
great hopes for him, but Charles Carroll of Homewood, so called
after the home Carroll constructed for him, was never able to
measure up, much to the disappointment of the parent. Catherine Carroll returned from the European trip desirably educated
for a young woman of sixteen and quite pretty. [19] After his

experience with Mary, Charles Carroll must have resolved not to undergo the same torture with Kitty, but the Carroll girls had a knack for bringing home young men who were not up to their father's expectations.

In 1798, at age twenty-two, she met Robert Goodloe Harper—like Caton, possessed of great charm and large debts—and Charles Carroll's troubles began all over again. It never occurred to either of these two young heiresses that a young man in debt might be smitten by their fiscal charms, for indebtedness never worried them as long as their father remained an inexhaustible font. Over the last twenty-three years of his life, he gave the three children some 305,000 dollars in the form of cash allowances, excluding gifts of property.[20] It was no small wonder that Kitty Carroll proved to be irresponsibly extravagant both before and after her marriage to Harper.

Charles Carroll put up a stubborn fight, and for a time Harper must certainly have been discouraged by the refusal to allow him to call at Doughoregan Manor. Throughout the fall of 1800, the prospective son-in-law was rebuffed in his attempts to convince Mr. Carroll that he was not a fortune-hunting adventurer but a good lawyer with a promising future and a serious suitor. Harper began by admitting to Carroll that he owed in excess of 14,000 dollars. Like any suitor, Harper stressed his positive points rather than his indebtedness. He swore that he had no intentions of using any of Kitty's fortune to pay off his debts, and Carroll assured him that this would be the case since her money was invested in lands which would be unproductive for the near future.

Carroll thought that Harper's estimate of his earnings as a beginning lawyer was unrealistic, and besides, it was insufficient to maintain Kitty in the style to which she was accustomed. Before he would even think of consenting to Harper's marriage to Kitty, "an event however not likely to happen, or at distant day, if ever," a house had to be purchased and furnished, a carriage procured and servants provided for. This was out of the question for someone as heavily indebted as Harper, and Carroll asked him to discontinue his attentions to Catherine.[21]

This may possibly have been a case of safeguarding the treasure after the crime had been committed, for Harper reacted to these rebuffs like a man extremely confident of eventual success. Kitty had, in all probability, already been swept off her feet by the gallant former congressman whose eloquence was as effective in the sitting room as in congressional debates. This must have been the case, for Miss Carroll's brother-in-law Richard Caton came rapidly to Harper's defense, possibly because he too had once felt Carroll's wrath regarding his debts, but also perhaps, because he had been asked to intercede by Miss Carroll herself.

The three-way entente proved too much for Carroll and he was gradually worn down until in January 1801 he consented to a spring wedding.[22] Throughout the entire difficult courtship, Carroll had not once offered Harper's lukewarm Protestantism as a major obstacle, although Carroll did feel that it might be a source of friction in the event of children. The real objection, all along, was the size of his daughter's dowry as compared to Harper's debts. Nevertheless, the nuptials were celebrated in Annapolis on May 23, 1801, with Bishop John Carroll present to perform the ceremony.[23]

The Harper marriage, while productive of more grandchildren for Charles Carroll, was nonetheless not the happiest of matches. Kitty's extravagant nature was made less endurable by what seems to have been abundant possession of the talents of a whining, nagging wife. She was forever ill, no doubt many times unfeignedly, but there are letters from wife to husband containing the most maudlin sentiments. "You must bear with patience & fortitude [the time he had to spend with her at home], a little while longer," she wrote, "Heaven will at last hear your prayer & remove the cause of your misery. . . ."[24] His law practice did keep him away a good deal of the time, either in Annapolis or Washington, but letters such as this one from Mrs. Harper must have constituted additional provocation. He was accused of not being happy at home, of not being appreciative, of begrudging her the small amount of time and attention she asked for, with the result that Harper stayed away even more. Indeed, one suspects that for Harper this was a marriage contracted on the rebound, so to speak, following that unsuccessful affair in Philadelphia.

The children, several of whom—including his favorite, Mary Diana—died tragically young, fared only slightly better with Harper than did their mother. No doubt he loved them, but like Carroll he never managed to accept and deal with them. His technique was to treat them as adults even earlier in life than was the custom of the times, and he adopted the harshest of disciplinarian approaches in his relationship with them. His letters to them, while they were boarded in parochial schools, are a mixture of nine parts criticism to one part parental affection. Yet, on the occasion of the death of fourteen-year-old Elizabeth he was so moved that he attempted to write a poetic final tribute.

> For she was as the lily pure.
> Sweet as the fragrance of the rose,
> and like its bloom her fleeting hours
> sped swiftly on to death's repose,
> and, ah! as transient as its bloom.[25]

Also like Carroll, Harper expected marvelous things from his children and sincerely tried, through his constant lecturing and his determination to see that they were well educated, to instill the necessary drive to fulfill their individual promise. He was not terribly successful, and the loss of Mary Diana, the oldest and most talented, must have been a crushing blow, especially since she died away from home while at school in Europe.[26]

Nevertheless, as was expected of the Carrolls and their relations, the family endured. "Oakland," the estate Harper eventually constructed on the Falls Road in northern Baltimore, became a social mecca at which the Harpers entertained grandly and lavishly. One guest recorded in his diary that at one affair the guests arrived for over two hours and then danced and promenaded under the shadows of the huge trees surrounding the estate, pausing only to refresh themselves with strawberries and cream, cherries and ices of all sorts. The dancing continued until sunset when the ladies removed to the house, where, after coffee, the ball continued until the late hours of the morning.[27] The estate was obviously quite handsome, with its dairy designed in the form of a Greek temple, complete with Ionic portico, and there is ample proof that Robert Goodloe Harper's marriage had, at the very least, provided him with much of the wherewithal required to live as he did.

During the course of her marriage to Harper, Catherine Carroll Harper received from her father at least 86,958 dollars in cash and this does not include any transfers of property, which were substantial but in Kitty's name alone. Harper's law practice was considerable and his fees must certainly have exceeded the ten to twelve thousand dollars annually that he had expected. Yet, as late as 1822, he had outstanding single debts as large as ten thousand dollars. In 1822, Carroll had to pressure Harper in order to have him set aside money to pay off an obligation for which the father-in-law was security. Carroll wished his daughter's husband to apply the 1,200 dollars annual interest on two of Harper's bonds, in Carroll's possession, toward the elimination of the debt.

Partly because he did not wish to relinquish his familial position, but also because he had a rather low opinion of the financial maturity of both his daughter and her husband, Carroll never surrendered his control over the income from Catherine's annuities, which amounted to more than five thousand dollars annually.[28] Mrs. Caton was similarly dealt with, and this continued long after they had growing families of their own. Their reaction to this sort of treatment from an aging parent took the form of open recriminations, but their husbands could do little more than quietly accept their father-in-law's eccentricities.

The point is that Harper, regardless of several sources of income, never seemed to have enough to satisfy his family's appetite and his own ambitious plans. The financial condition in which his death left the family was not really as bad as it would have been had Kitty not been one of the Carroll heirs. Harper's son wrote from Paris in the 1830s, complaining that the family's fortunes had dwindled away to nothing and that it was "really hard thus to be striped of the luxuries to which we have been accustomed from our infancy and reduced to poverty. . . ."[29] "Poverty," to this rather spoiled young man, was something quite apart from the state described by the usage then current in Baltimore. He was, after all, studying in Paris, and the family did somehow manage to scrape by and to absorb the rather high cost of his education complete with all extraordinary extracurricular expenses.

Considering the income he realized, including the supplement from Carroll, Robert Goodloe Harper died a man of relatively modest means, especially in terms of the social circle in which the family moved. The inventories of his estate, after nearly five thousand dollars for a debt owed to the Baltimore merchant Robert Oliver, and the many smaller debts, were paid, show a balance of slightly over ten thousand dollars. This represents his total worth, excluding land, but counting the twenty-seven slaves, servants rather than hands, belonging to the estate. Harper lived very well, often close to the financial borderline, and perhaps he did so because his family was always assured the security of the Carroll fortune in the event of his death.[30]

It was not in the field of financial affairs that Harper could have been expected to make his place in Maryland. Rather it was always in the law that this former master of political oratory was destined to succeed, and he became one of the giants of an exceptionally talented early nineteenth-century Maryland bar. His marriage was partly responsible for attracting to his offices the great and the wealthy, but he was at the same time a highly gifted debater, with that background in the classics so highly prized by his generation, and he possessed a first-rate command of law.[31] His base of operation was, of course, the Baltimore area but he practiced before the Supreme Court of the United States and the lesser federal courts as well as the Maryland state courts.

The Baltimore-Annapolis bar was a closed fraternity dominated by a small group of powerful attorneys. Considering that Maryland remained a Federalist stronghold well into the Republican period, there was a surprising absence of partisanship among the members of this select group. William Wirt as United States attorney general practiced often in Baltimore, and Wirt was a good Republican. Yet, he happily observed that regardless of the fact that most of the Baltimore bar was Federalist, it made little difference in their professional and personal relations with him. As a matter of fact, after his first case before the Baltimore Federal Court, several of the Maryland Federalist lawyers, who had represented the other side, came to visit the new attorney general and congratulated him on the handling of his first case. Wirt did have a complaint about the tendency of these otherwise splendid gentlemen to be excessively long-winded in court, and he expressed the opinion that Maryland trials always lasted longer than those elsewhere. Arguments that should have required part of one day consumed an entire week.[32]

The worst offender was the great William Pinkney, whose ·oratory simply knew no limits. Nicknamed "Orlando Furioso" by Wirt, Pinkney would invariably promise to speak for two and one-half hours and then hold forth for two or three days, much to the delight of the spectators, while not only causing chagrin among his fellow lawyers who had to sit and listen but also slowing down the judicial machinery already overburdened with a heavy docket. Pinkney's technique was not merely built upon his ability to overwhelm the court but also depended every bit as much on his talents and the preparation that went into such an onslaught. The only real rival Pinkney had in Maryland was Robert Goodloe Harper, and a contest involving them on opposite sides of a case was certain to attract a large gathering of

Marylanders, who loved every minute of this nineteenth-century spectator sport.[33]

Harper was perfectly cast in such a role, dressed in dark blue outercoat, buff waistcoat, and brilliantly polished boots. With immaculately trimmed bristling sidewhiskers, he was a handsome man even in his later years. His law office attracted bright young men eager to serve as clerks and study under his direction, perfectly willing to tolerate the office discipline administered by their teacher. Becoming more autocratic with age, Harper "reviewed his law students as a commander would his troops." They were not only instructed in the law but strongly admonished to pursue their other studies as well and equally avidly. Spencer's *Faerie Queene* was every bit as much a part of their education as Blackstone, and they were advised to try writing poetry and, under no circumstances, to neglect their Latin.[34]

Harper's desire for military glory and high rank, which had been frustrated in two earlier wars, was finally realized ironically enough during a war which he had opposed. Harper's Anglophilia was of quite ancient standing long before the advent of the 1812 crisis. Like so many other Federalists, the war was repugnant to him for a host of philosophical reasons, in addition to an emotional involvement in the English-French struggle, an involvement that dated from the 1790s not the nineteenth century. He was scarcely able to discuss the war hawks or James Madison calmly. His correspondence with the British minister Augustus James Foster, after the latter was declared persona non grata by the American Department of State, would have left Harper open to prosecution under his own Logan Act of 1798 had the Madison administration been aware of the Maryland Federalists's activities.[35]

Nonetheless, Harper did not deserve the appellation "Blue Light Federalist" tied to his coattails by the dissident Taney faction of the Maryland Federalist party, which supported the Madison administration.[36] The "Blue Light Federalists" were supposed to be the most obnoxious of the "British Men," the "Monocrats," who, during the war, were accused of sending, by signaling with blue lights, traitorous messages to British warships standing offshore at night and advising the enemy of the most opportune attack approaches.

Such charges were patently without foundation, and Harper, along with countless other "antiwar" Marylanders, rushed to Baltimore's defenses when the Chesapeake region was invaded by a British expeditionary force in late August 1814. Harper was appointed a general in Samuel Smith's hastily constructed Baltimore defenses, and he commanded troops in the crucial North Point engagement on September 13 and 14. It was the failure of the British General Ross's attack upon Baltimore via North Point that necessitated the futile frontal assault on Fort McHenry and saved the city from what the British considered its proper deserts as a "nest of pirates."

It was long in coming and brief, to be sure, but Robert Goodloe Harper's military chance finally arrived. The enemy had not been, perhaps, the one he had most desired, neither had the war occurred when it ought to have, nor had he been in agreement with the validity of the Republican justification for or conduct of the affair; but it was a war nonetheless. For the rest of his life, he was customarily addressed as "General Harper," out of respect and no doubt because he reacted more favorably to that title than any other. Very few other important Federalists, northern or southern, managed to oppose the war as Harper had and yet emerge from the unfortunate struggle as both a patriot and a hero. His was not the stigma of hinted dismemberment of the Union that touched everyone who came near the convention in Connecticut, whether they were moderate or extremist. In an odd way, perhaps he was fortunate that his city was attacked by the enemy, for he was given the opportunity, or was forced, to help repel the invader. He may have been right for the wrong reasons, but in contrast to many other Federalists of his persuasion and passion, Harper's opposition to the war and the Republican regime literally stopped at the water's edge.

The citizens of his adopted city were sincerely saddened by the general's sudden death in January, 1825, and their parting tribute was splendid to witness.

All told nearly "2,000 soldiers, volunteers [since] there are no regulars in the city [marched in the funeral procession]; there were three bands of music with muffled drums; each company having a peculiar dress made their appearance quite novel! Two companies wore plaid uniforms and all were garbed in frock jackets. Many sported ostrich feathers in their caps, 'which gave them much the appearance of the ancient Spanish dress.' The General's horse, bearing his sword and boots, followed the hearse. Then came the mourning coaches, companies of riflemen, and the procession ended with a great number of hackney coaches and thousands of pedestrians" following at a respectful distance to the cemetery where burial with full military honors took place.[37]

The English visitor who recorded these impressions of the "grand parade," although accustomed to the pageantry of English state affairs, was truly impressed by the dignity and majesty which marked the event.

Robert Goodloe Harper would have loved it!

NOTES

1. Johann David Scoepf, 1783, quoted in Raphael Semmes, *Baltimore as Seen by Visitors, 1783-1860*. Studies in Maryland History No. 2 (Baltimore: Maryland Historical Society, 1953), pp. 2-3.
2. Luigi Castiglioni, "Description of Baltimore, 1785-1787," quoted in Semmes, p. 4.
3. Mederic L. E. Moreau de St. Mery, quoted in Semmes, p. 8.
4. Hamilton Owens, *Baltimore on the Chesapeake* (New York: Doubleday, Doran & Co., 1941), pp. 141-142.
5. Thomas Scharf, *History of Maryland from the Earliest Period to the Present Day* (Baltimore: J. B. Piet, 1879), II, 605. Also, "Federal Census of 1790 and 1800," Adam, Seybert, *Statistical Annals of the U. S.* (Philadelphia: no publisher, 1818), p. 47, as quoted in Thomas P. Abernethy, *The South in the New Nation, 1789-1819*, Vol. IV in *A History of the South* (Baton Rouge: Louisiana State University Press, 1961), p. 13.
6. Scharf, Alexander Hamilton to Governor Lee, September 6, 1794, II, 585-586.
7. *Maryland Gazette*, September 18, 1794.
8. Morris I. Radoff, *The Old Line State, A History of Maryland* (Baltimore: Historical Record Association, 1956), II, 55. Also, Chilton Williamson, *American Suffrage: From Property to Democracy 1760-1860* (Princeton: Princeton University Press, 1960), pp. 110-121. Williamson disagrees with Radoff and maintains that the requirement was only thirty pounds sterling.
9. Williamson, p. 110. Williamson also sees a very close connection between suffrage reform and the agitation for paper money emission in Maryland during the same period. His point is that if the requirements for voting could not be lowered then emission of paper money would, in effect, reduce the visible property requirement. He contends that paper money depreciation nullified the ten-pound qualification in Georgia, the thirty-pound qualification in Maryland, and the fifty-pound requirement in New Jersey. Ibid., p. 121. One wonders, however, if Williamson is correct, how we explain the necessity for

the reform furor of 1801 and the suffrage extension movement led by Michael Taney and desperately fought by the conservatives.

10. Enoch Mason Esq., of Virginia, to RGH, September 1, 1800, quoted in a letter from RGH to Robert Smith, December 3, 1800, Harper-Pennington Papers.

11. RGH to Mercer, October 21, 1800, John Eager Howard to RGH, October 24, 1800, ibid.

12. RGH to C. T. Thomas, October 27, 1800, to Howard, October 28, Howard to RGH, October 28, 1800, ibid.

13. Mercer to John Ross Key, October 31, 1800, ibid.

14. RGH to John Eager Howard, November 9, 1800, ibid.

15. RGH to Mercer, November 11, Mercer to RGH, November 11, and RGH to Mercer, November 12, ibid.

16. RGH to Robert Smith, December 3, to Mercer December 18 and 19; Mercer to Smith, December 5, to RGH, December 19, ibid.

17. RGH to Mercer, December 19, 1800, ibid.

18. Ellen Hart Smith, *Charles Carroll of Carrollton* (Cambridge: Harvard University Press, 1942), pp. 219-222.

19. Ibid., pp. 234-247.

20. Ibid., pp. 301-304, also the small collection of Carroll Miscellaneous Estate Papers in the Library of Congress.

21. Charles Carroll to Richard Caton, September 18, 1800. This material is also contained in the Harper-Pennington Papers.

22. RGH to Caton, October 2, 1800; Carroll to Caton, October 4, 1800. RGH included a resume of his financial condition in his Autobiography, which was written for Carroll. The Autobiography is dated January 10, 1801, indicating that Carroll held out through December.

23. Smith, *Carroll of Carrollton*, p. 264.

24. Catherine Harper to RGH, Friday [no date], Harper-Pennington, III.

25. Harper-Pennington Papers, III.

26. Mary Diana's trip was supervised by the Albert Gallatins, and it seems that at least socially, the old wounds had been healed. Harper-Pennington MSS, 1817-1818.

27. "Robert Gilmore's Diary, 1826-1827," *Maryland Historical Magazine*, Vol. XVII (September 1922), quoted in Semmes, p. 94. Oakland was destroyed by fire in the last century and almost no accurate physical details of the estate survive, except for the temple dairy.

28. Harper-Pennington MSS, III.

29. RGH, Jr., to Catherine Harper, December, 1832, ibid.; also Charles Carroll to Roger B. Taney, January 4, 1831, Charles Carroll of Carrollton Papers, Box I, L.C.

30. The writer could find no record of a will, which seems a remarkable oversight in the case of a trained lawyer. The estate information is contained in Baltimore County Inventories of Estates 1826-28 Liber

DMP, p. 36, Baltimore County Inventories, 1828-29 Liber DMP, p. 37, Administrative Accounts Folio 329 Book N24, Administrative Accounts 1829 Folio 93 Book N27. This material is deposited in the Hall of Records, Annapolis.

31. Carroll-Harper Papers, Maryland Historical Society.
32. William Wirt to Elizabeth Wirt, July 24, 1818, Wirt Papers, Box 5, Maryland Historical Society.
33. Wirt to Elizabeth Wirt, April 7, 1821, Wirt Papers, Box 6.
34. Kennedy, *Life of William Wirt*, pp. 25-26.
35. In the Harper-Pennington Papers and the Alexander Contee Hanson Family Papers in the Maryland Historical Society are several of the most extraordinary letters in all of Harper's manuscripts. Dating from June of 1812 is the draft of remarks Harper obviously intended to give to someone respecting the course England ought to follow if the United States declared war, "which unfortunately appears too probable." Harper detailed the course Great Britain must follow if the war was to be kept limited and hopefully brief. He wrote, "there can be no doubt that the war . . . is contrary to the feelings and wishes of a great majority of the people." He warned that if England launched an invasion that "the nation will be united in support of the war; its friends will be returned in the approaching elections." "We shall rush headlong into the arms of France. . . ." "But all these mischiefs may be averted, if Great Britain should confine herself to a maritime war against us, and a defensive system in Canada." Harper emphasized that the opposition to the war, given the right environment, would grow sufficiently to capture the state legislatures, the Senate, and perhaps even the presidency. Offensive British actions, coastal attack, unleashing of the Indian tribes against the frontier, etc., would only "strengthen the hands of the war party."

    Also in the collection is a letter from Hanson to RGH, June 8, 1812, informing the latter that Augustus John Foster, British Minister to the United States, "would gladly receive and converse with you freely upon any subject." Foster does not plan to come to Baltimore but asks Hanson, "Will you direct a letter to me under cover to Major Lewis in whose room I stay, saying whether you can be here on Saturday evening? The interview and paper which you talked of drawing up may do great good—"
36. Alexander Contee Hanson Family Papers, Maryland Historical Society; also Swisher, pp. 68-69, 70-76.
37. Joseph Pickering, quoted in Semmes, pp. 77-78. Also, William Wirt to Laura H. Wirt, January 14, 1825. "The town has been much shocked this morning by the sudden death of General Harper. He had eaten his breakfast as usual and was standing by the fire reading a news-

paper when . . . he dropped and it is supposed died before he reached the floor. It is easy to conceive the agony and horror of his family; for he was an excellent private as well as public character. Poor Mrs. Harper, it is said, . . . swallowed laudanum with the intention of killing herself. . . . The shock seems to have paralized all the business of the town."

Notes on the Sources

Robert Goodloe Harper left no great body of manuscripts to posterity, and thus one is forced to put together the bits and pieces of the man which have survived, and in the case of Congressman Harper, to depend heavily upon the public record.

Considering the fact that Harper uprooted himself and moved to a distant part of the country four times it is surprising that any papers have survived. The collection is richest after he settled permanently in Baltimore and the largest single collection of manuscripts is in the Maryland Historical Society. The RGH materials are contained in several related collections: the RGH Papers, the Harper-Pennington Papers, the Harper-Speed Letters, the Leakin Papers, and the Mary Diana Harper Papers. The Carroll family manuscripts also are invaluable, consisting primarily of the Carroll Papers, the Carroll-Harper Papers, and the Carroll-McTavish Papers. Also in the MHS collection are the Samuel Chase Papers, the Alexander Contee Hanson Collection, the James McHenry Papers, the William Patterson Papers, and the William Wirt Papers.

In the Manuscript Division of the Library of Congress, of particular significance to this study are the Adams Papers, microfilm edition, the Galloway-Maxcy-Markoe Papers, Robert Goodloe Harper Papers, Izard Papers, James McHenry Papers, Samuel Smith Papers, William Loughton Smith Papers, William Sullivan Papers, and William Wirt Papers.

Materials relating to Harper's estate, wealth, and business are found in the Maryland Hall of Records, Annapolis, in the Administrative Accounts and the Baltimore County Inventories of Estates.

In South Carolina, of particular significance to this study is the splendid public records collection at the South Carolina Archives, Columbia containing the County Land Records, Civil Court Records, the Journal of the South Carolina House, Land Grant Indexes, and the South Carolina Legislative Papers. In addition, a small collection of Harper Papers is contained in the collection of the South Caroliniana Library of the University of South Carolina. The John Rutledge, Jr. Papers, Southern Historical Collection of the University of North Carolina Library was most valuable, as were the Timothy Pickering and Theodore Sedgwick Papers in the Massachusetts Historical Society.

Among the most important published correspondence from the period covered by this study are: George Gibbs, (ed.) *Memoirs of the Administrations of Washington and John Adams from the Papers of Oliver Wolcott*, (2 vols.; New York: William Van-Norden, 1846); John C. Hamilton, (ed.) *The Works of Alexander Hamilton*, (7 vols.; New York: Charles Francis Co., 1850-1851); Robert Goodloe Harper, *Select Works of Robert Goodloe Harper, Consisting of Speeches on Political and Forensic Subjects*, (Baltimore: O. H. Neilson, 1814) [Two volumes were projected but only the first was published.]; Henry P. Johnston, (ed.) *Correspondence and Public Papers of John Jay*, (4 vols.; New York: G. P. Putnam's Sons, 1890-1893); Henry C. Lodge, *The Works of Alexander Hamilton*, (12 vols.; New York: G. P. Putnam's Sons, 1903); "Letters of William Barry Grove," Edited by H. W. Wagstaff, *Federalism in North Carolina*, Vol. IX, No. 2, in the James Sprunt Historical Publications, (Chapel Hill: University of North Carolina Press, 1910); Bernard C. Steiner, *The Life and Correspondence of James McHenry*, (Cleveland: The Burrows Brothers Co., 1907); Anne C. Morris, (ed.) *The Diary and Letters of Gouverneur Morris*, (2 vols.; New York: Charles Scribner's Sons, 1888); "Papers of James A. Bayard, 1796-1815," Edited by Elizabeth Donnan, *Annual Report of the American Historical Association for the Year 1913*. (Vol. II; Washington, 1915); "South Carolina Federalist Correspondence, 1789-1797." Edited by Ulrich B. Phillips, *American Historical Review*, Vol. XIV (1909). Also valuable were the following diaries: "Diary of Timothy Ford, 1785-1786." *South Carolina Historical and Genealogical Magazine*, XIII (1912); James F. Jameson (ed.) "The Diary of Edward Hooker, 1805-1808," *Annual Report of the American Historical Association for 1896*. (Washington: 1897); and "Robert Gilmore's Diary, "*Maryland Historical Magazine*, XVII (September, 1922); Samuel E. Morrison, *Life and Letters of Harrison Gray Otis*, (Boston: Houghton Mifflin, 1913).

Several of Harper's political pamphlets are of special interest: *RGH, An Address to the People of South Carolina—By the General Committee of the Representative Reform Association at Columbia*. (Columbia: 1794); RGH, *Legislative Choice of Elec-*

tors in Maryland, Bystander. (Baltimore: 1800); RGH, *Observations on the Dispute Between the United States and France.* (Charleston: 1797); RGH, *Speech on the Foreign Intercourse Bill.* (1798).

The major published source for RGH as a southern Federalist Congressman was, of course, the *Debates and Proceedings in the Congress of the United States.* (Washington: Gales and Seaton, 1851) referred to as the *Annals of Congress.*

Secondary material is quoted where used in the text but several items deserve special attention. One must begin in southern history with Ulrich B. Phillips, and particularly important to this study were "South Carolina in the Election of 1800," *American Historical Review,* IV (October, 1898); and "The South Carolina Federalists," *American Historical Review,* XIV (1901). John H. Wolfe, *Jeffersonian Democracy in South Carolina,* (Chapel Hill: University of North Carolina Press, 1940) is a classic and offers countless insights into South Carolina in the Federal period. William A. Schaper, "Sectionalism and Representation in South Carolina," *Annual Report of the American Historical Association for 1900,* I (1901), was also of value.

Several state and local histories even though dated were important as sources of background information and detail. David Duncan Wallace, *South Carolina: A Short History 1520-1948.* (Columbia: University of South Carolina Press, 1961); J. Thomas Scharf, *History of Baltimore, City and County from the Earliest Period to the Present Day.* (2 vols.; Philadelphia: L. H. Everts, 1881)were the most important of these.

Two recent studies were markedly influential as this work progressed. Lisle A. Rose, *Prologue to Democracy: the Federalists in the South, 1789-1800.* (Lexington: University of Kentucky Press, 1968) is the beginning point for anyone who would understand the southern Federalist party. George C. Rogers, *The Evolution of a Federalist, William Loughton Smith of Charleston, 1758-1812.* (Columbia: University of South Carolina Press, 1962) is a model biographical study of the individual who had a great influence upon Harper during his first term in Congress. James Morton Smith, *Freedom's Letters, The Alien and Sedition Laws and American Civil Liberties,* (Ithaca: Cornell University Press, 1956) is indispensible, as are Alexander DeConde, *Entangling Alliance: Politics and Diplomacy Under George Washington,* (Durham: Duke University Press, 1958) and *The Quasi War: The Politics and Diplomacy of the Undeclared War With France,*

(New York: Charles Scribner's Sons, 1966). Marvin R. Zahniser, *Charles Cotesworth Pinckney: Founding Father* (Chapel Hill: University of North Carolina Press, 1967), provides a perceptive recent view of a member of the South Carolina Federalist establishment.

Index

226